Send Help!

A Collection of Marooned Cartoons

EDITED BY

JON ADAMS AND ELLIS ROSEN

VORACIOUS

LITTLE,
BROWN

New York Boston London

Voracious / Little, Brown and Company, Hachette Book Group, 1290 Avenue of the Americas, New York, NY 10104. littlebrown.com. First Edition: November 2021. Voracious is an imprint of Little, Brown and Company, a division of Hachette Book Group, Inc. The Voracious name and logo are trademarks of Hachette Book Group, Inc. The publisher is not responsible for websites (or their content) that are not owned by the publisher. The Hachette Speakers Bureau provides a wide range of authors for speaking events. To find out more, go to hachettespeakersbureau.com or call (866) 376-6591. Cover design by Kirin Diemont. Cover illustration by Jon Adams. Book design by Jon Adams. ISBN 978-0-316-26279-8, LCCN 2021939613, 10 9 8 7 6 5 4 3 2 1, LSC-C. Printed in the United States of America. Don't worry! If you need more reading material because you're currently marooned on an island, here's all the fine print again. Copyright © 2021 by Jon Adams and Ellis Rosen. Art copyright © 2021 by Jon Adams, Ellis Rosen, and the individual artists credited. Hachette Book Group supports the right to free expression and the value of copyright. The purpose of copyright is to encourage writers and artists to produce the creative works that enrich our culture. The scanning, uploading, and distribution of this book without permission is a theft of the authors' intellectual property. If you would like permission to use material from the book (other than for review purposes), please contact permissions@hbgusa.com. Thank you for your support of the authors' rights. Voracious / Little, Brown and Company, Hachette Book Group, 1290 Avenue of the Americas, New York, NY 10104. littlebrown.com. First Edition: November 2021. Voracious is an imprint of Little, Brown and Company, a division of Hachette Book Group, Inc. The Voracious name and logo are trademarks of Hachette Book Group, Inc. The publisher is not responsible for websites (or their content) that are not owned by the publisher. The Hachette Speakers Bureau provides a wide range of authors for speaking events. To find out more, go to hachettespeakersbureau.com or call (866) 376-6591. Cover design by Kirin Diemont. Cover illustration by Jon Adams. Book design by Jon Adams. ISBN 978-0-316-26279-8, LCCN 2021939613, 10 9 8 7 6 5 4 3 2 1, LSC-C. Printed in the United States of America. Don't worry! If you need more reading material because you're currently marooned on an island, here's all the fine print again. Copyright © 2021 by Jon Adams and Ellis Rosen. Art copyright © 2021 by Jon Adams, Ellis Rosen, and the individual artists credited. Hachette Book Group supports the right to free expression and the value of copyright. The purpose of copyright is to encourage writers and artists to produce the creative works that enrich our culture. The scanning, uploading, and distribution of this book without permission is a theft of the authors' intellectual property. If you would like permission to use material from the book (other than for review purposes), please contact permissions@hbgusa.com. Thank you for your support of the authors' rights. Voracious / Little, Brown and Company, Hachette Book Group, 1290 Avenue of the Americas, New York, NY 10104. littlebrown.com. First Edition: November 2021. Voracious is an imprint of Little, Brown and Company, a division of Hachette Book Group, Inc. The Voracious name and logo are trademarks of Hachette Book Group, Inc. The publisher is not responsible for websites (or their content) that are not owned by the publisher. The Hachette Speakers Bureau provides a wide range of authors for speaking events. To find out more, go to hachettespeakersbureau.com or call (866) 376-6591. Cover design by Kirin Diemont. Cover illustration by Jon Adams. Book design by Jon Adams. ISBN 978-0-316-26279-8, LCCN 2021939613, 10 9 8 7 6 5 4 3 2 1, LSC-C. Printed in the United States of America. Don't worry! If you need more reading material because you're currently marooned on an island, here's all the fine print again. Copyright © 2021 by Jon Adams and Ellis Rosen. Art copyright © 2021 by Jon Adams, Ellis Rosen, and the individual artists credited. Hachette Book Group supports the right to free expression and the value of copyright. The purpose of copyright is to encourage writers and artists to produce the creative works that enrich our culture. The scanning, uploading, and distribution of this book without permission is a theft of the authors' intellectual property. If you would like permission to use material from the book (other than for review purposes), please contact permissions@hbgusa.com. Thank you for your support of the authors' rights. Voracious / Little, Brown and Company, Hachette Book Group, 1290 Avenue of the Americas, New York, NY 10104. littlebrown.com. First Edition: November 2021. Voracious is an imprint of Little, Brown and Company, a division of Hachette Book Group, Inc. The Voracious name and logo are trademarks of Hachette Book Group, Inc. The publisher is not responsible for websites (or their content) that are not owned by the publisher. The Hachette Speakers Bureau provides a wide range of authors for speaking events. To find out more, go to hachettespeakersbureau.com or call (866) 376-6591. Cover design by Kirin Diemont. Cover illustration by Jon Adams. Book design by Jon Adams. ISBN 978-0-316-26279-8, LCCN 2021939613, 10 9 8 7 6 5 4 3 2 1, LSC-C. Printed in the United States of America.

Printing 1, 2021

Foreword

Emma Allen, *New Yorker* Cartoon Editor

On very rare occasions, even cartoonists can't come up with a joke. Tragedy plus time may eventually equal comedy (though I've always been suspicious of that equation: guy steps on a land mine—wait for it...). But in the immediate aftermath of something truly terrible, there tends to be a yawning, agonizing pause as we all try to find something, anything, to say, let alone laugh at. As the harsh reality of the global pandemic sank in, my email inbox was, unsurprisingly, pretty bare. Then time passed, and I got a few timid jokes about running out of toilet paper. "First thoughts are not always the best thoughts" is a humor maxim I stand by one hundred percent.

Next, something strange happened. I started receiving droves of desert island cartoons. If there were as many desert islands as desert island cartoons I was fielding in late March 2020, one could puddle-hop around the world, across a sea-spanning archipelago. There were jokes about stranded men and women turning down a cruise ship's offer of a (contagion-riddled) lift. There were jokes about desert islanders not wanting to return to civilization under lockdown—some palm-frond shade and a coconut sure look nice if you've been cooped up with Craigslist roommates in an illegal sublet, rationing ramen. With outdoor space and easily maintained social distancing at a premium, the cartoon desert island—a trope created back when being marooned by a shipwreck was, I guess, a constant communal anxiety—suddenly seemed quite deluxe. Cartoonist Colin Tom captured another element of the weirdness of how we've lived recently—his drawing of a stranded guy with a fleet of messages in bottles washing up on his micro-shore is captioned, "Now everyone wants to talk."

New Yorker cartoon tropes or clichés often persist for decades, with cartoonists riffing on riffs on riffs on a theme—be it the grim reaper or Rapunzel or the first bluebird of spring (which I honestly don't know that anyone at this point gets; I don't, really). But what's continuously amazing and surprising about them is that they find new relevance in different historical moments.

In November of 2016, cartoons about clueless kings on the ramparts became fraught with specific meaning—whether that was the cartoonist's intention or not. I remember, around that time, revisiting a Robert Weber desert island cartoon from 1997, featuring one shipwrecked man asking another, "What's our immigration policy?," as a third man swims toward them. I don't remember 1997 that well, as I was nine, but boy oh boy, did it feel darkly relevant twenty years later. Given that we have, what, five years left before the planet goes kaput due to climate change, even jokes about the weather—the seemingly most neutral conversational fodder of all—have become loaded. Soon it may be unsafe to make jokes about the New York Mets (*toi toi toi*—spit three times).

But back to the first-bluebird-of-spring conundrum—not all tropes are built to be immortal. William Shawn, *The New Yorker*'s editor from 1951 till 1987, purportedly banned desert island cartoons for at least some of his time as head honcho, and I've heard a grumble or two from David Remnick when I show him too many gags on the illustrious theme in our weekly cartoon meeting.

It's true that, as the years pass, it becomes harder and harder to come up with an original desert island cartoon. The genre, unlike the island, is densely overpopulated. So many things have been done with the island's lone tree—it's been chopped down or refashioned into swings, rafts, and clothing; it's gotten a surveillance camera affixed to it; it's been given a bad haircut.

New Yorker cartoon tropes, at their best, allow a joke to be both timelessly relatable and highly specific to its time (consider the evolving outfits, topics of conversation, quirks of vernacular speech, and dynamics between the sexes on our otherwise little-changed isle). While bluebirds may migrate away (don't fact-check that), for now, at least, the desert island seems to be staying put. Maybe soon—or even between the writing of this and the book's publication—the desert island will stop connoting quarantine and isolation. Maybe desert island cartoons will start to be about all of the tropical vacations we're going to go on, just as soon as it's safe. As I imagine such a thrilling, mask-tan-line-less future, I am reminded of an old Chon Day desert island cartoon. A woman and man sit huddled beneath the signature palm tree as rain pours down. The woman says, "I hope it clears up for the weekend."

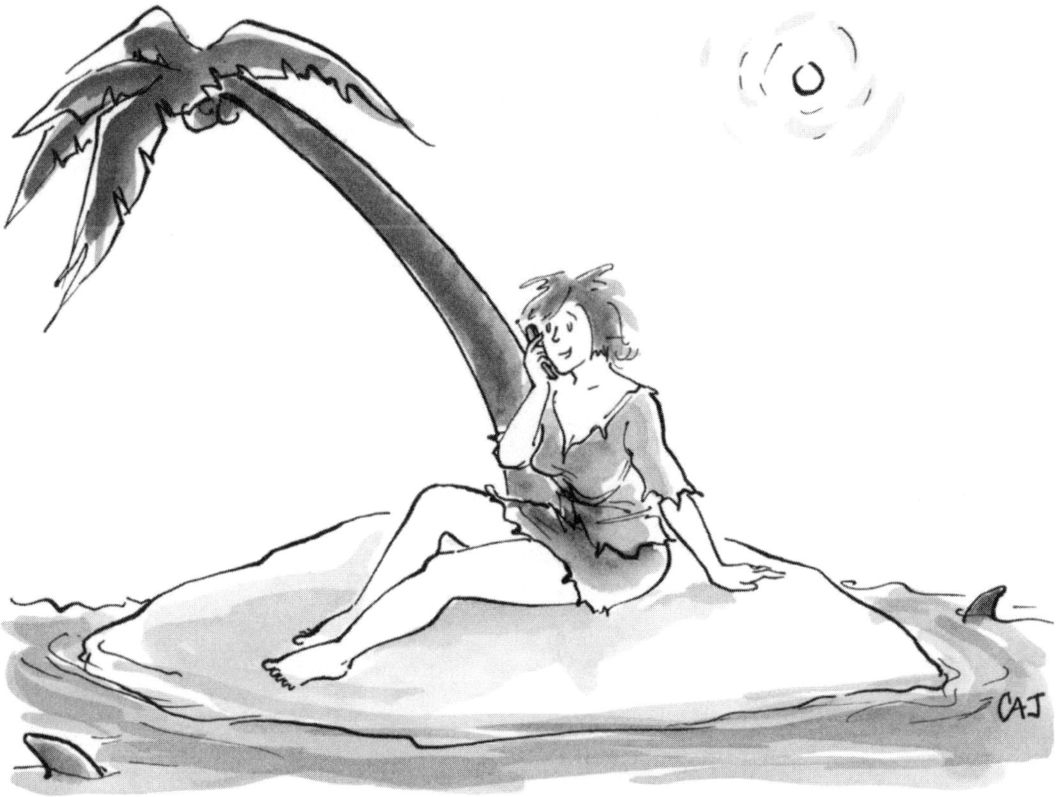
CAJ

"Wait—I almost forgot why I called."

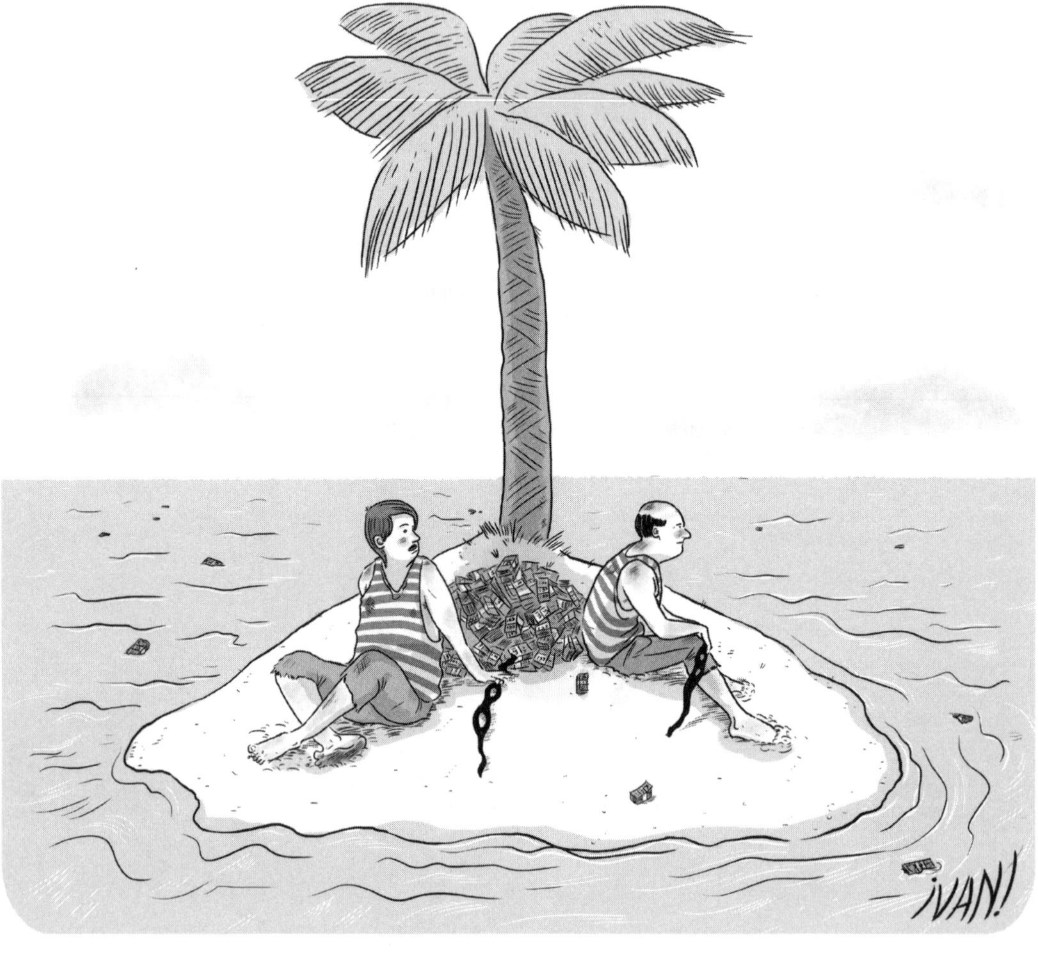
¡VAN!

"In my defense, we did technically get away with it."

"But enough about me..."

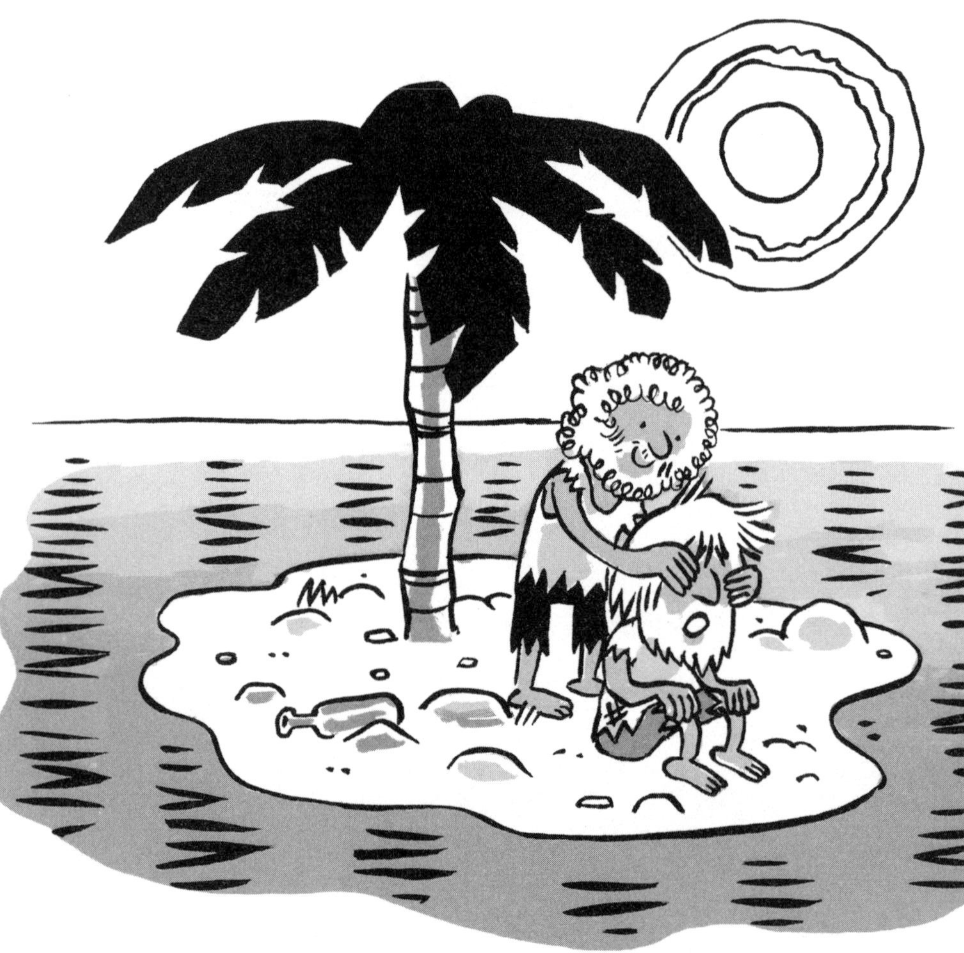

"I give up, who?"

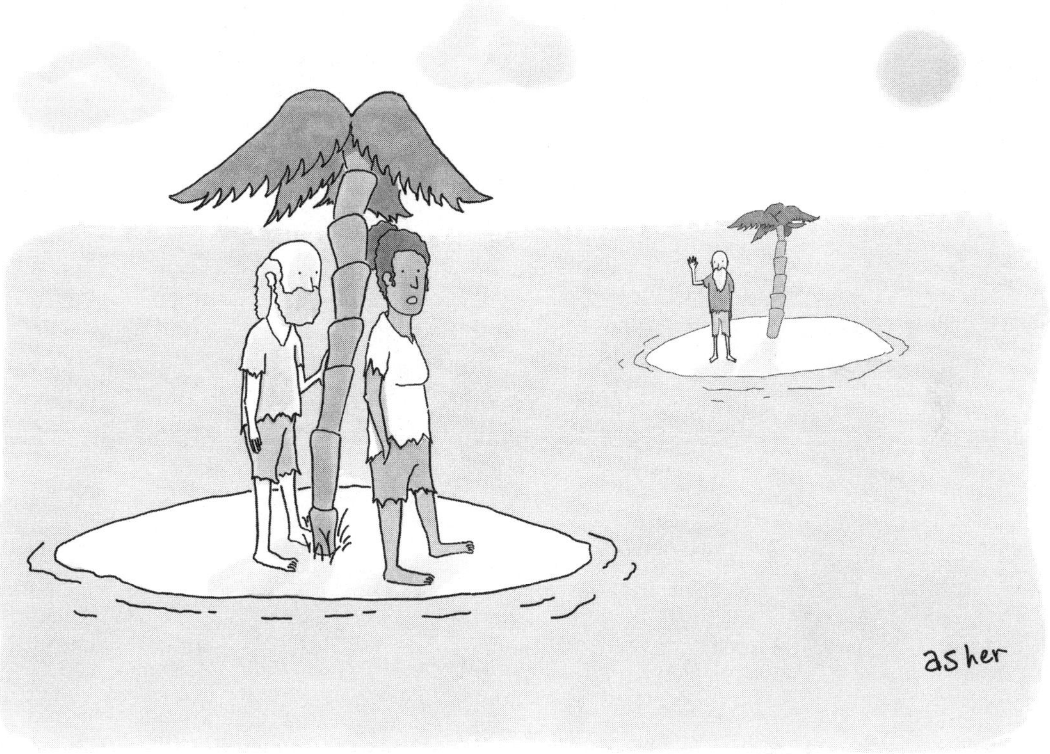
asher

"Shoot, I can never remember this guy's name."

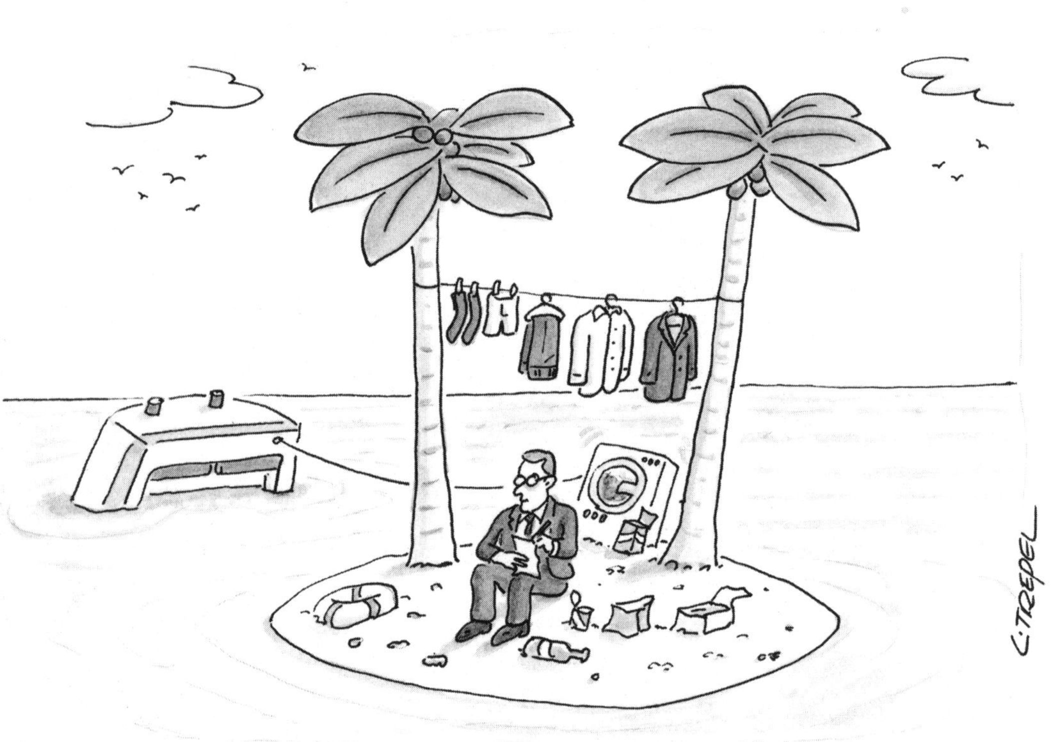
C.TREPEL

"DAY 174: OUT OF FOOD, NO SIGN OF HELP. BUT STILL LOOK GOOD."

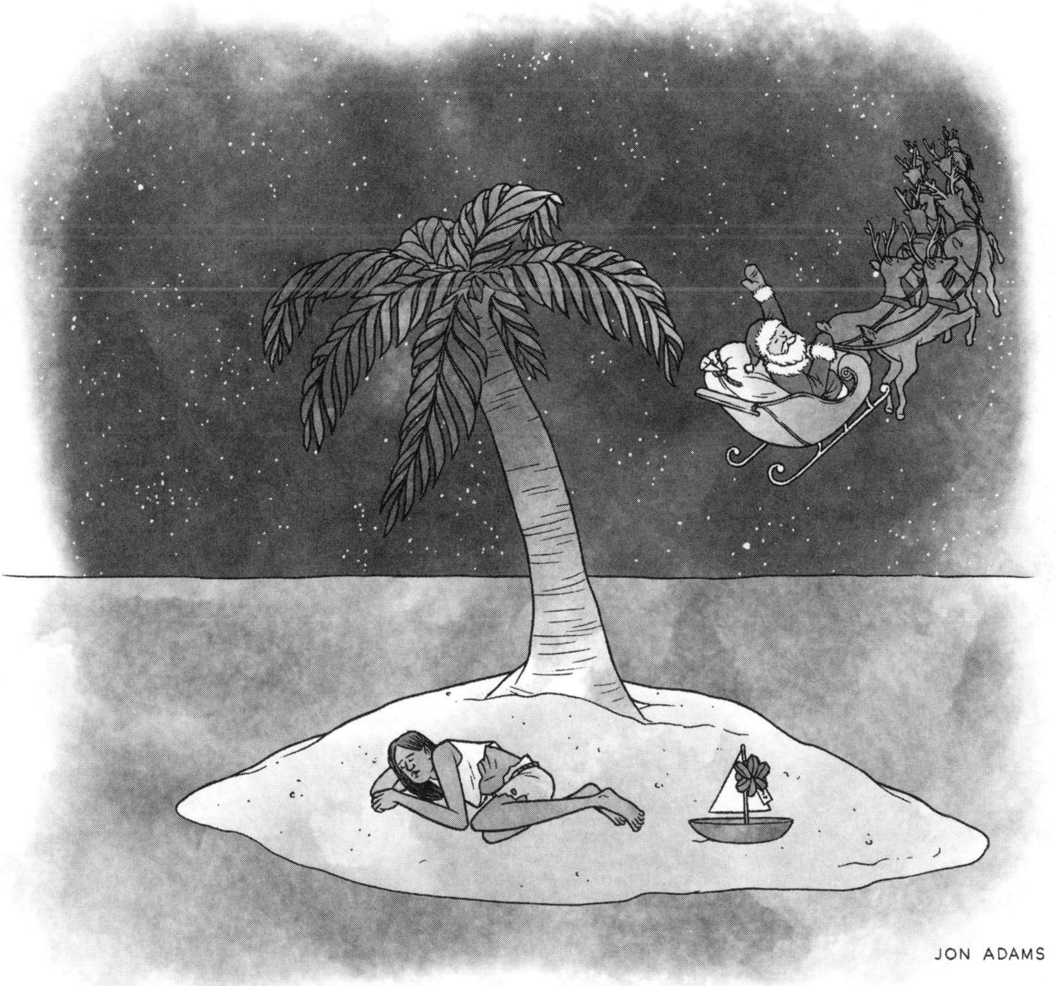
JON ADAMS

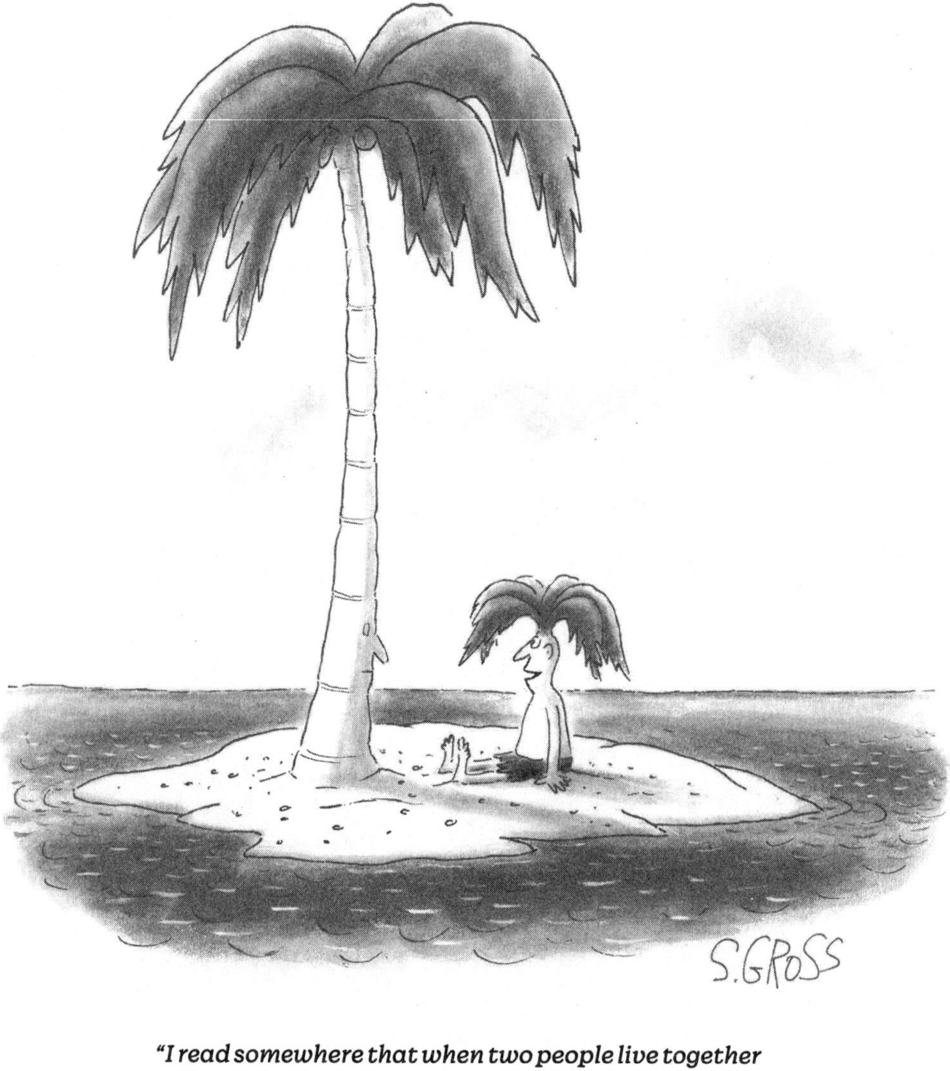
S.GROSS

"I read somewhere that when two people live together for a long time, they start to look like each other."

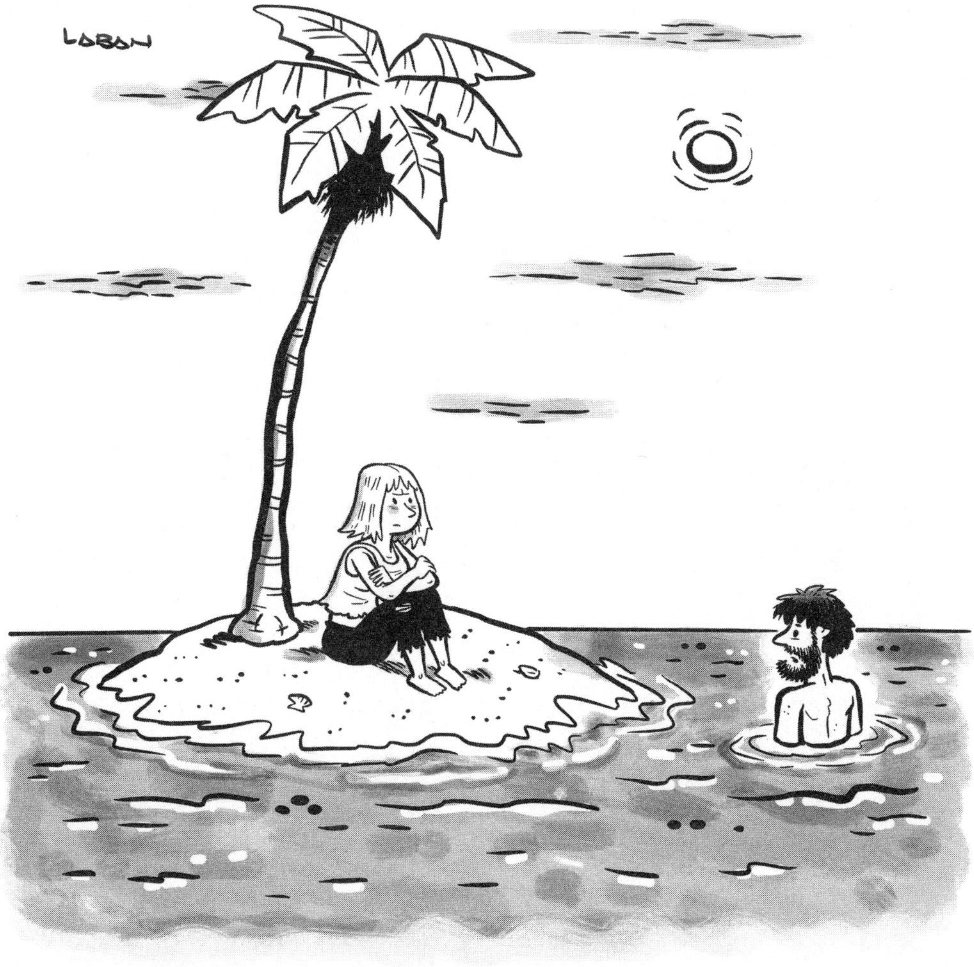
LABAN

"I have issues with commitment."

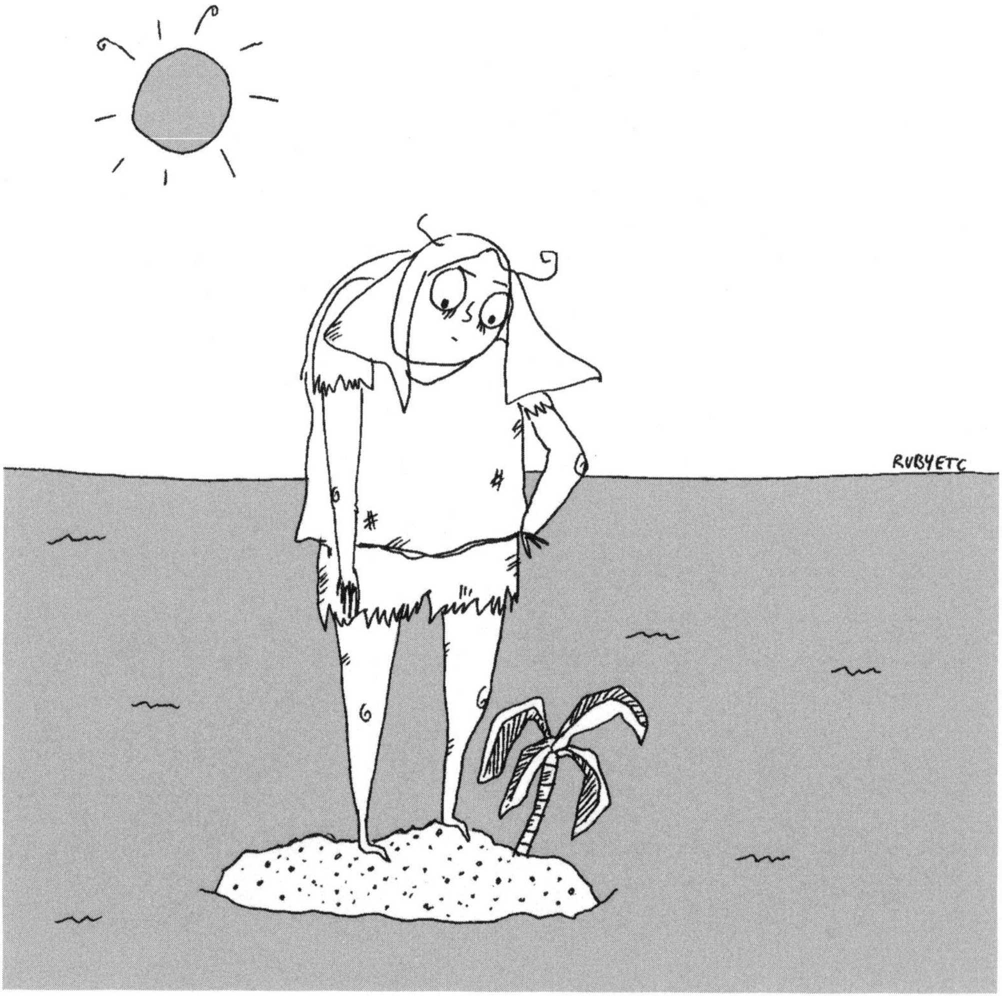
RUBYETC

"It seemed so much bigger when I was a shipwrecked child."

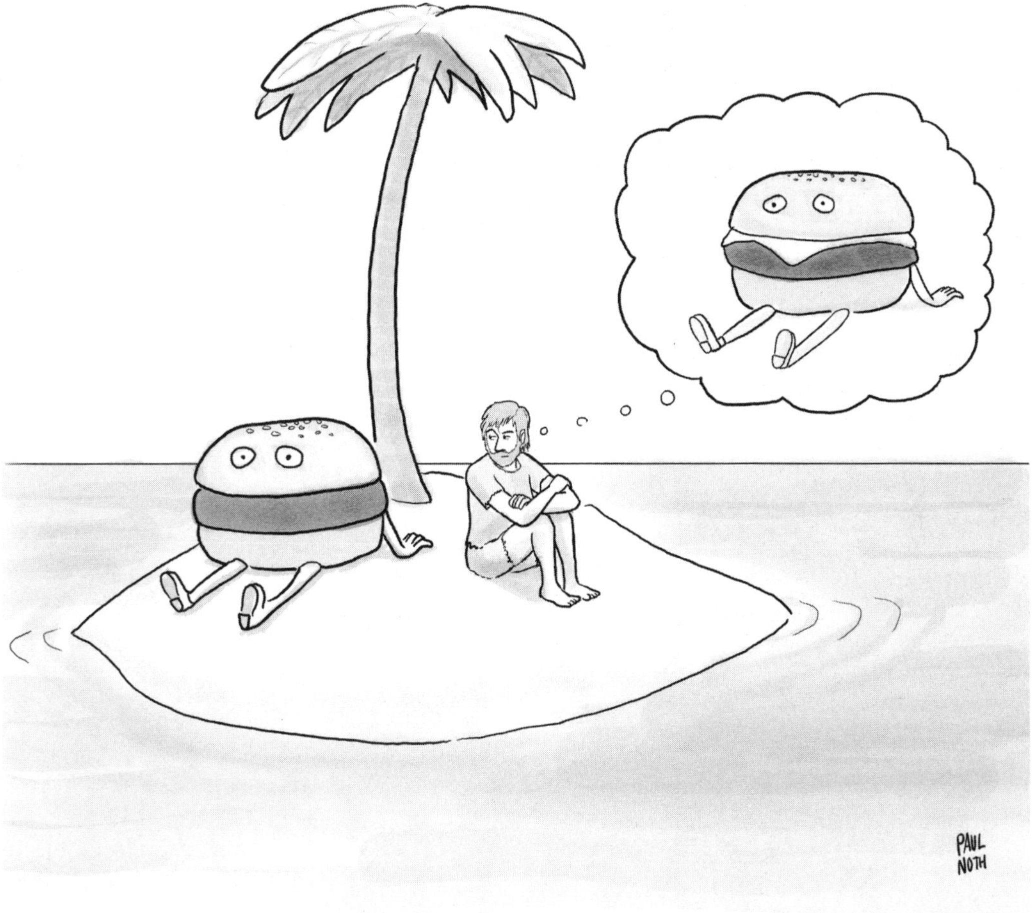
PAUL
NOTH

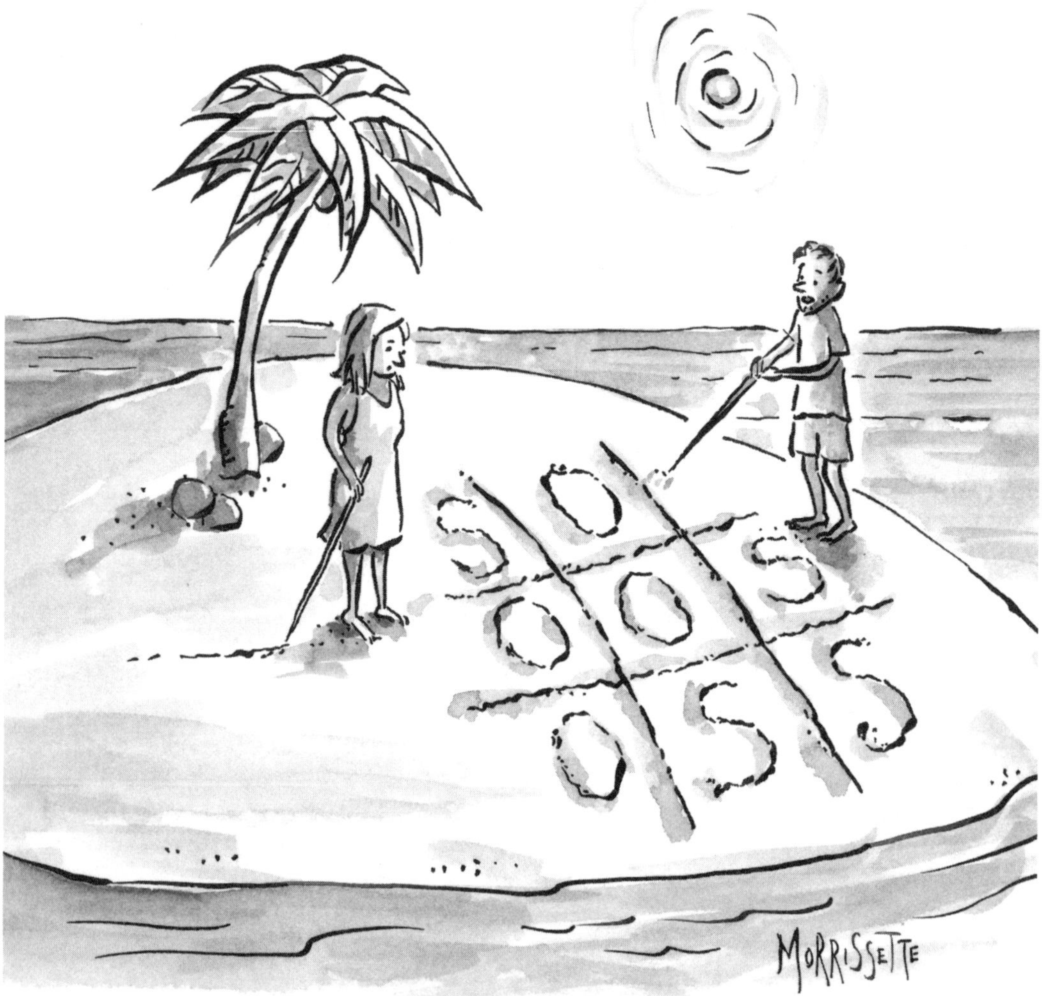
MORRISSETTE

"Do you remember what we were supposed to be doing?"

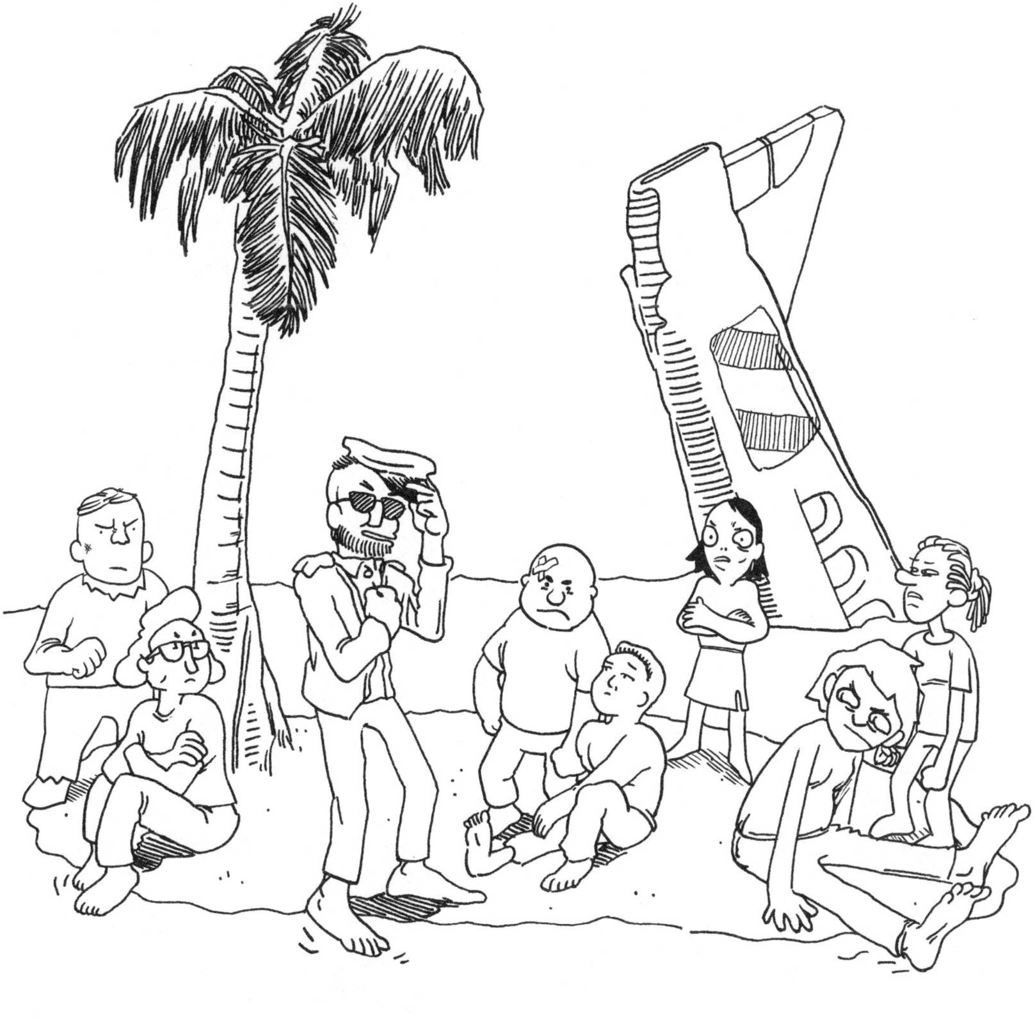

"Ladies and gentlemen, this is your captain speaking. At this time we are beginning our descent into madness."

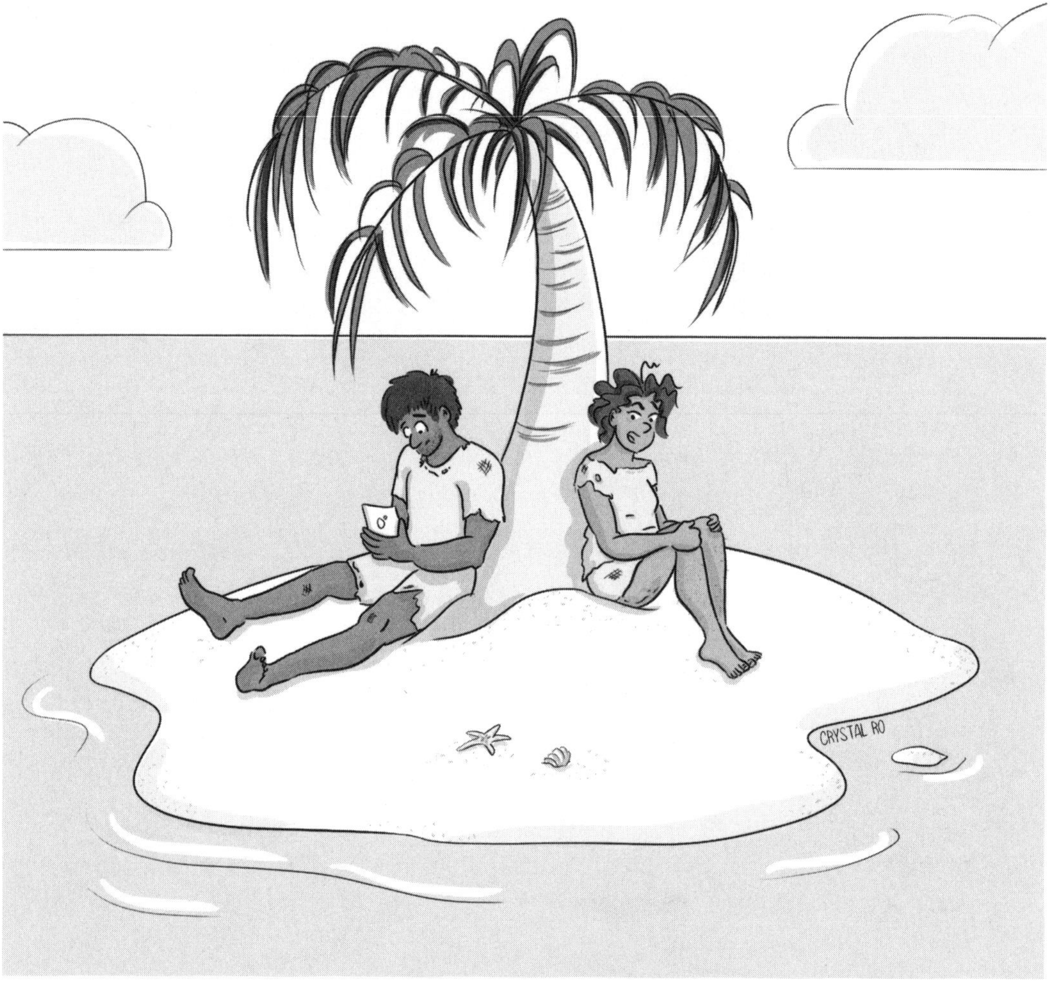
CRYSTAL RO

"Shipping is how much?"

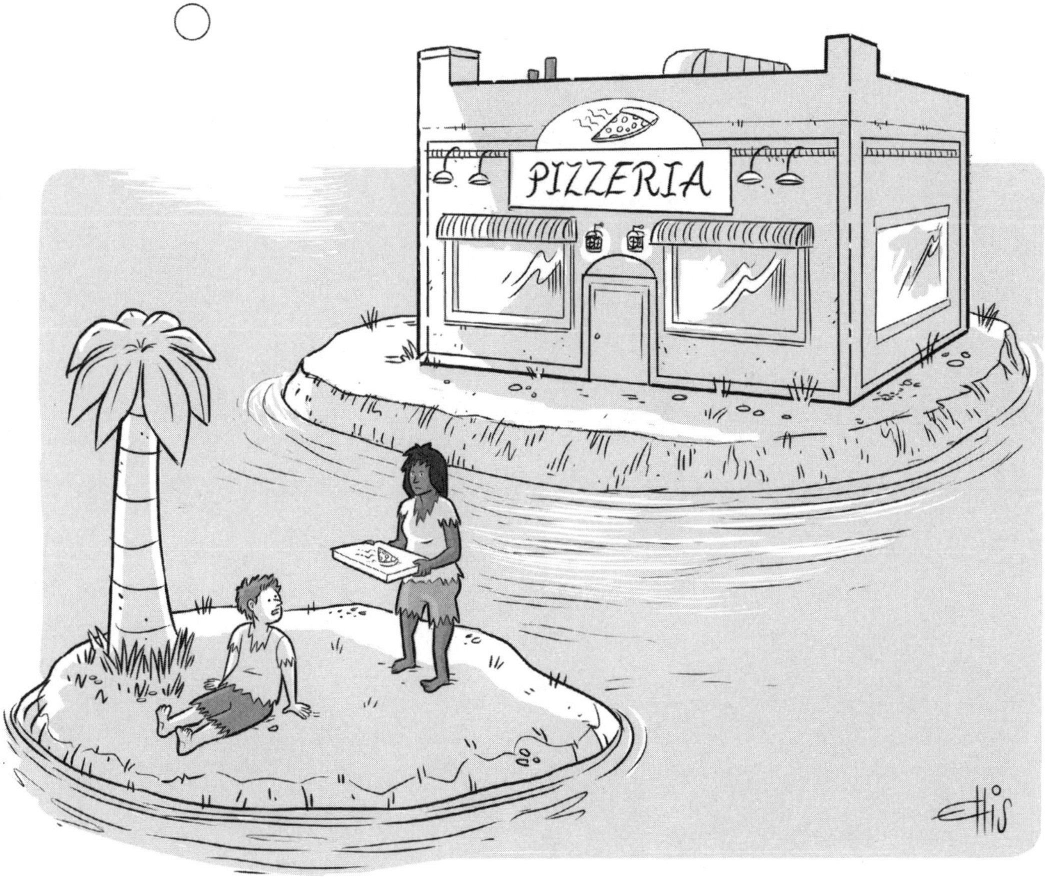
PIZZERIA

"Pizza again?"

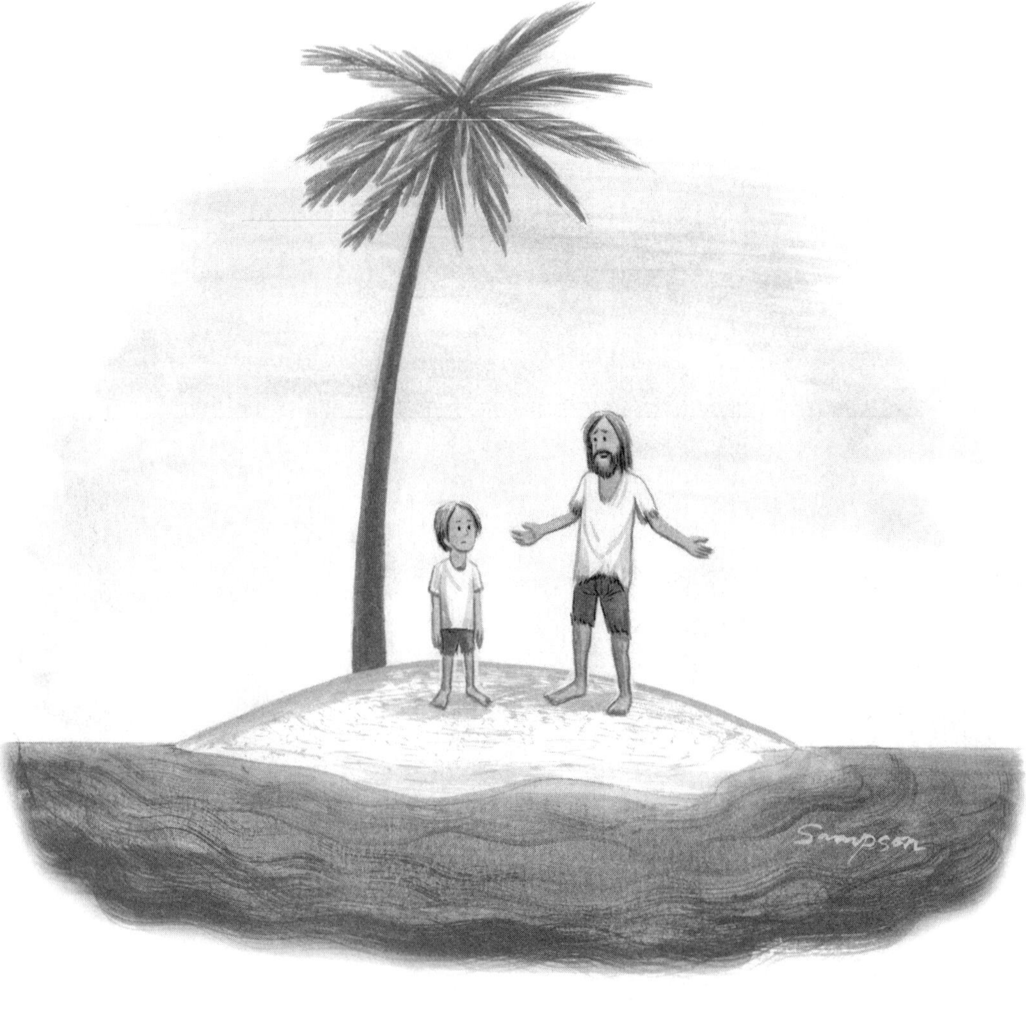
Sampson

"Someday, son, this will be all yours."

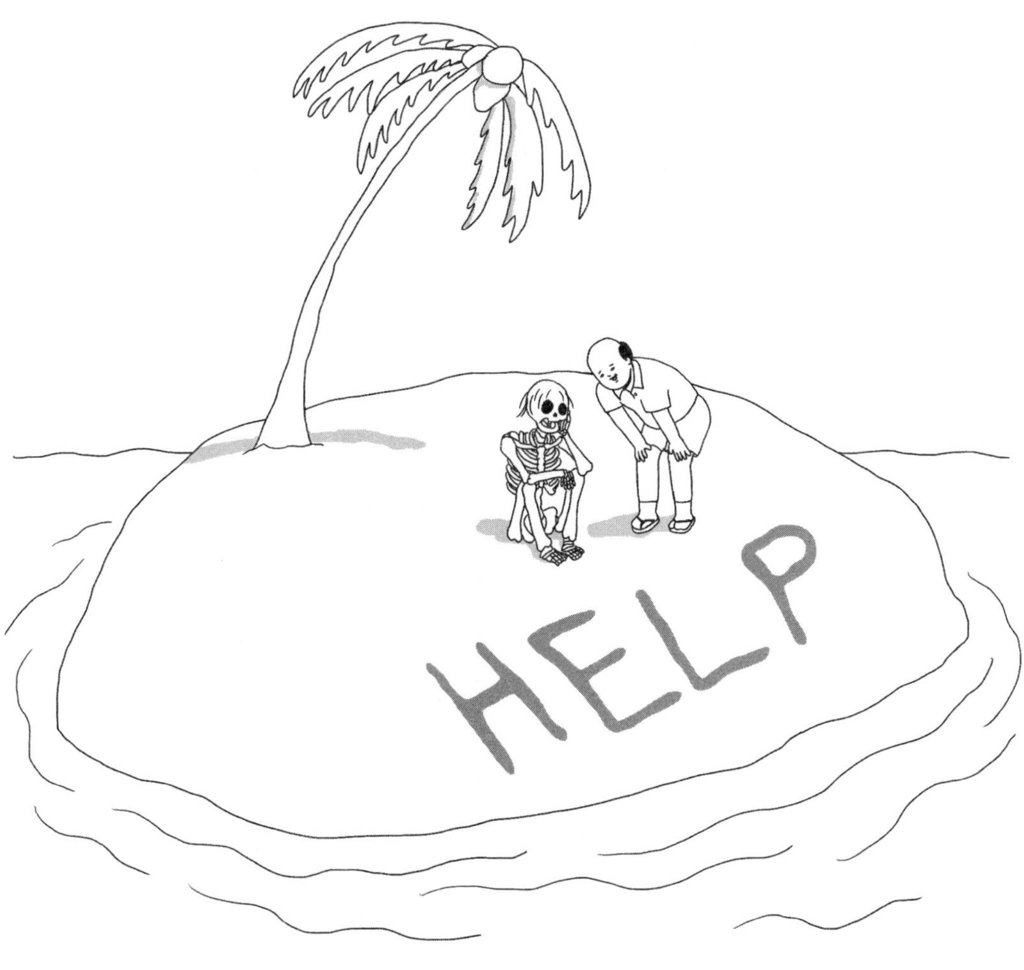
HELP

"Excuse me, sir, is that the wifi password?"

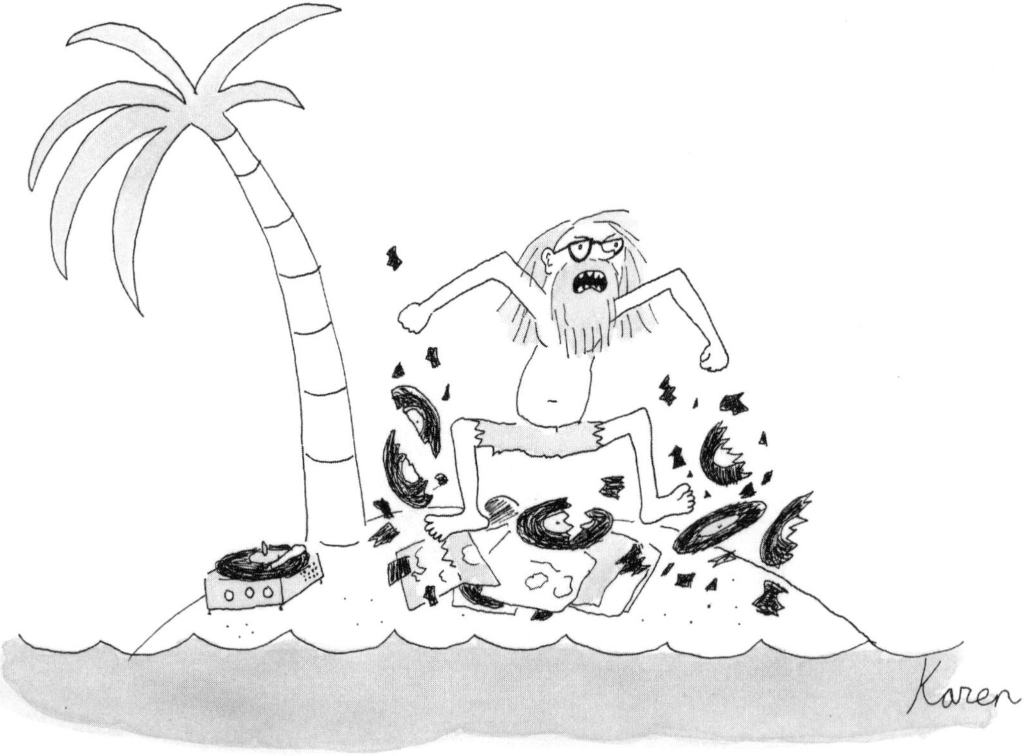
Karen

"Argh, I'm sick of these ten goddamn records!"

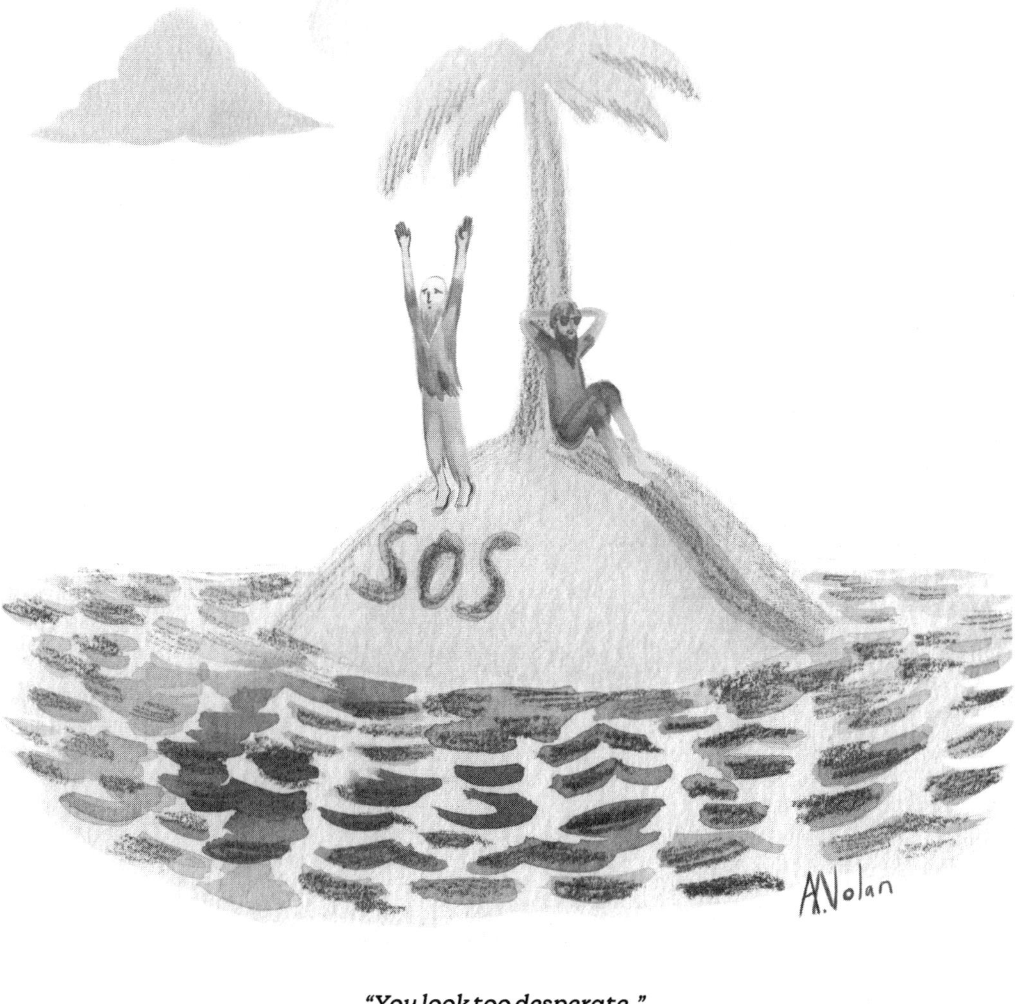
SOS
A. Nolan

"You look too desperate."

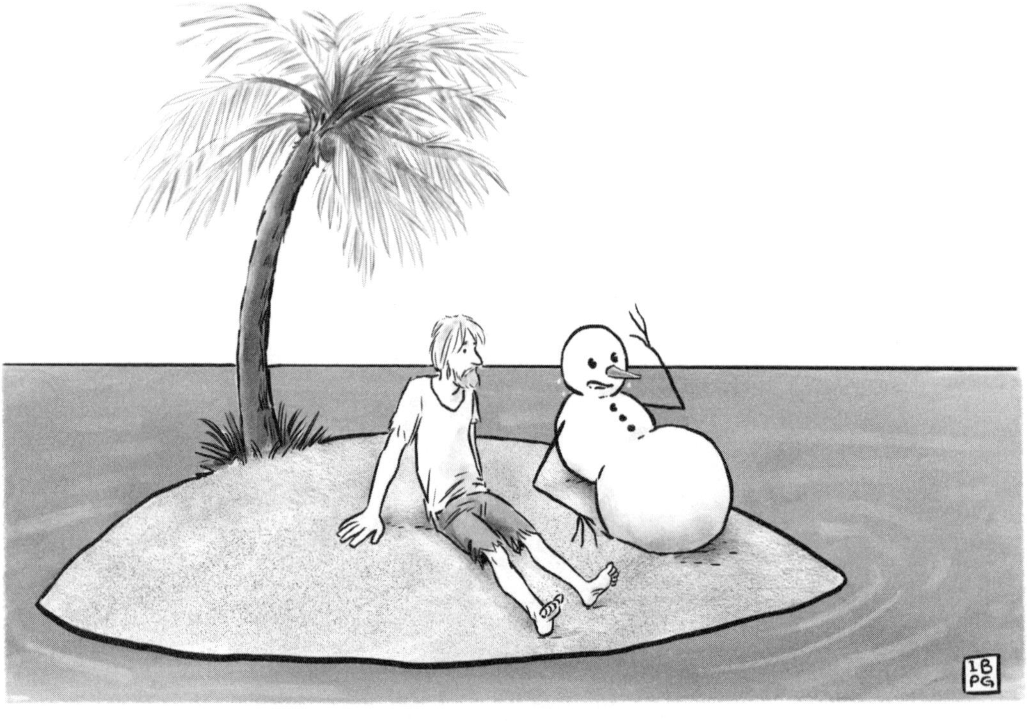
IB
PG

"You think you've got problems!"

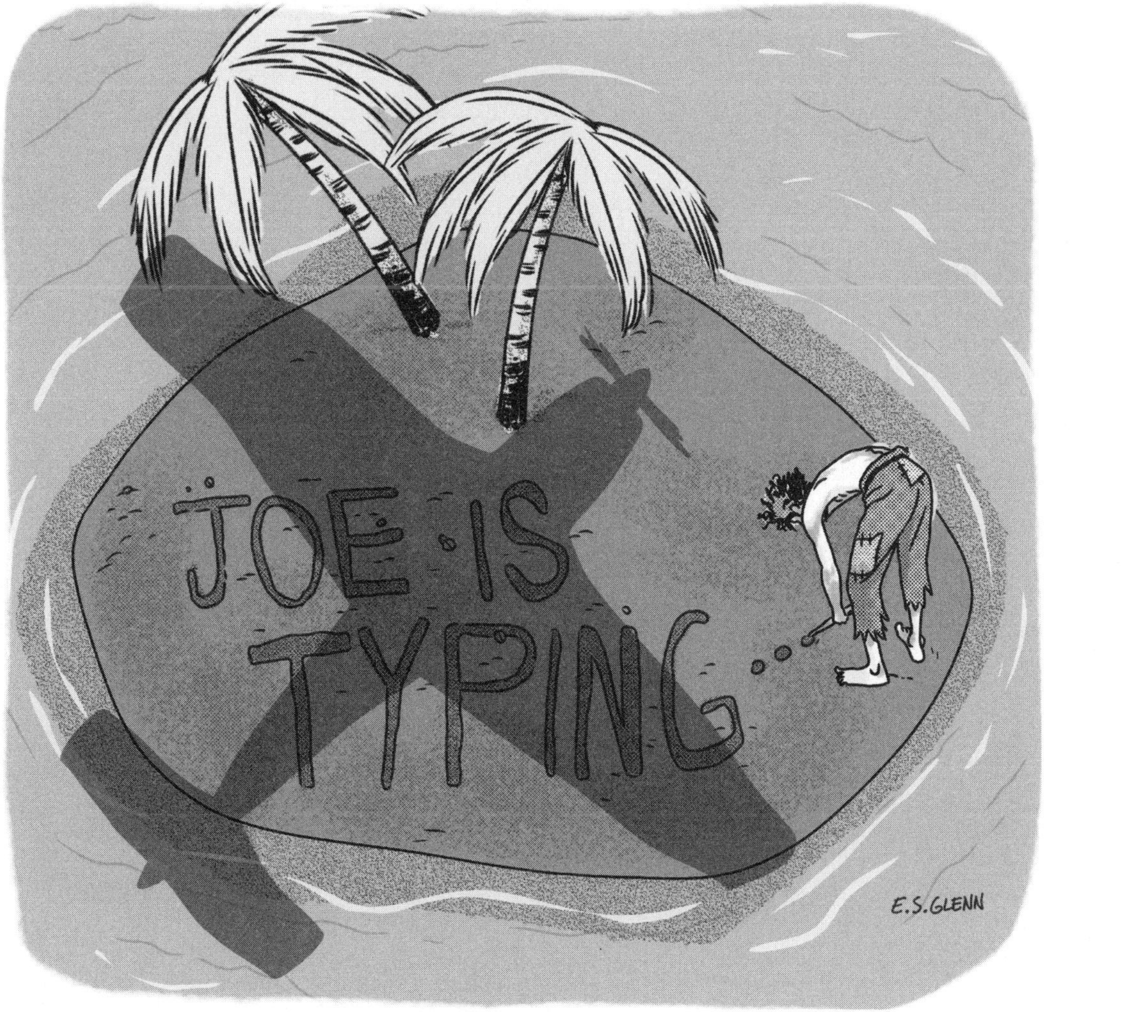
JOE IS TYPING
E.S.GLENN

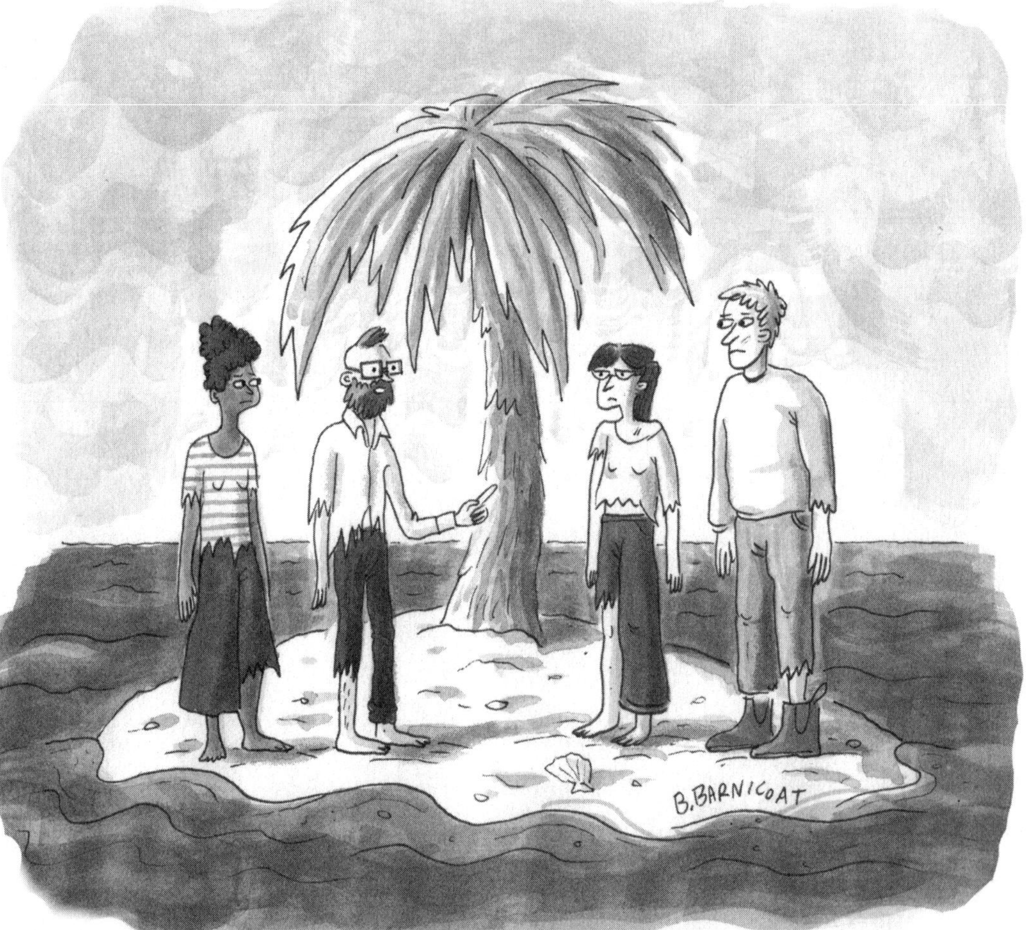
B.BARNICOAT

"So wait—Dana can ferment kombucha, Jason took a spoon-whittling course, I'm a barista, and Lisa has bookshop experience. We're going to be fine."

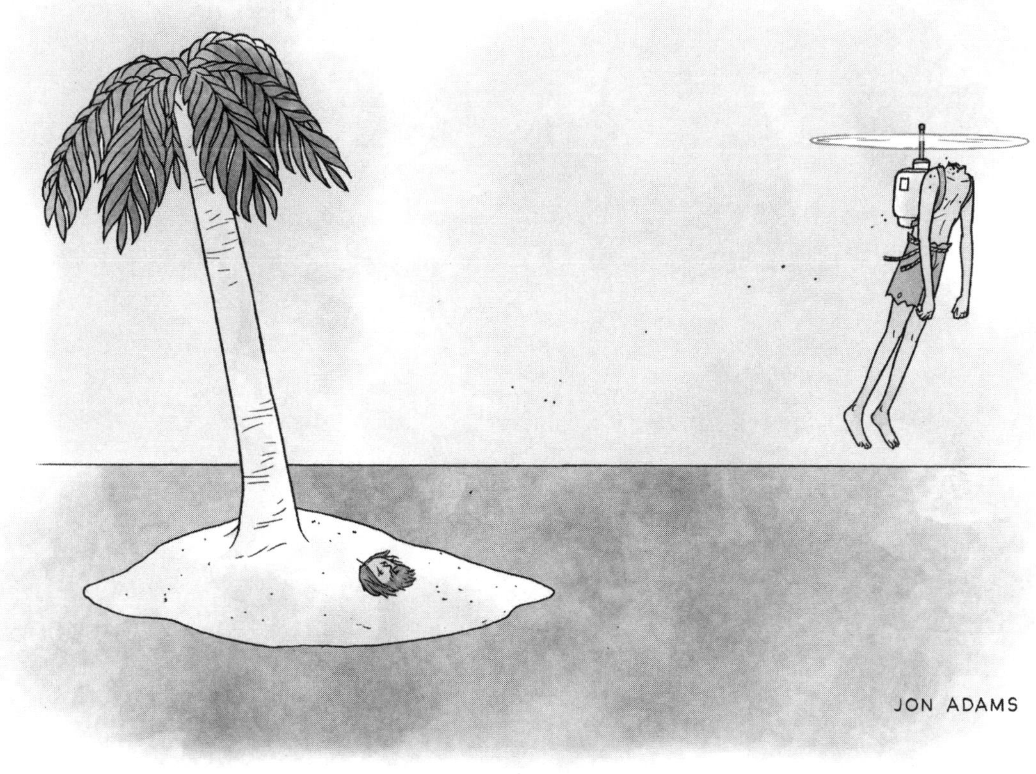
JON ADAMS

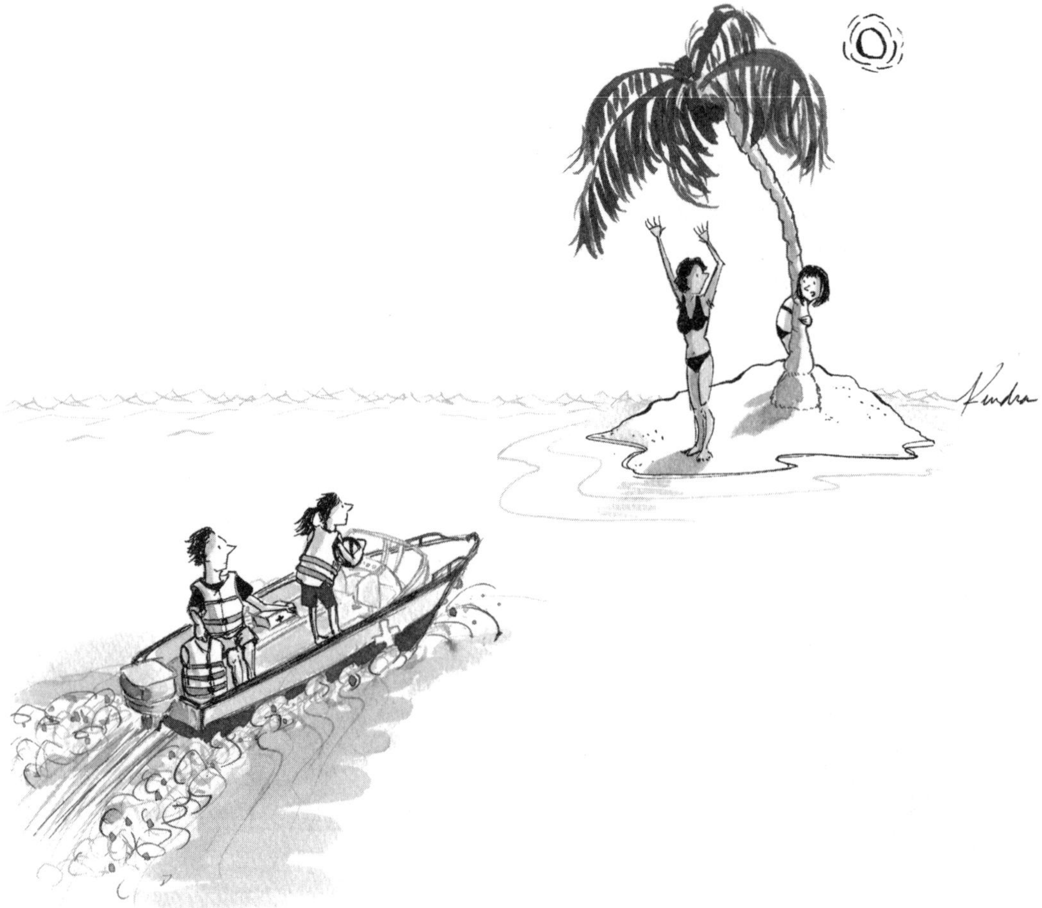
Kendra

"Shoot, I hooked up with that guy once. Just pretend I'm not here."

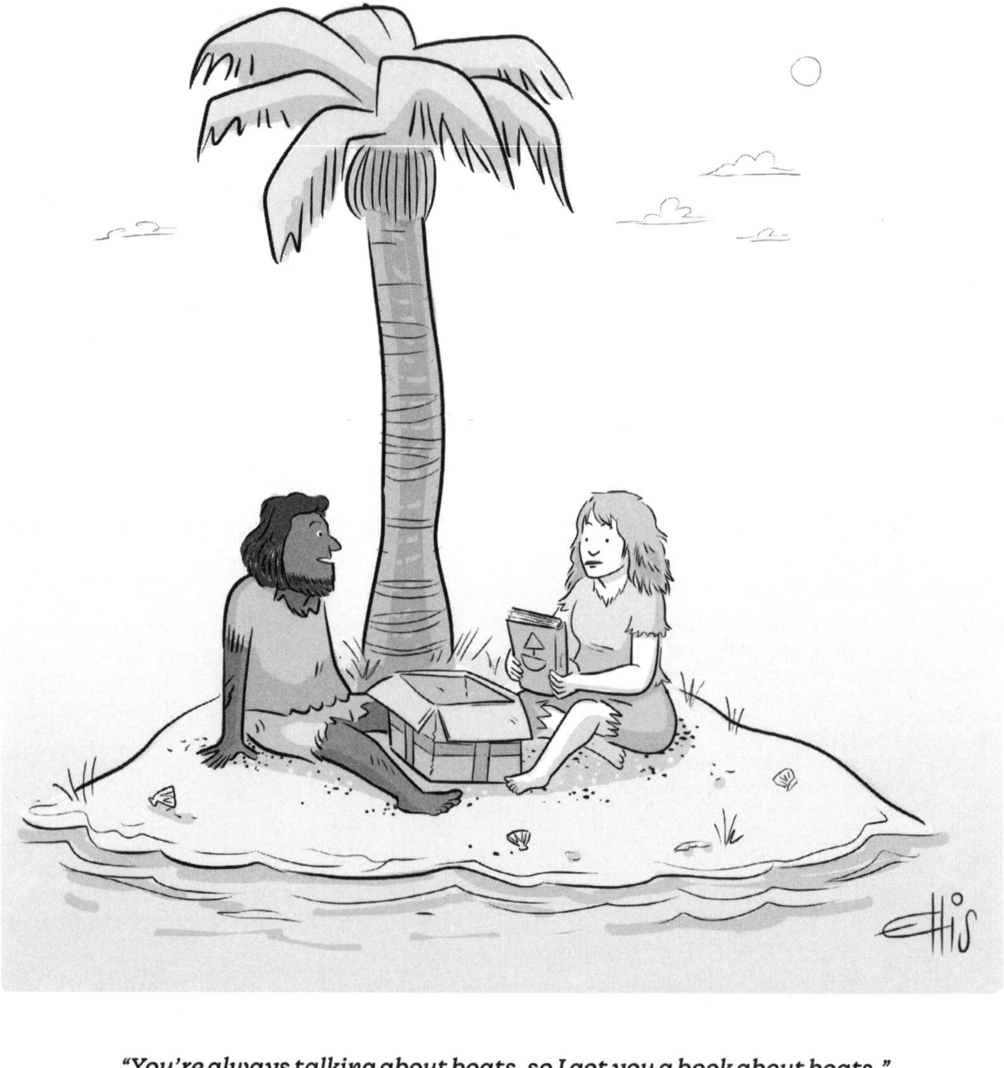

"You're always talking about boats, so I got you a book about boats."

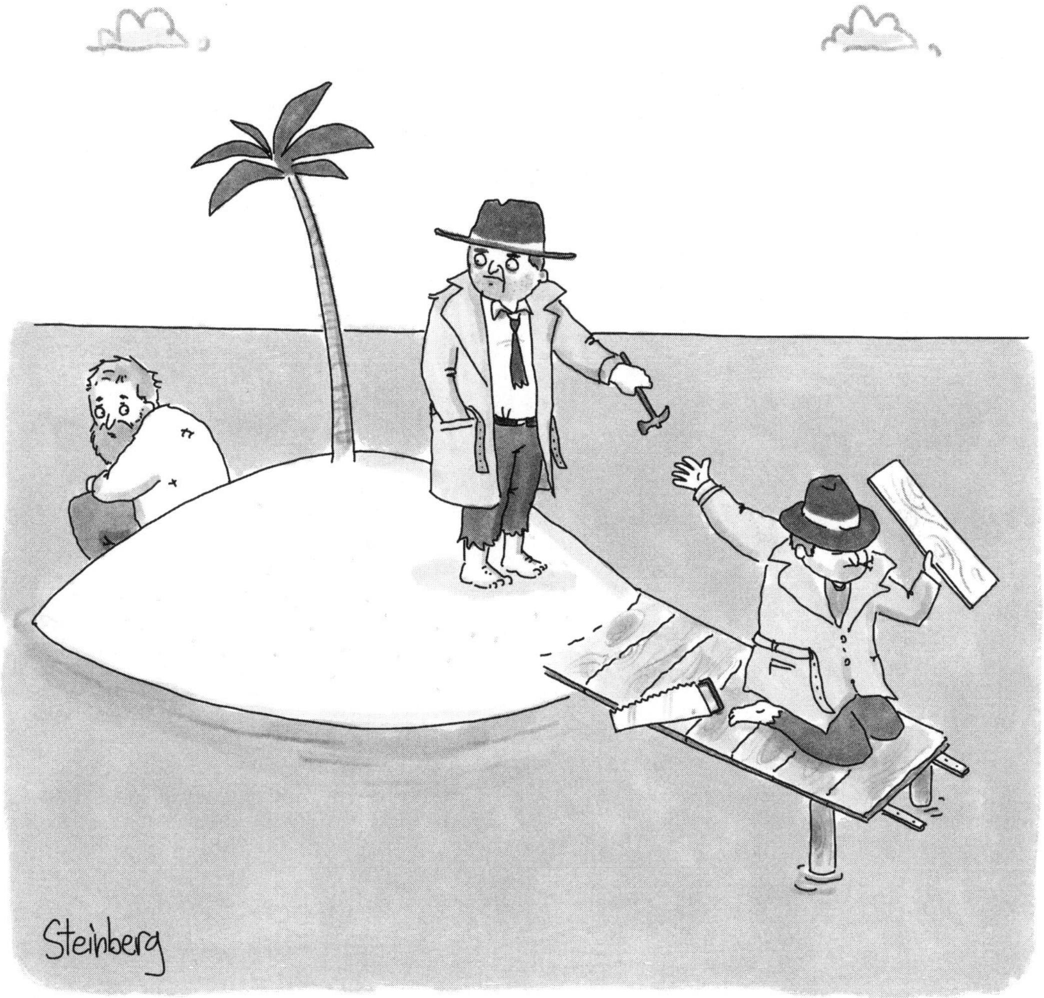
Steinberg

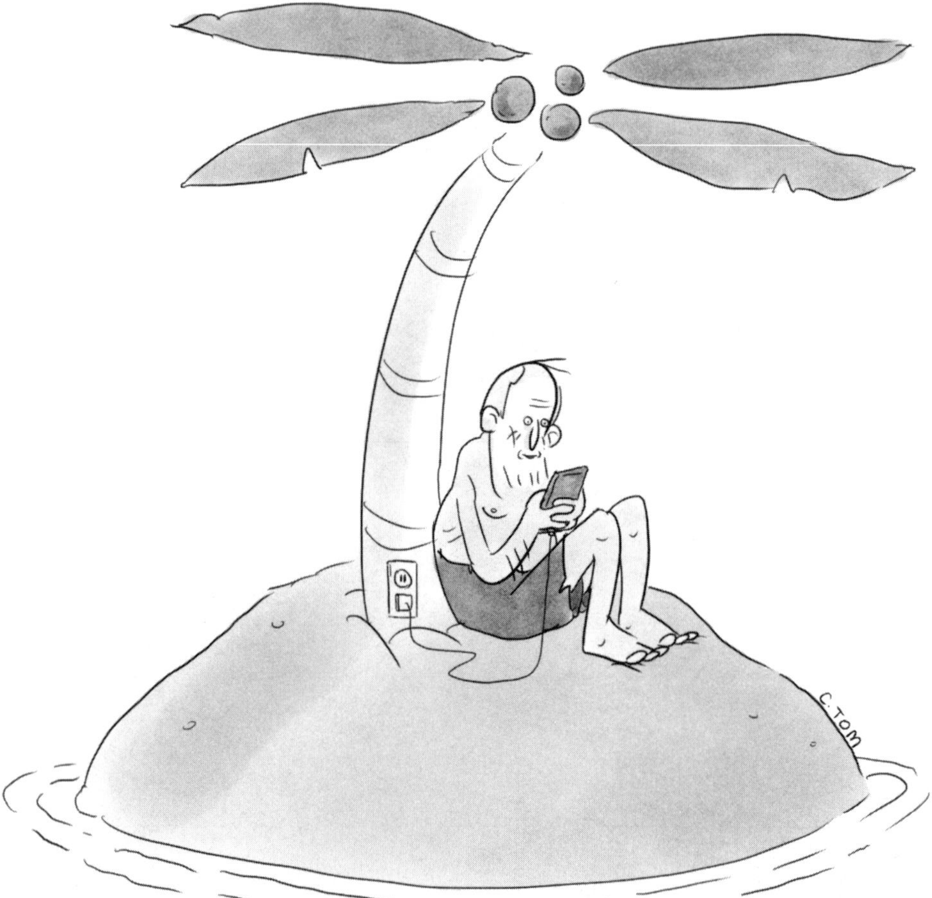
C.TOM

PARADISE

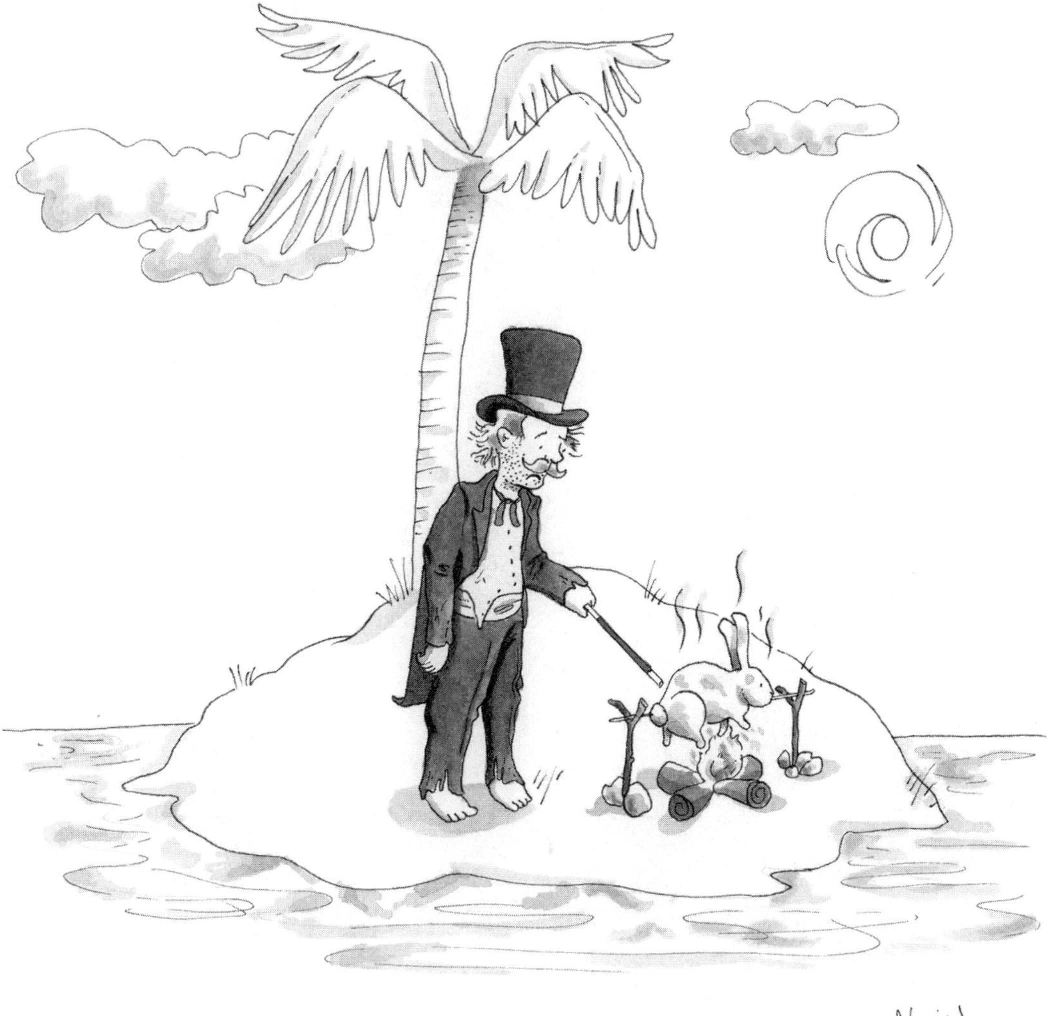
Navied

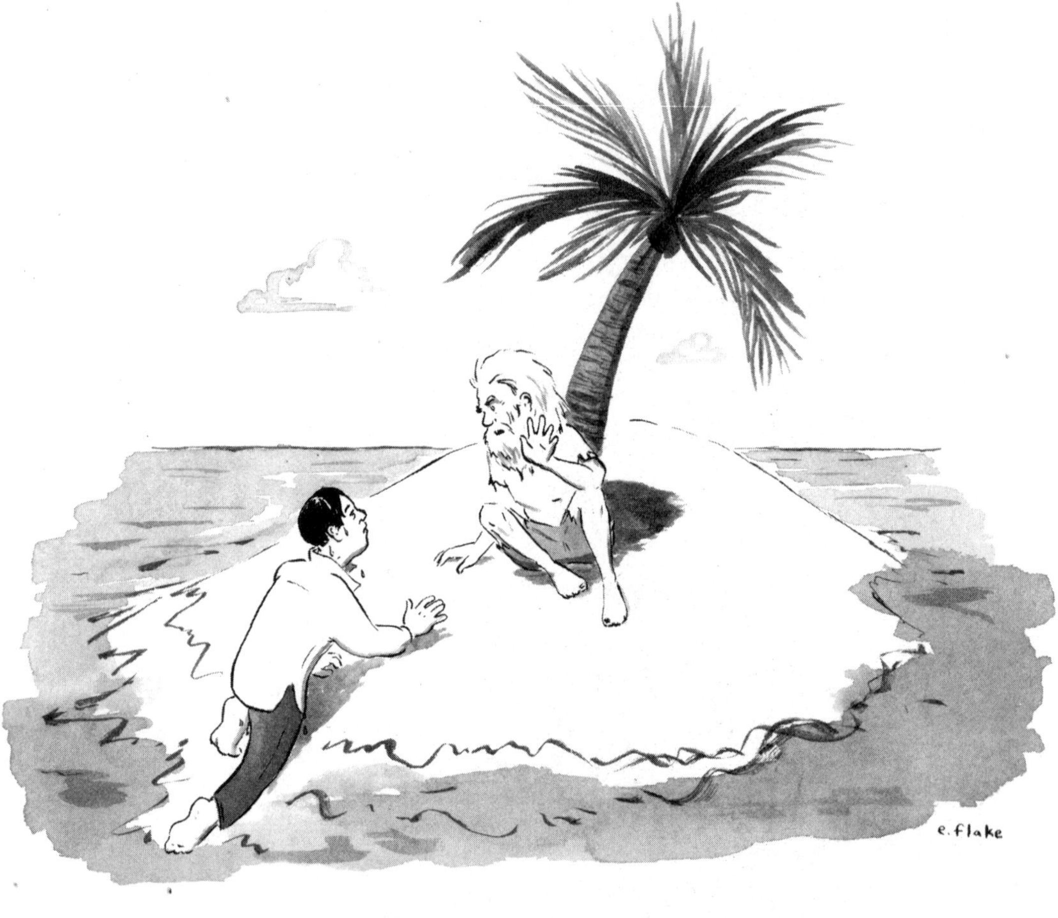
e. flake

"Before you say anything, let me tell you which TV shows I don't want spoilers on."

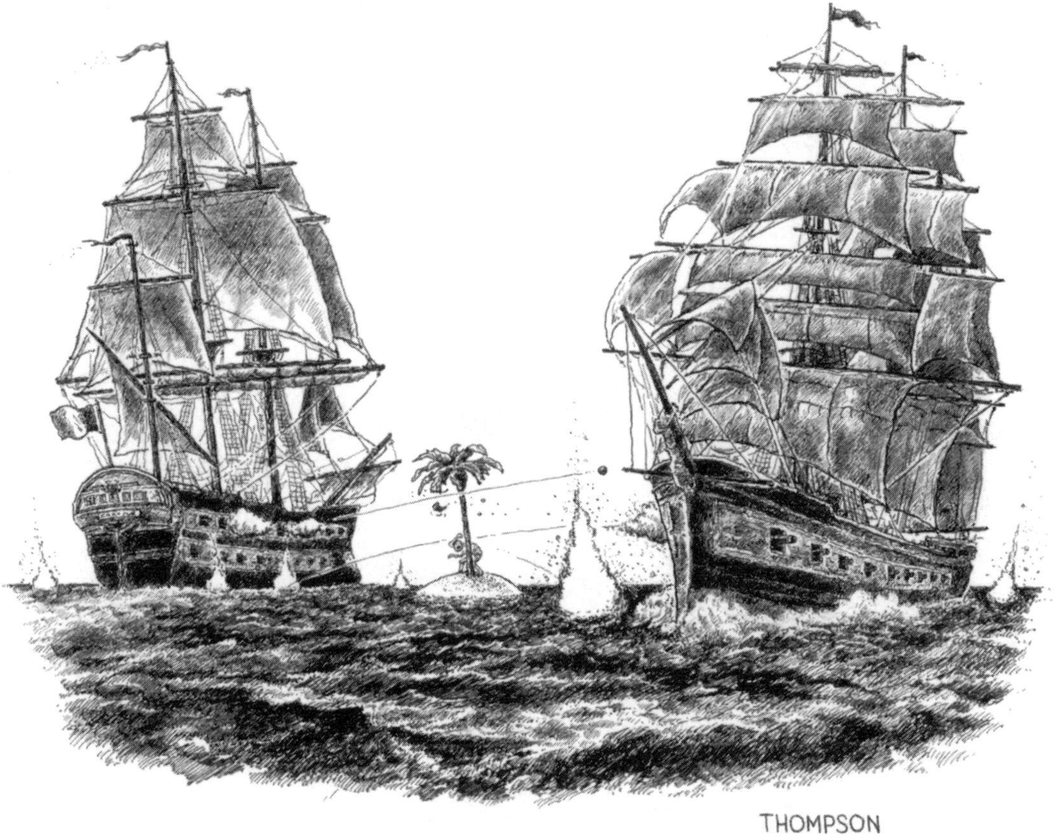

THOMPSON

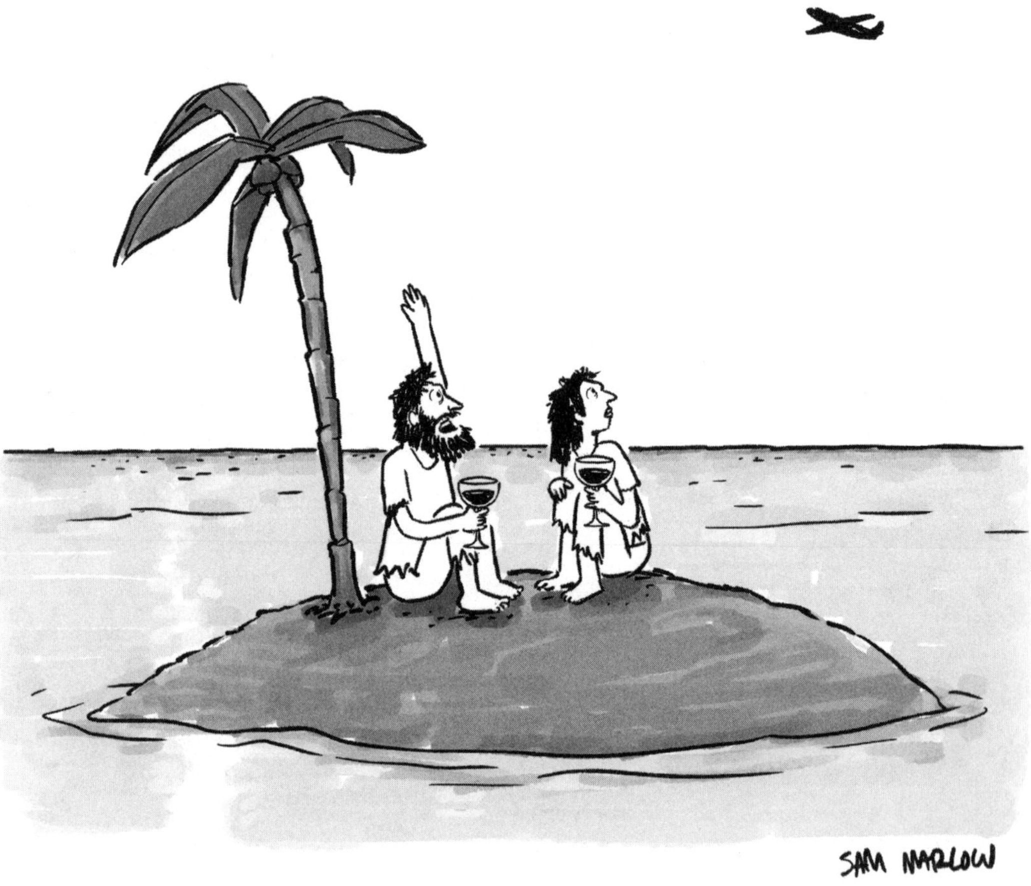
SAM MARLOW

"Send anecdotes!"

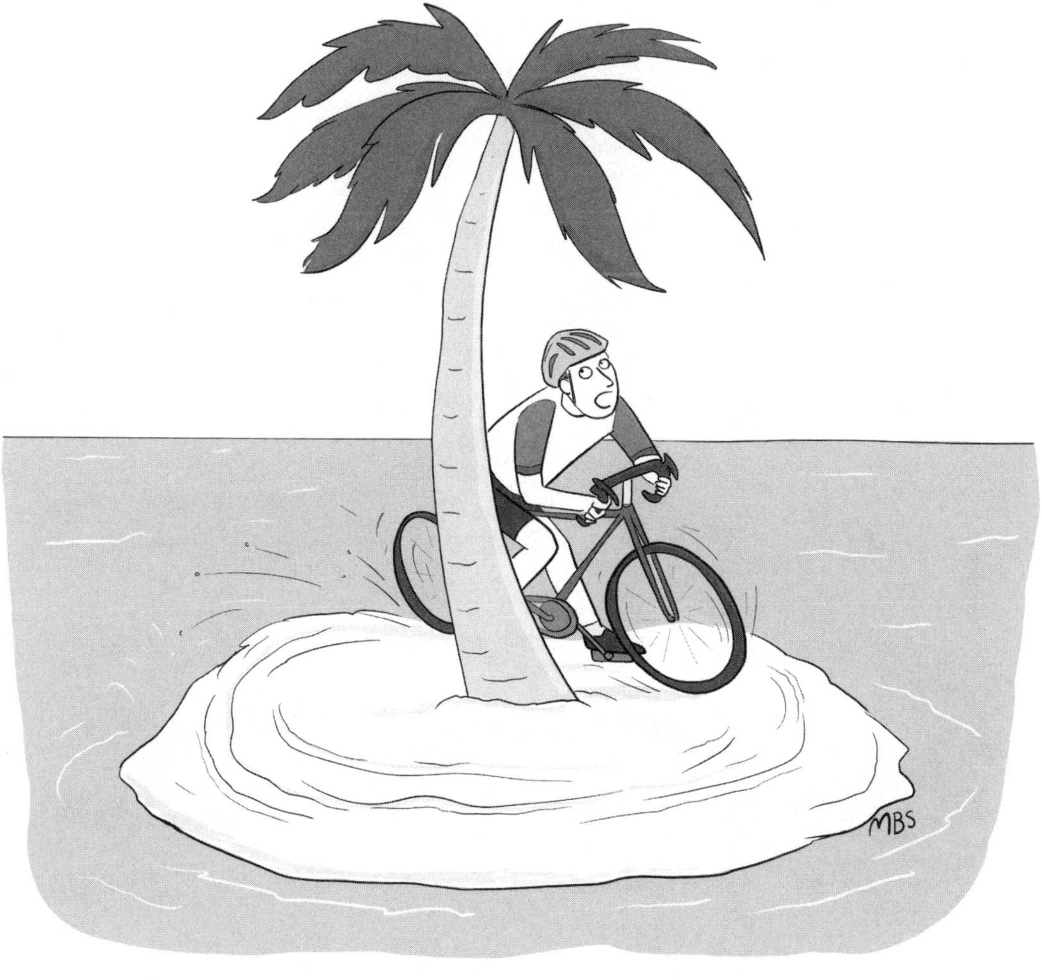
MBS

"And again on your left."

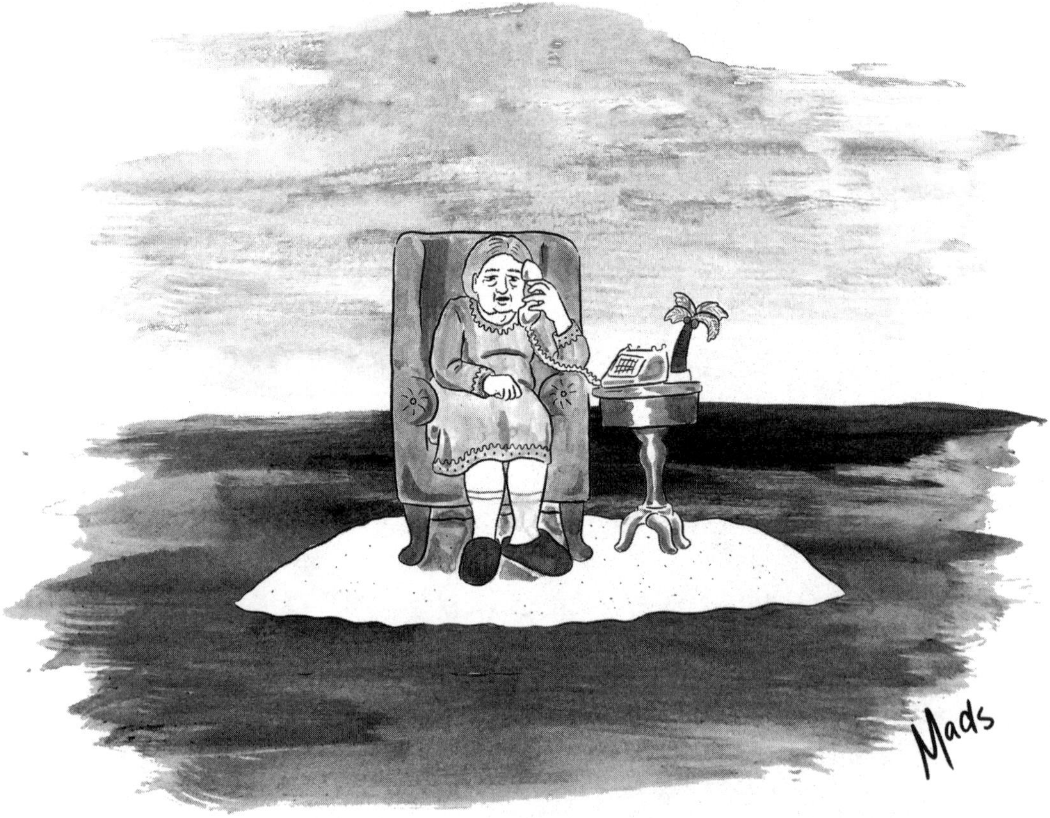
Mads

"No, no, you don't need to rescue me. I'll just stay here and sunburn to death."

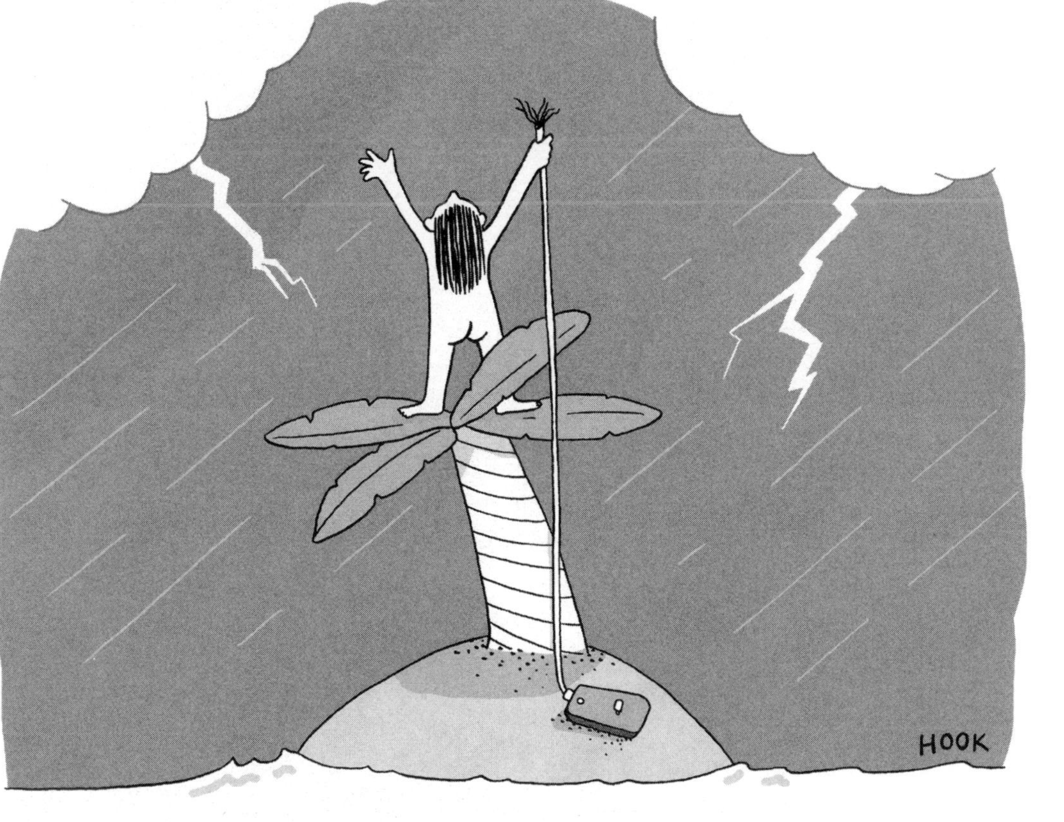
HOOK

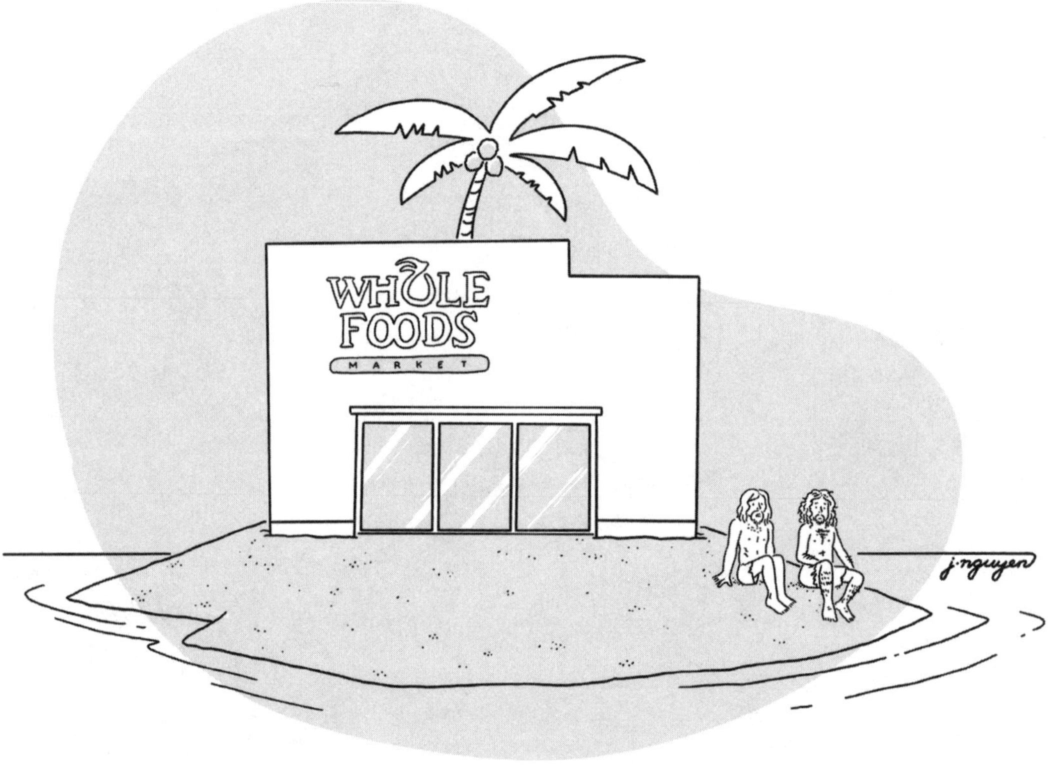
WHOLE FOODS
MARKET
j. nguyen

"We can't afford to be stranded here anymore."

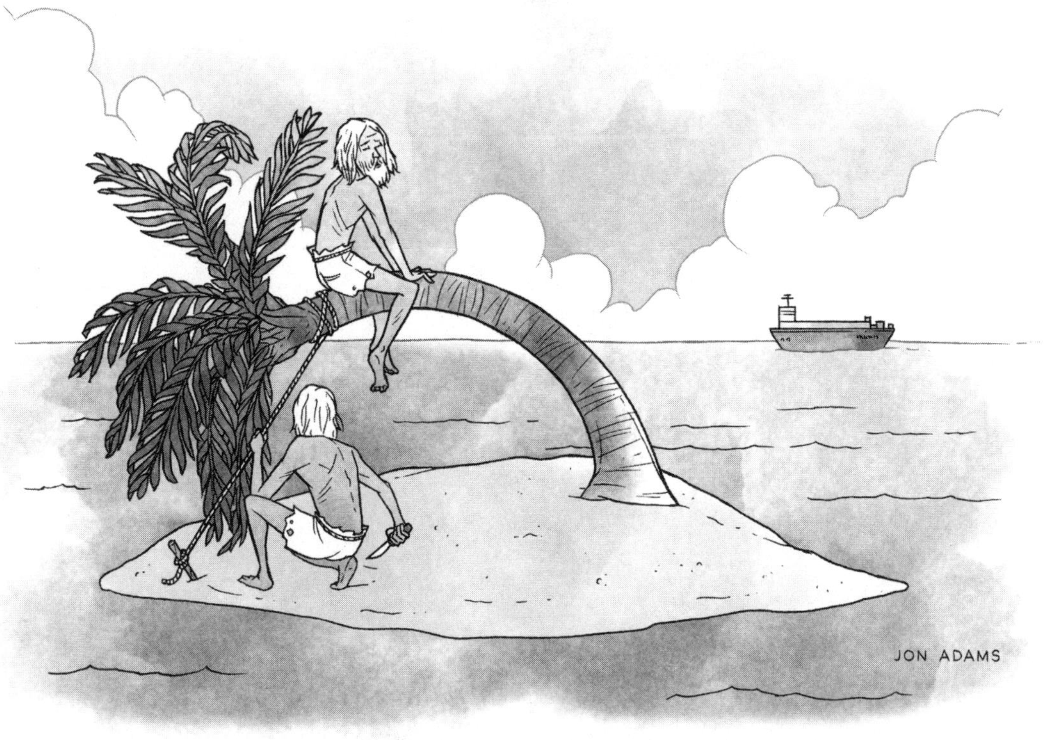
JON ADAMS

"If I don't come back for you, it's because our friendship was one of circumstance."

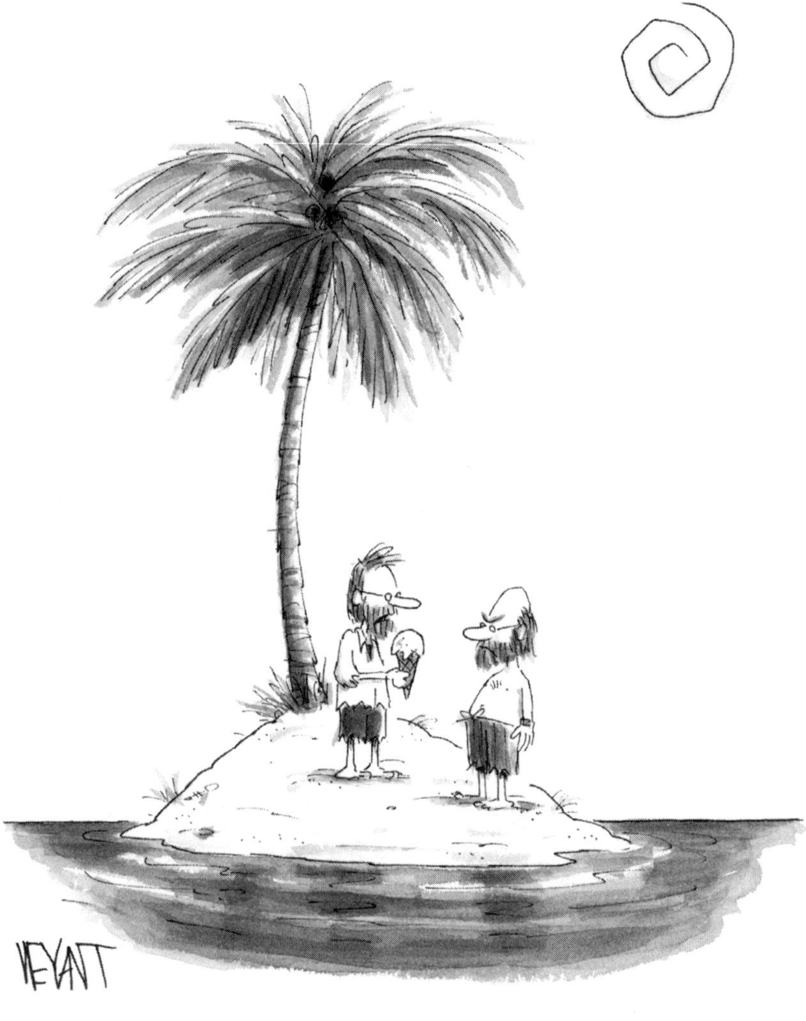

"Why, did you want one?"

bob

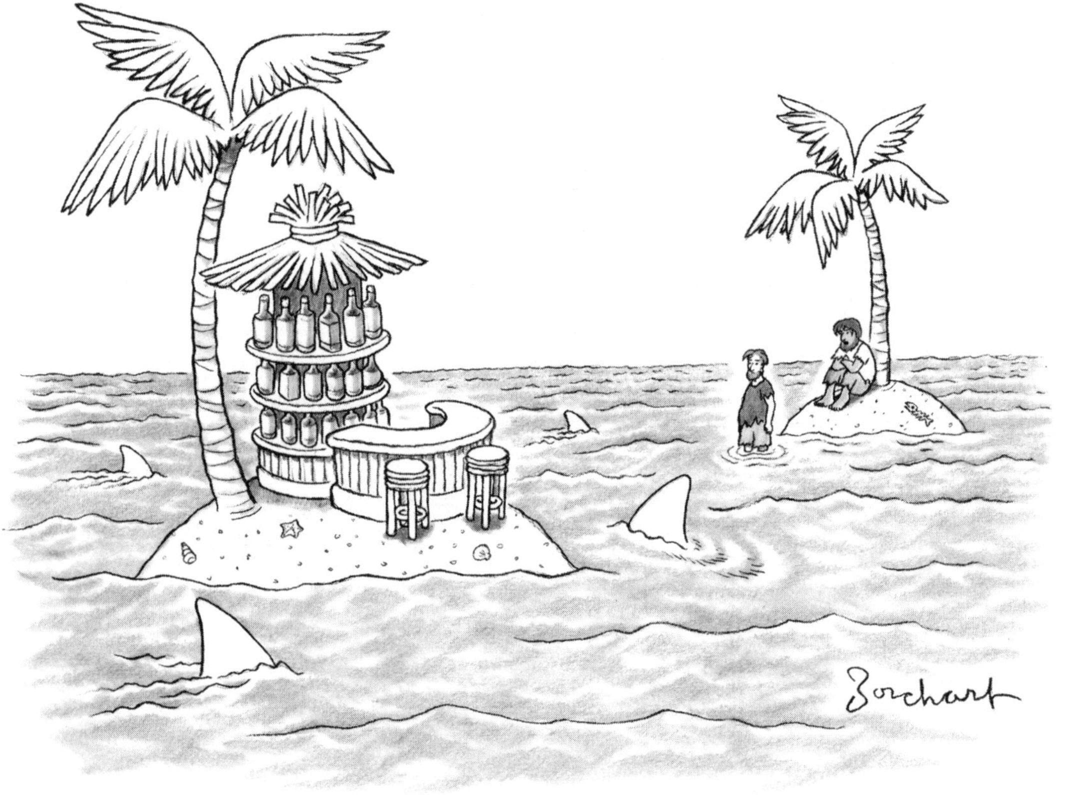
Borchart

"Keep in mind that it was put there by the sharks."

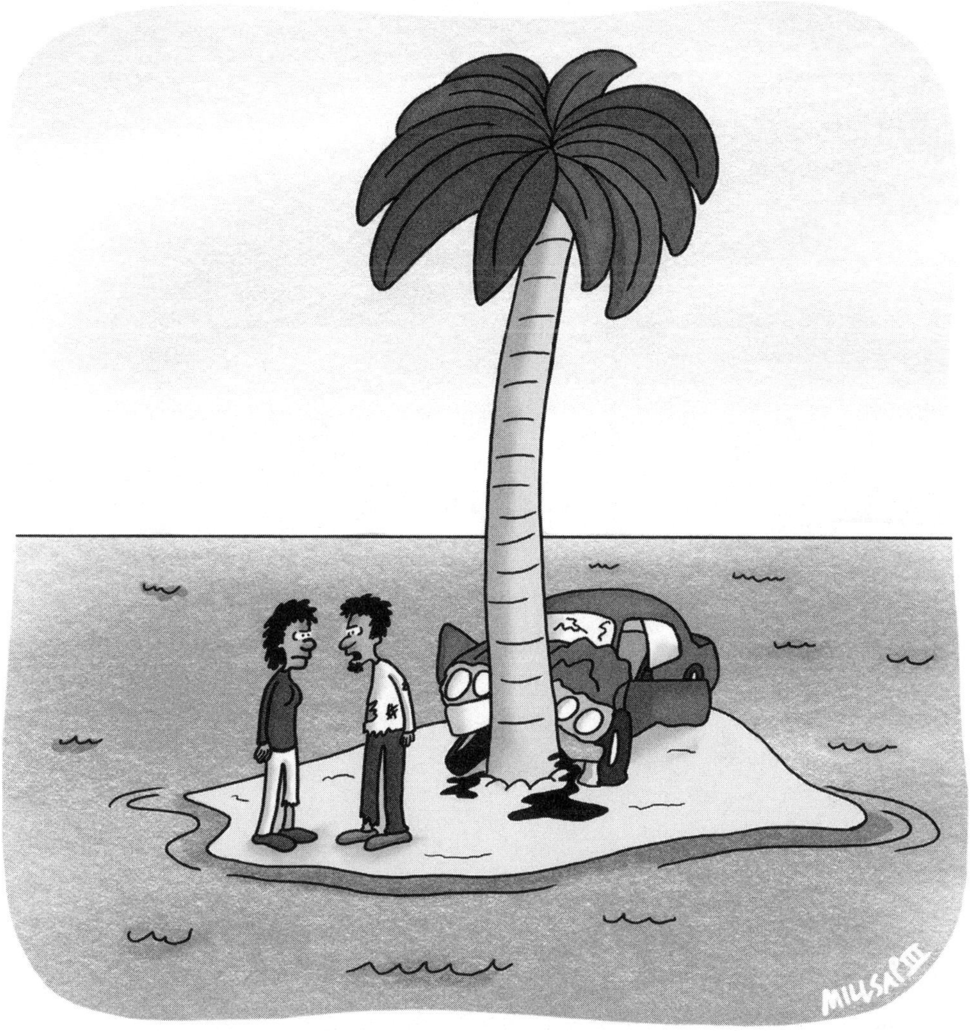
MILLSAP III

"I just looked down for a second."

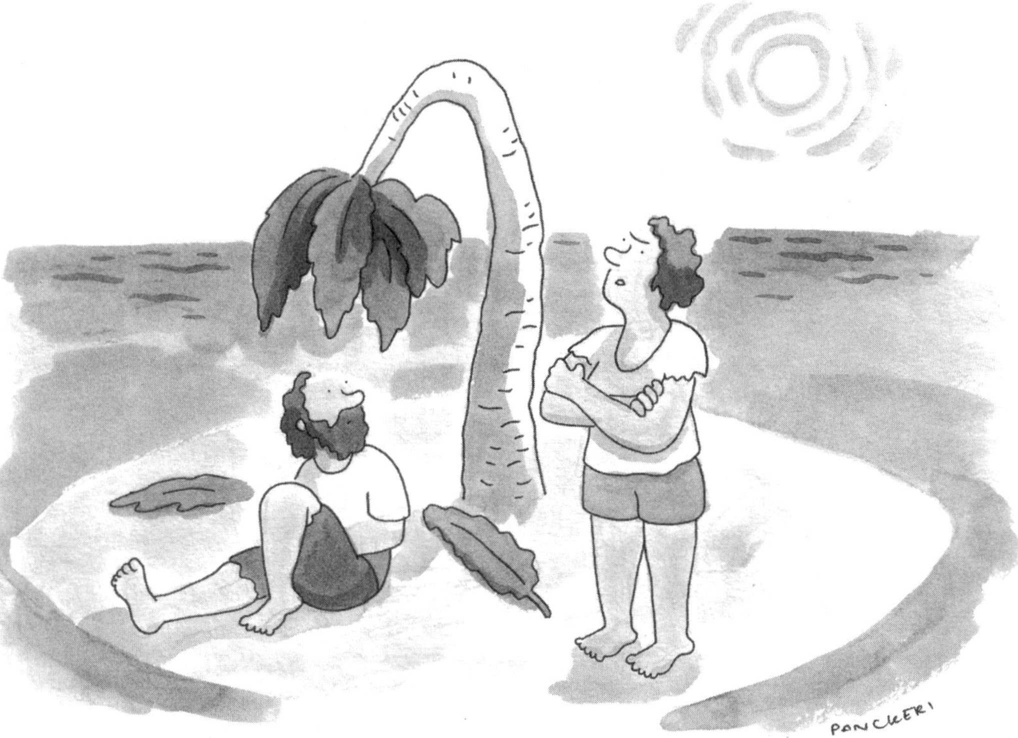
PANCKERI

"Damn it, I can't keep any plants alive."

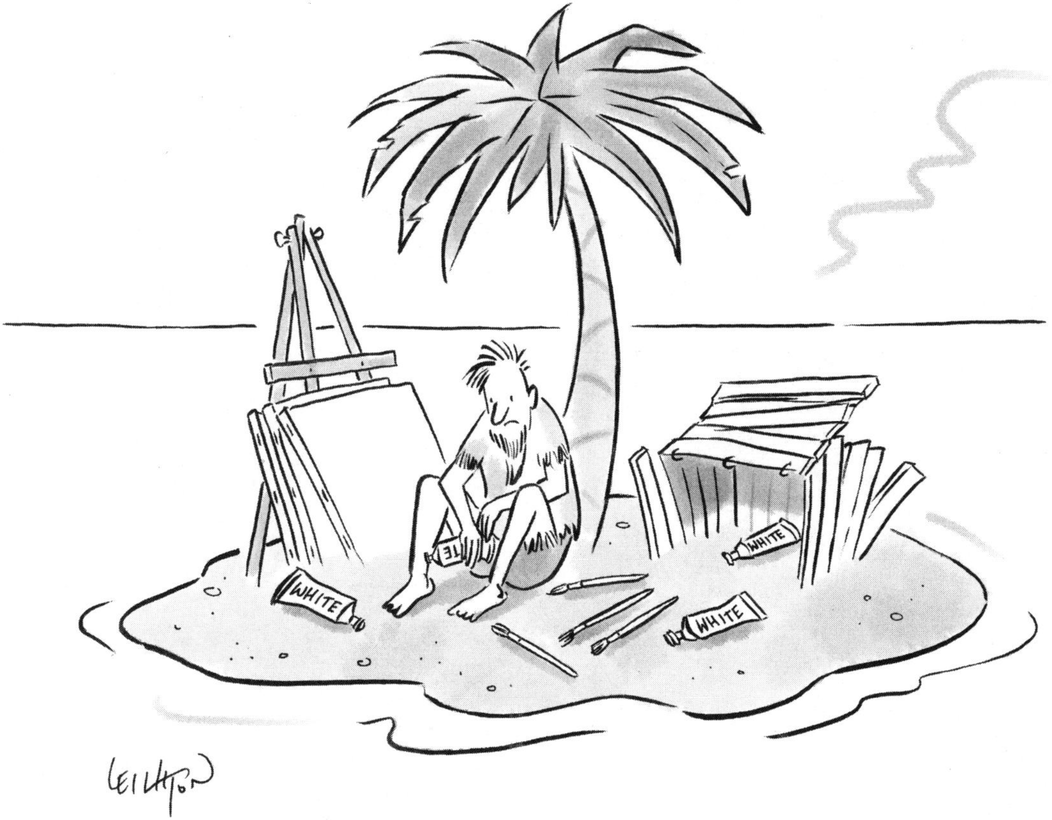
WHITE
WHITE
WHITE

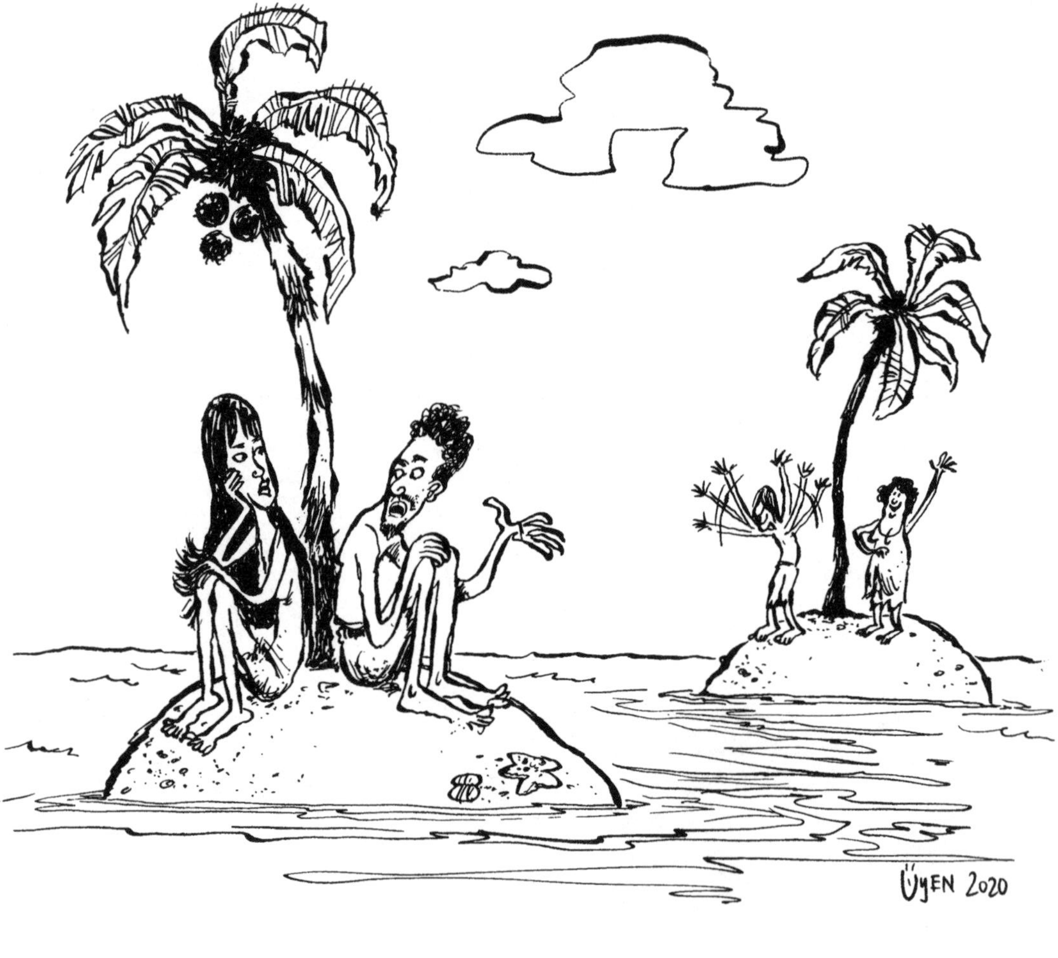
ÜYEN 2020

"They always tell the same sob story. I mean, hello! We were on the same boat."

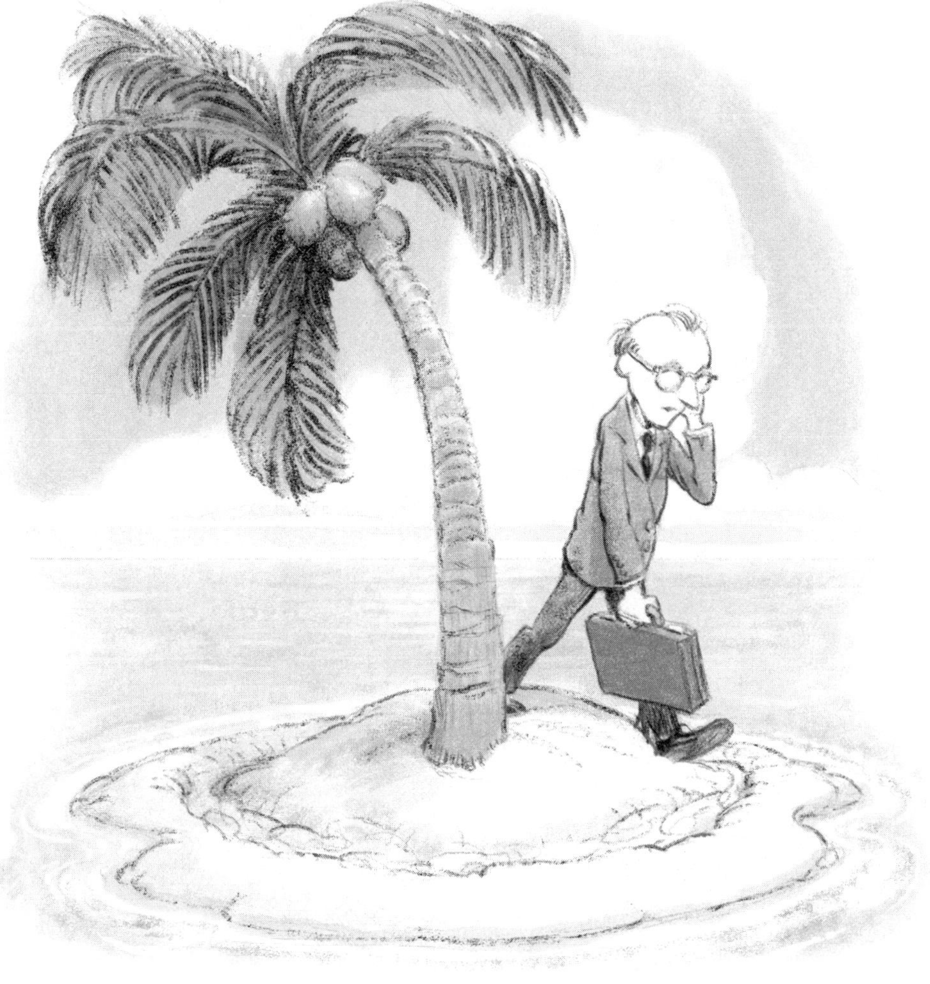

"I can't talk right now. I'm just holding my hand to my ear."

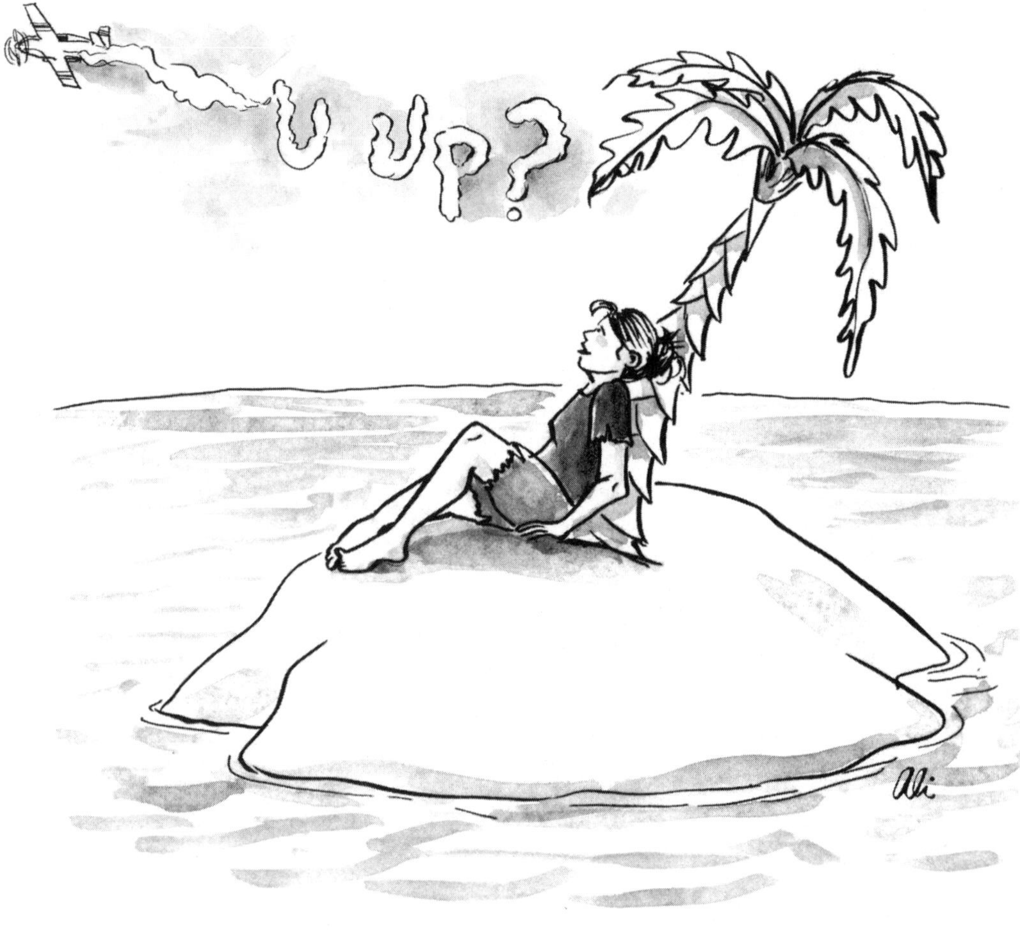
U UP?
Ali

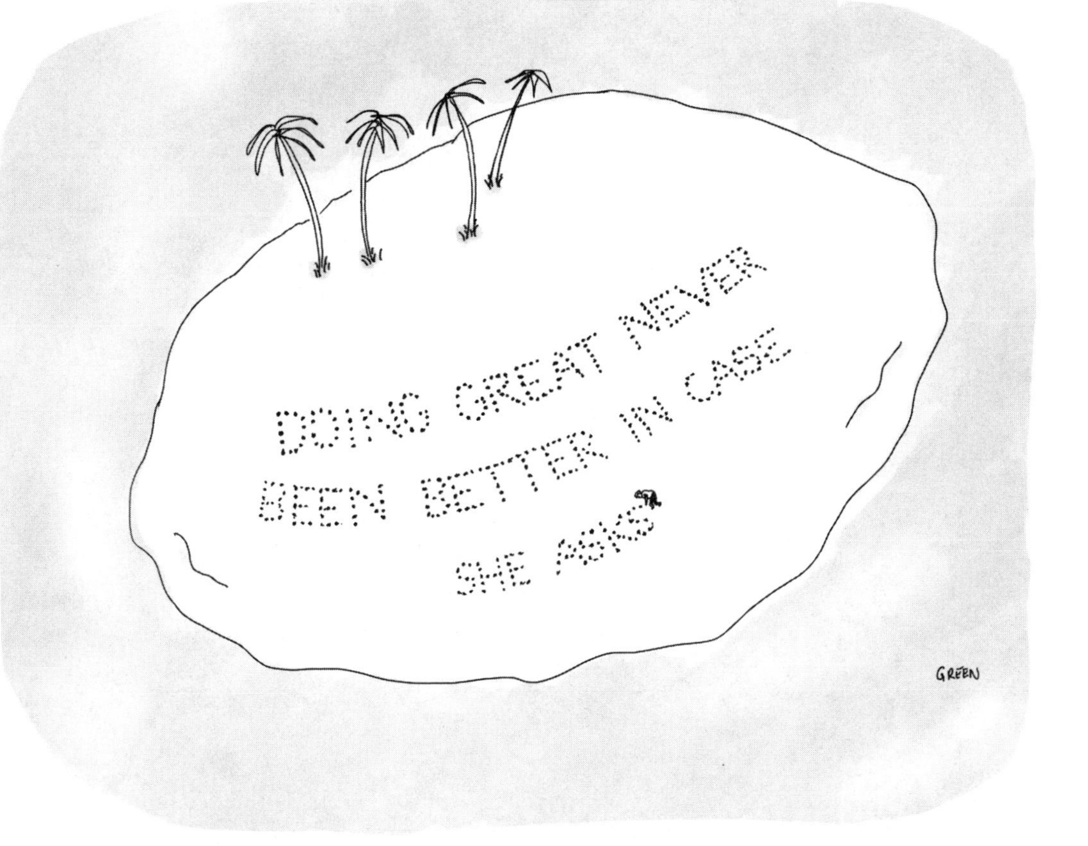
DOING GREAT NEVER
BEEN BETTER IN CASE
SHE ASKS
GREEN

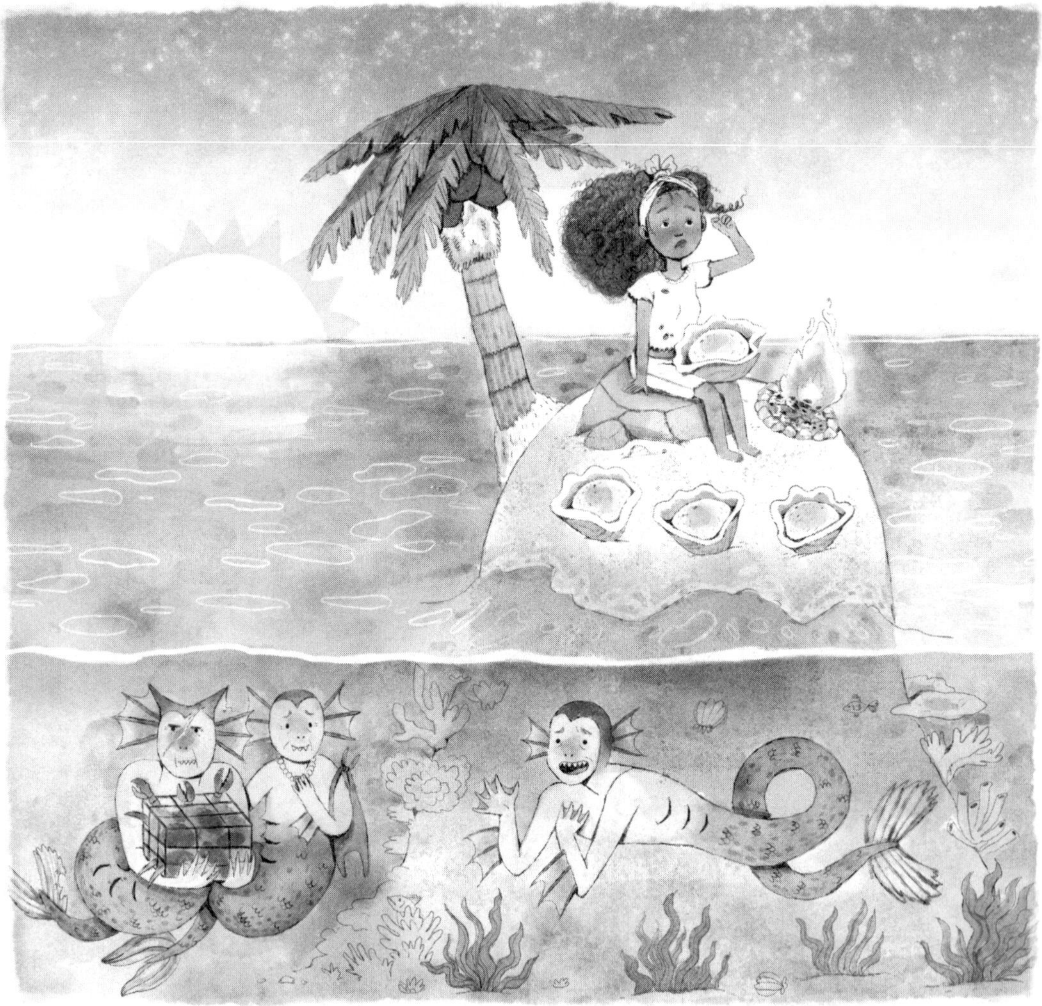

"This dinner is important to me, so don't say anything weird about her being a human."

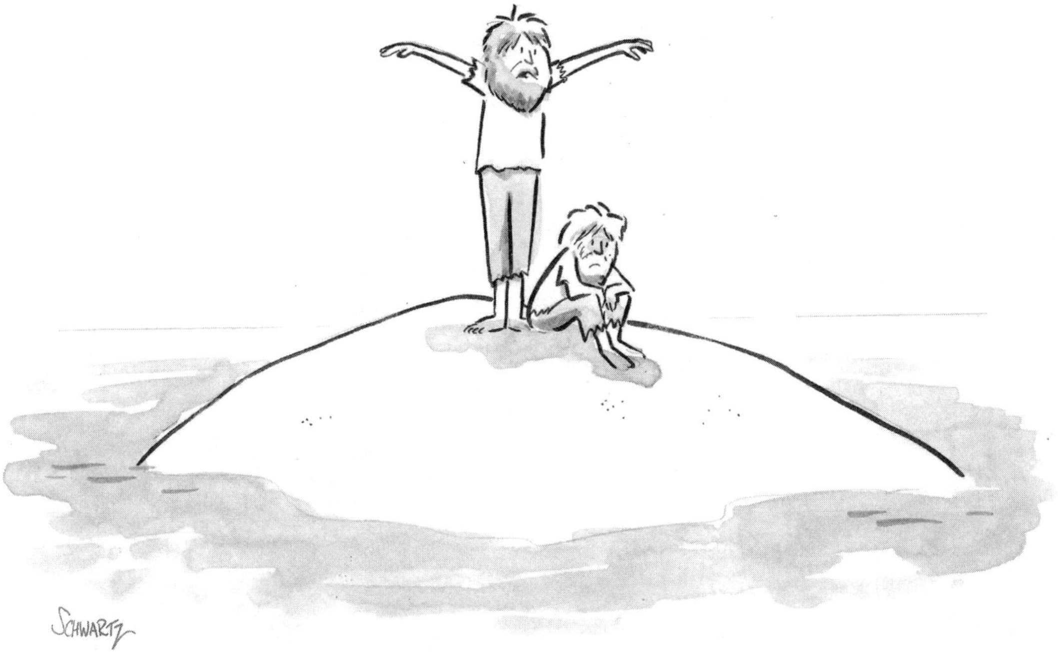
SCHWARTZ

"Okay, now you're the tree."

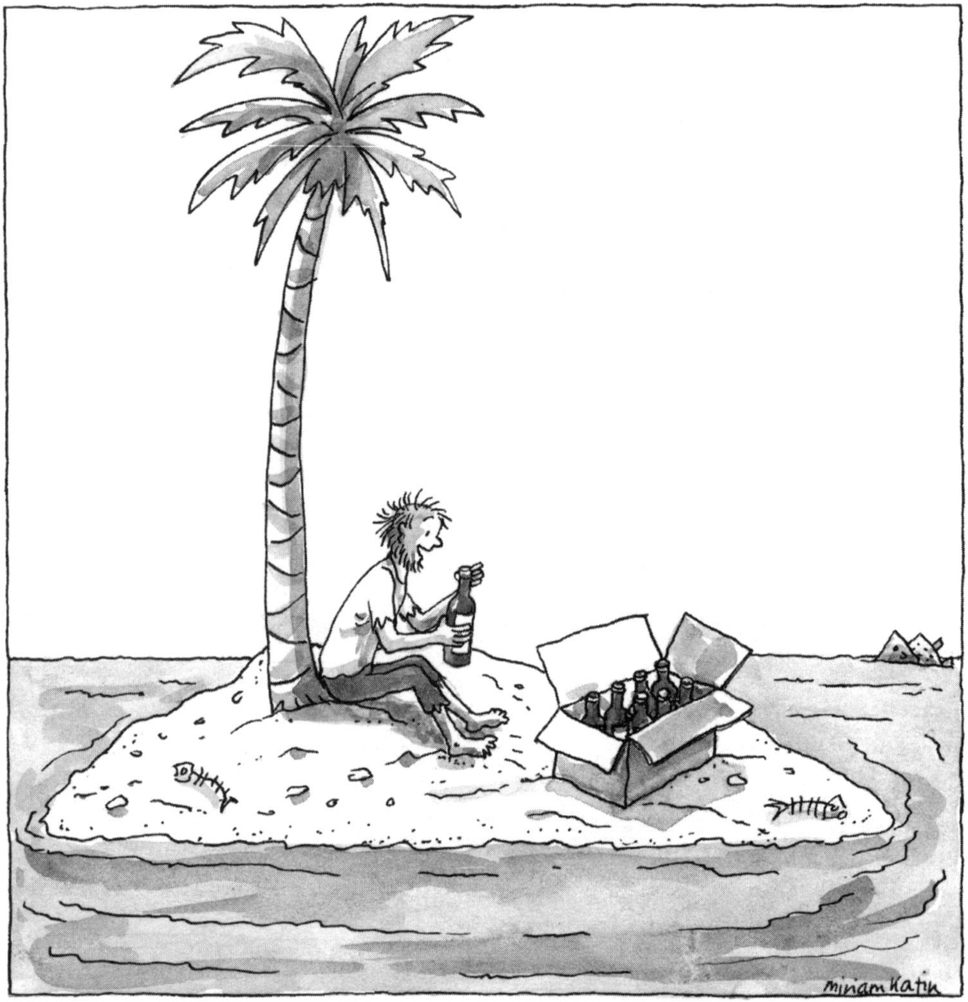
miriam Katin

"Thank god for screwcaps."

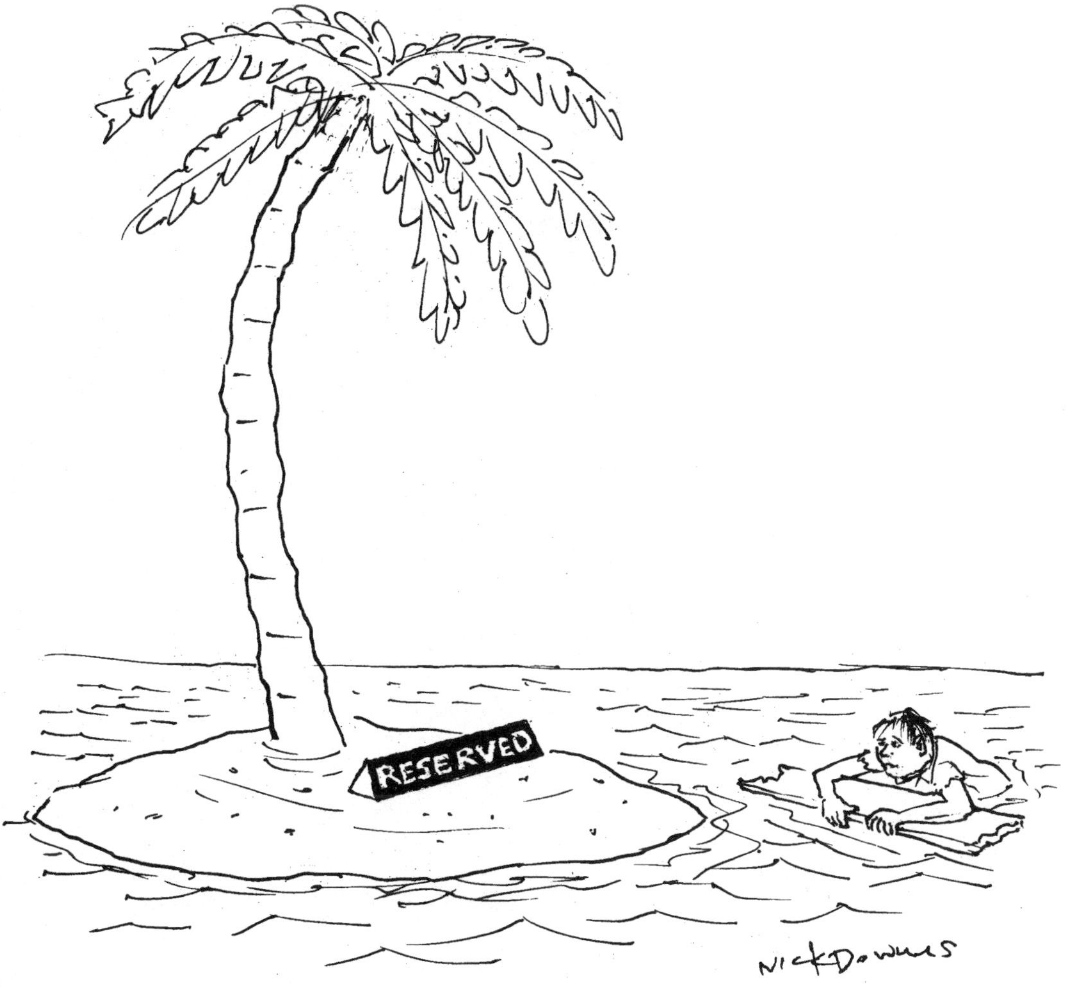
RESERVED
NICK DOWNES

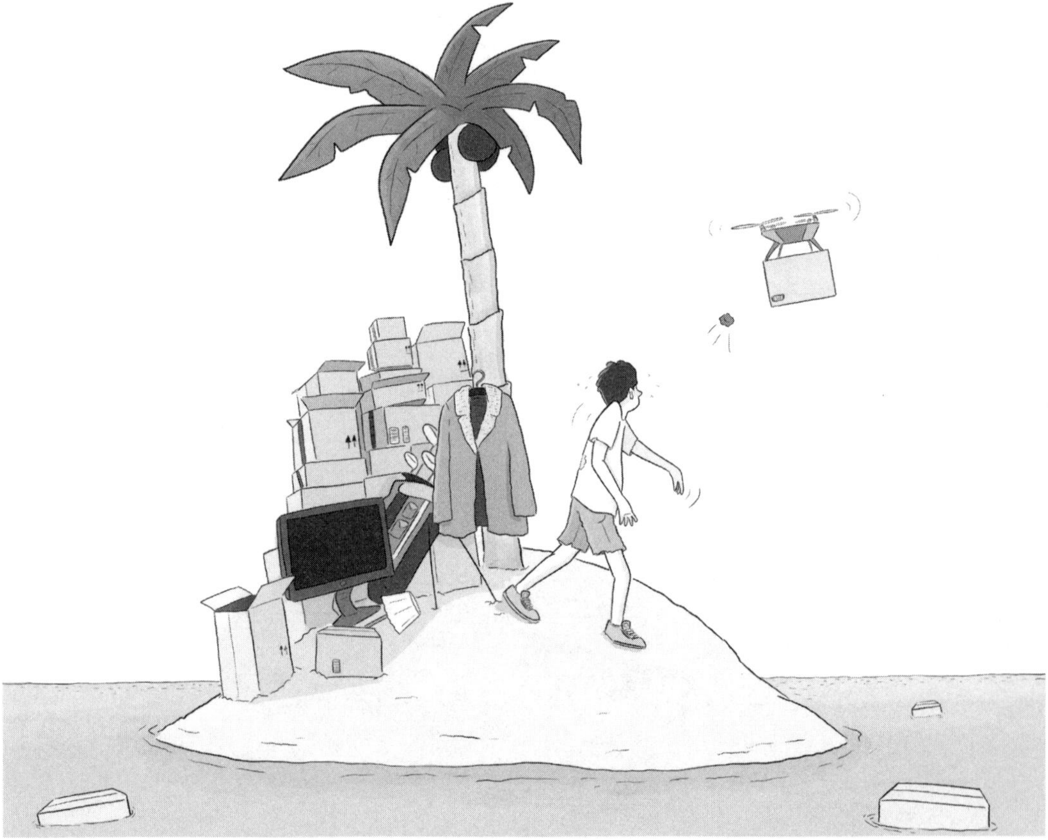

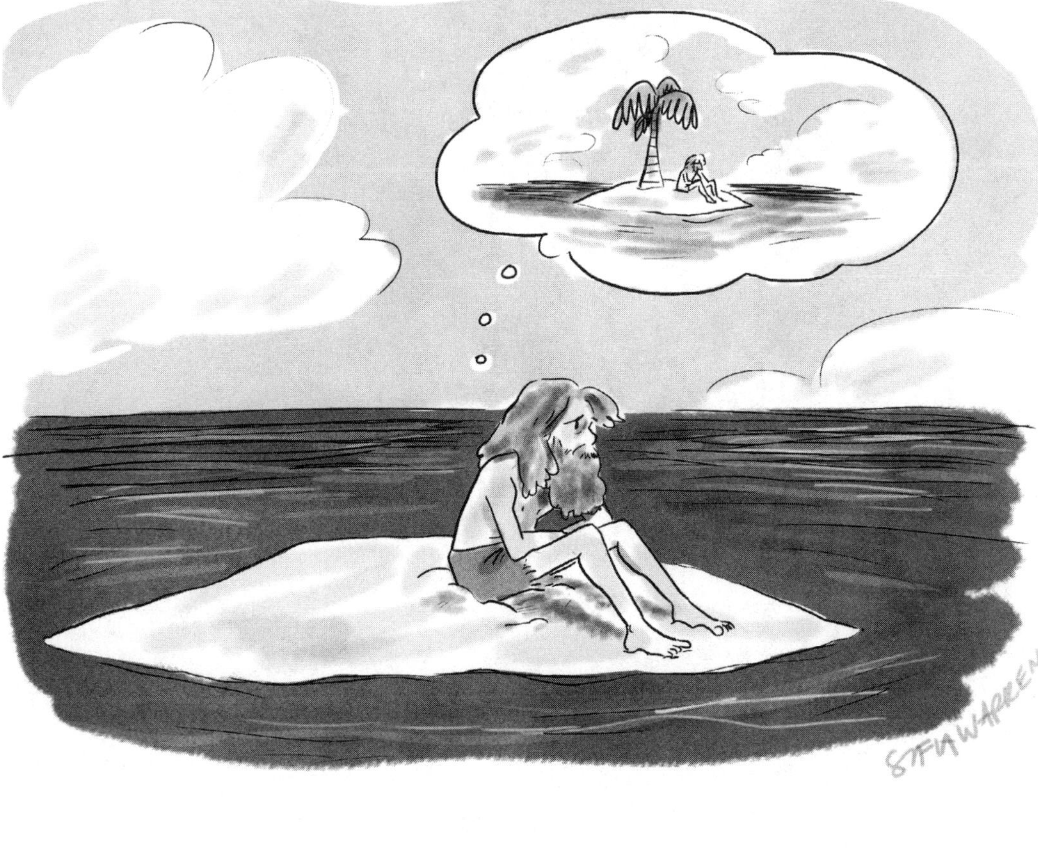

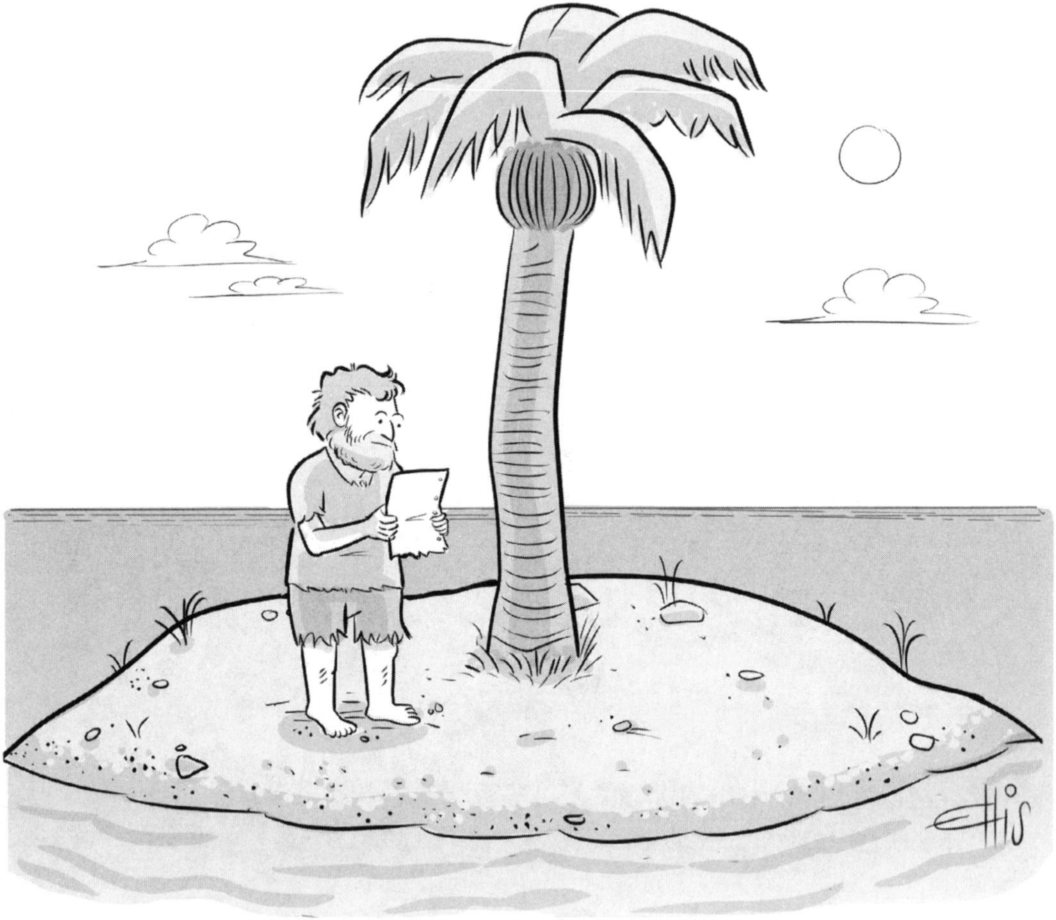

"We came to rescue you but you were sleeping so soundly and we didn't want to wake you. Love, Mom and Dad."

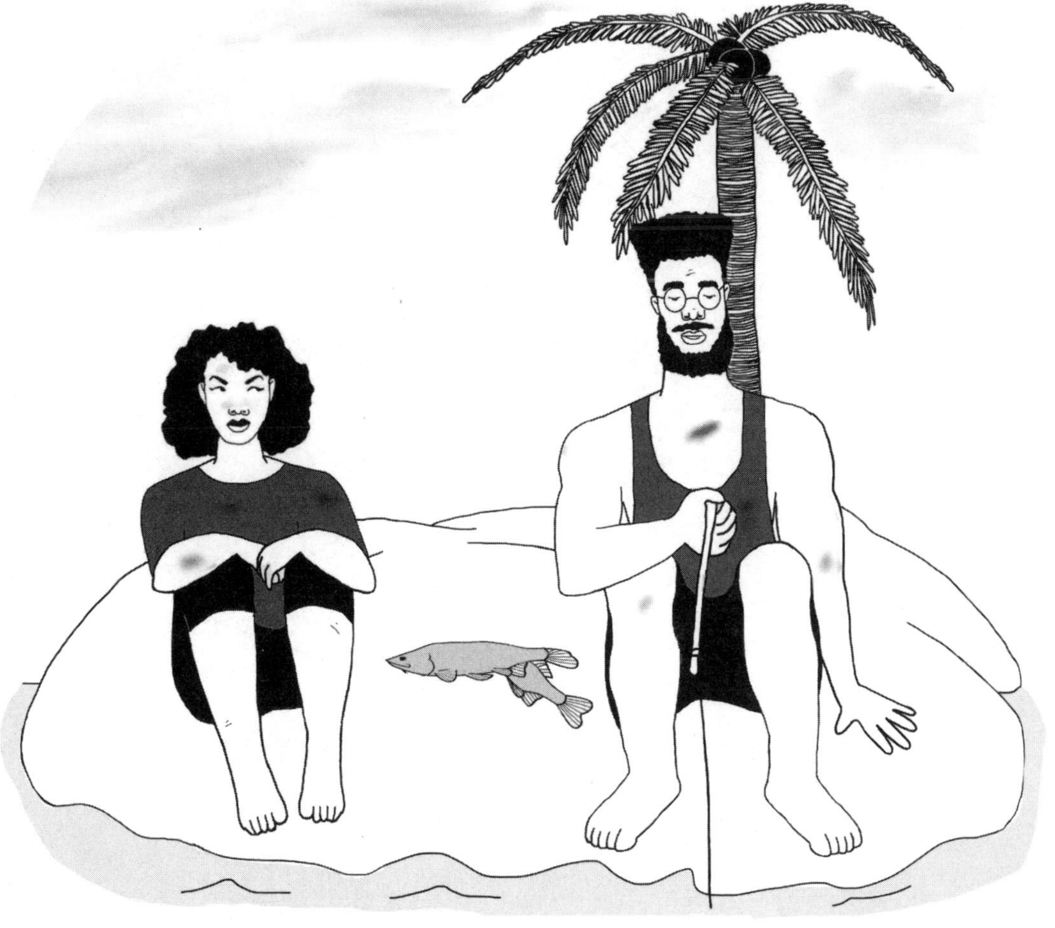

"The only good thing to come of this is that you always know what you want to eat."

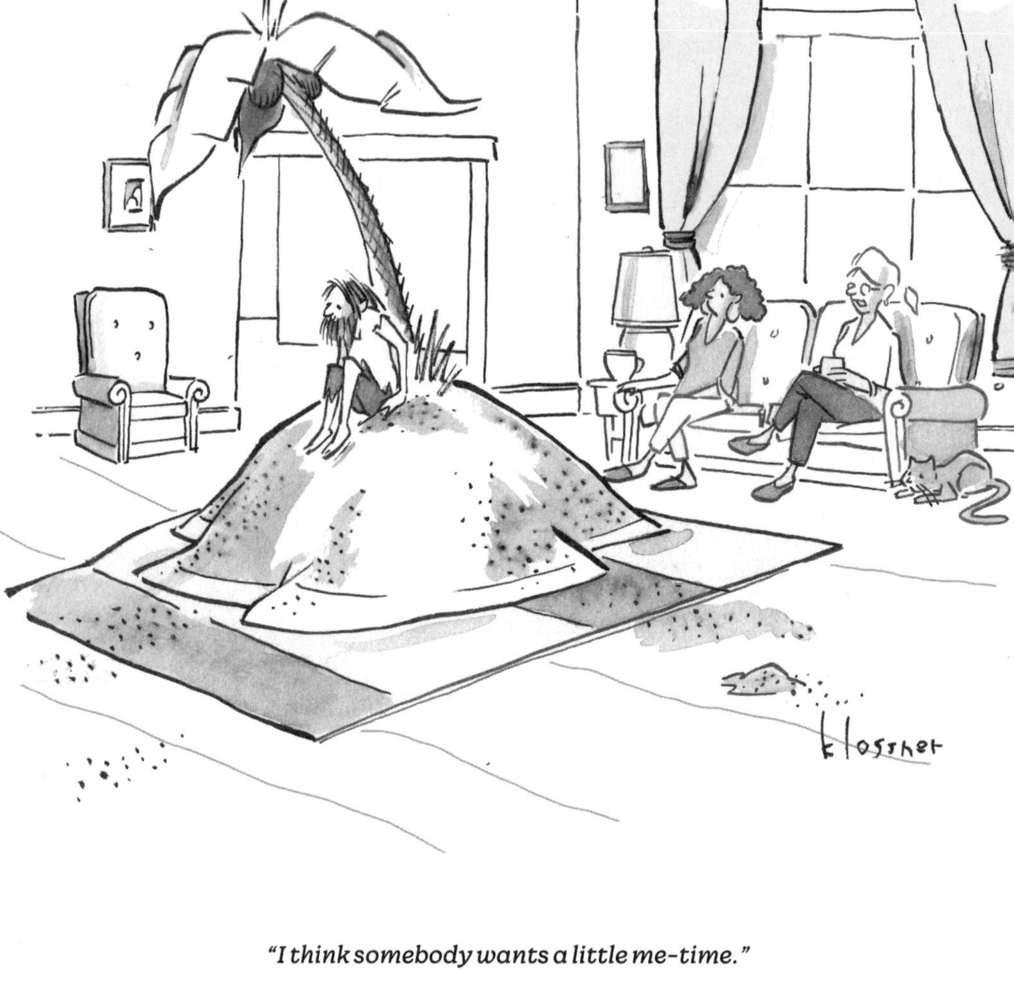
klossner

"I think somebody wants a little me-time."

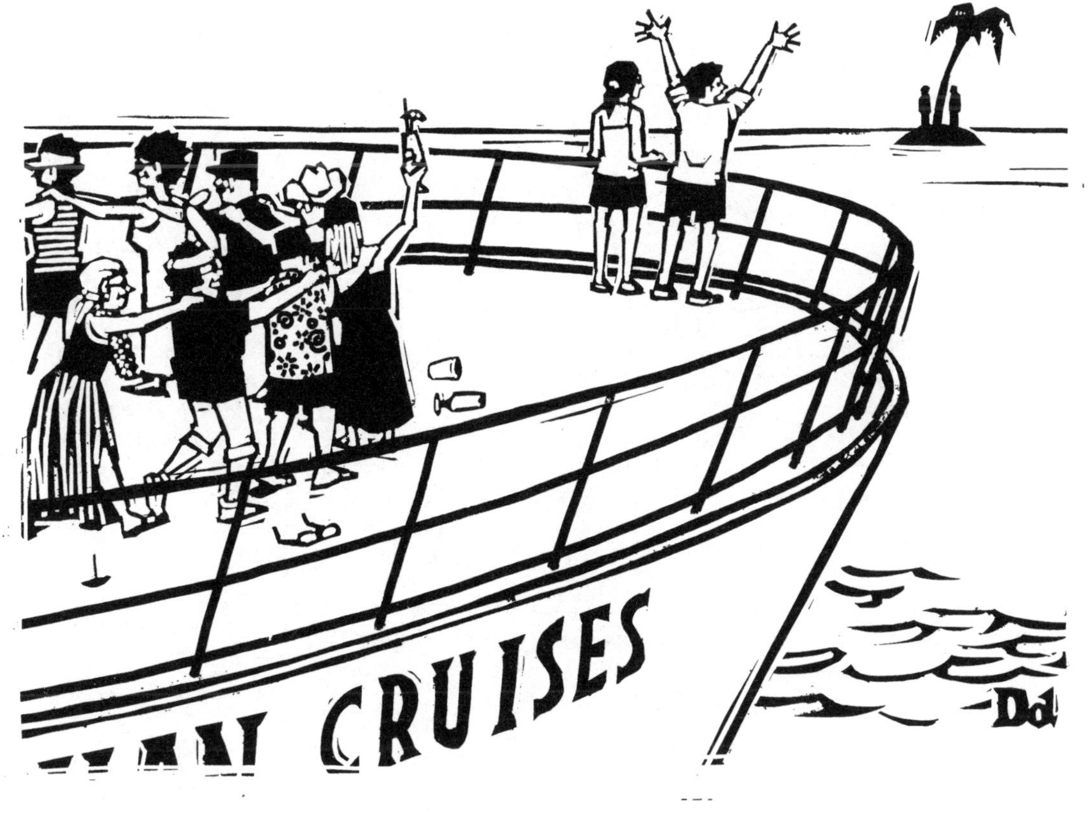
CRUISES

"Wave your hands! Those people might be able to save us!"

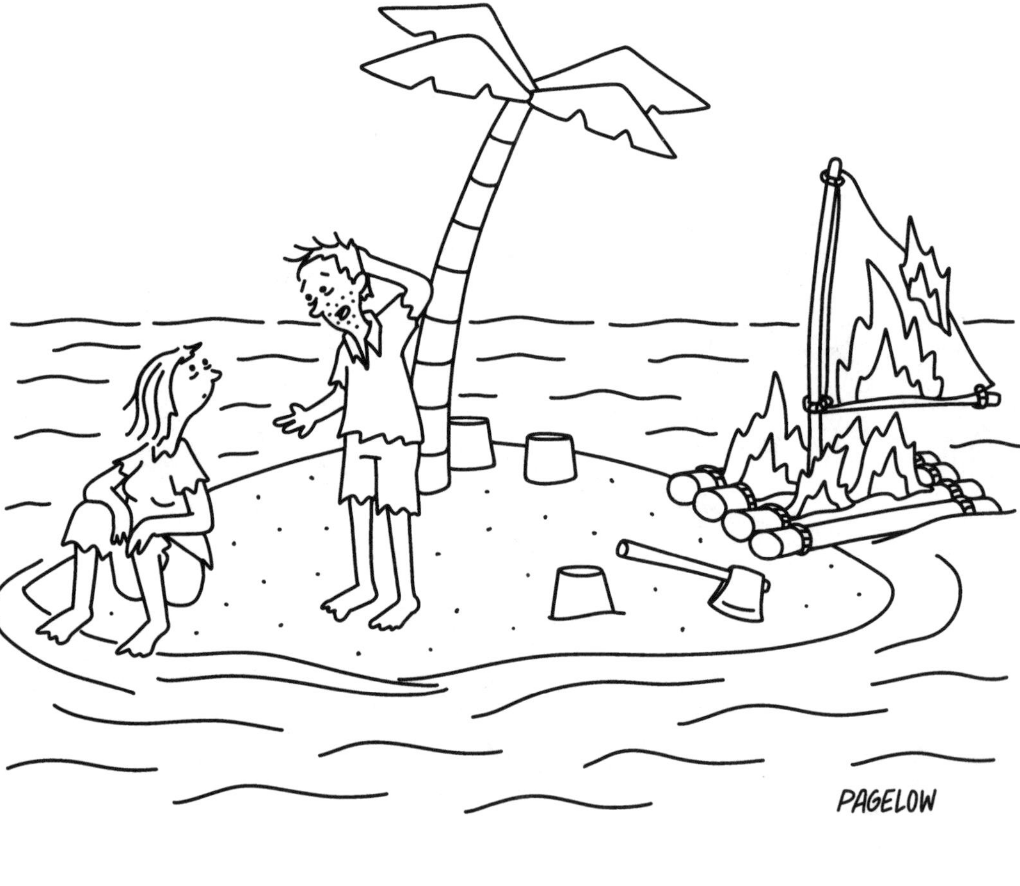
PAGELOW

"So, first the good news. I finally got a fire going."

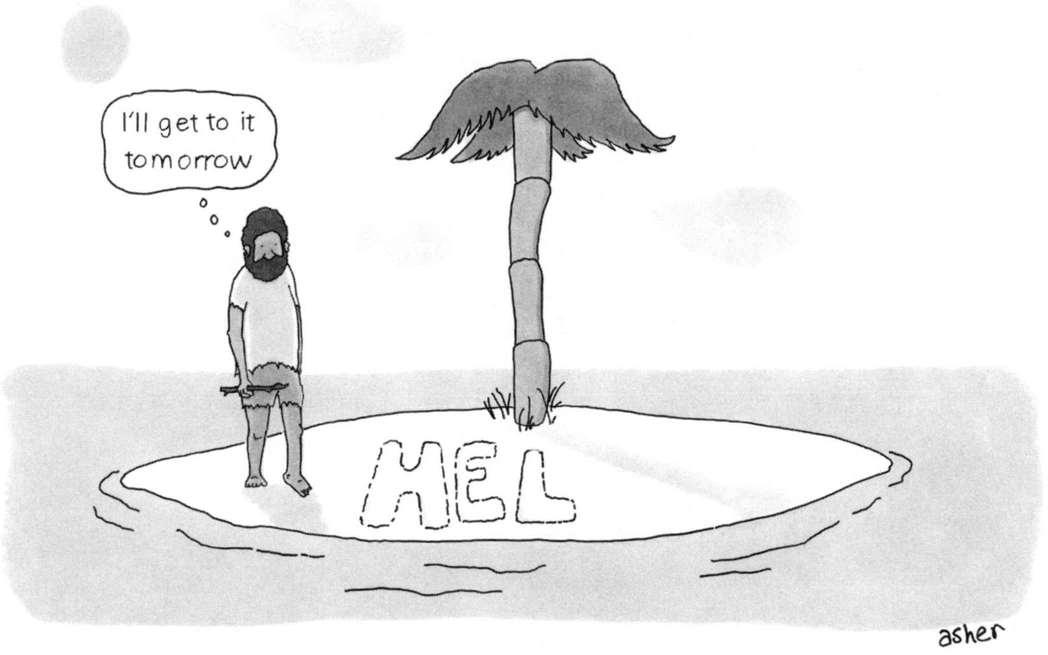
I'll get to it tomorrow
MEL
asher

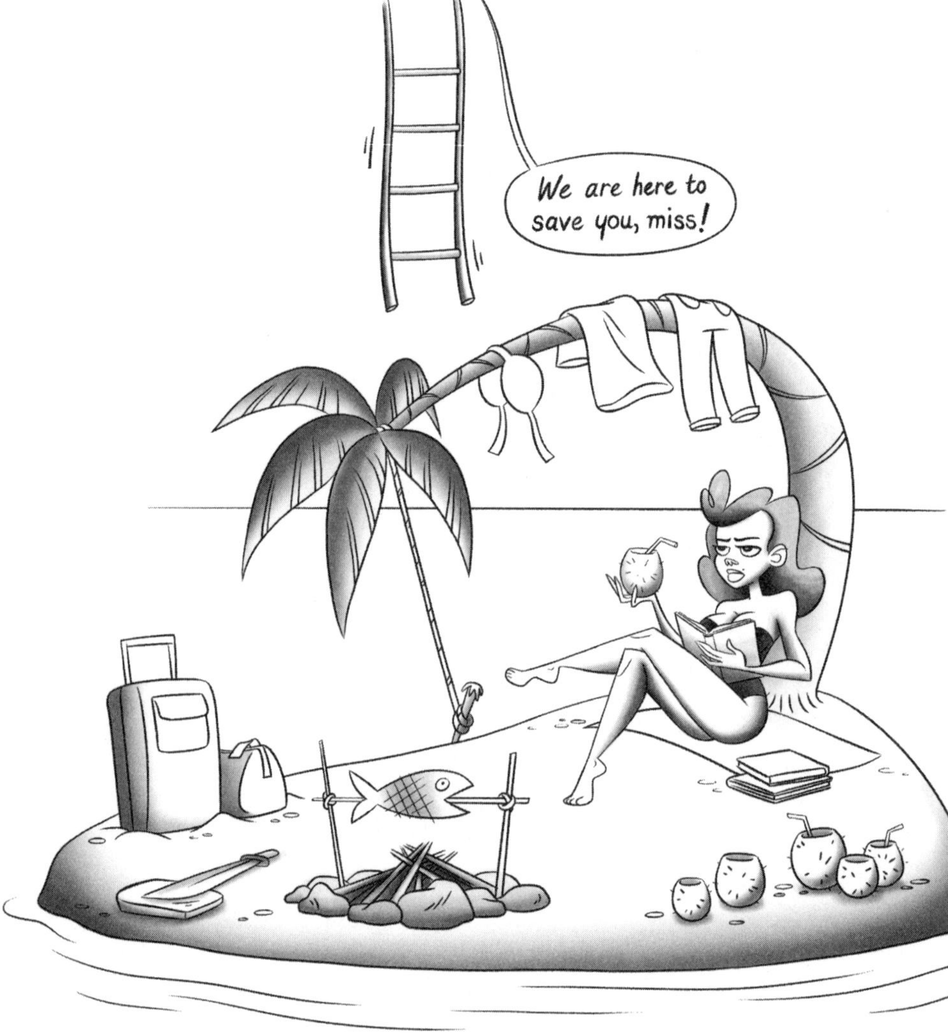
We are here to save you, miss!

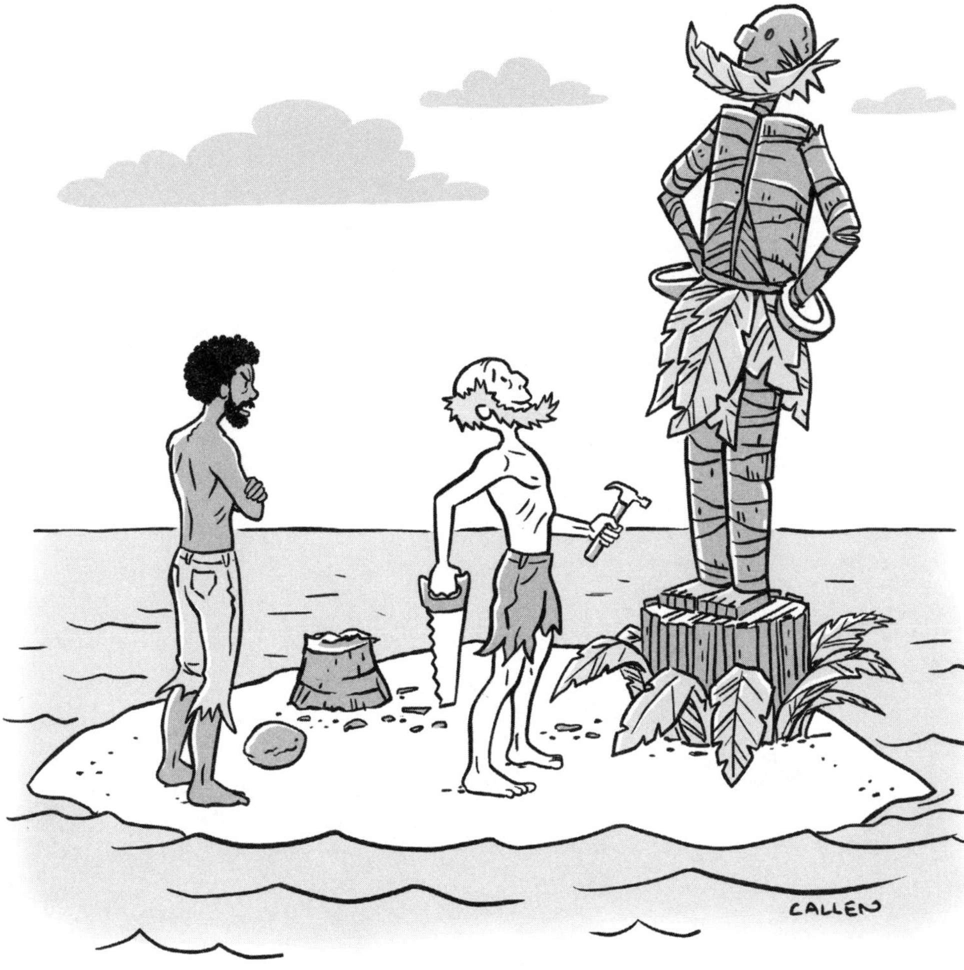
CALLEN

"Or, you could have built a boat."

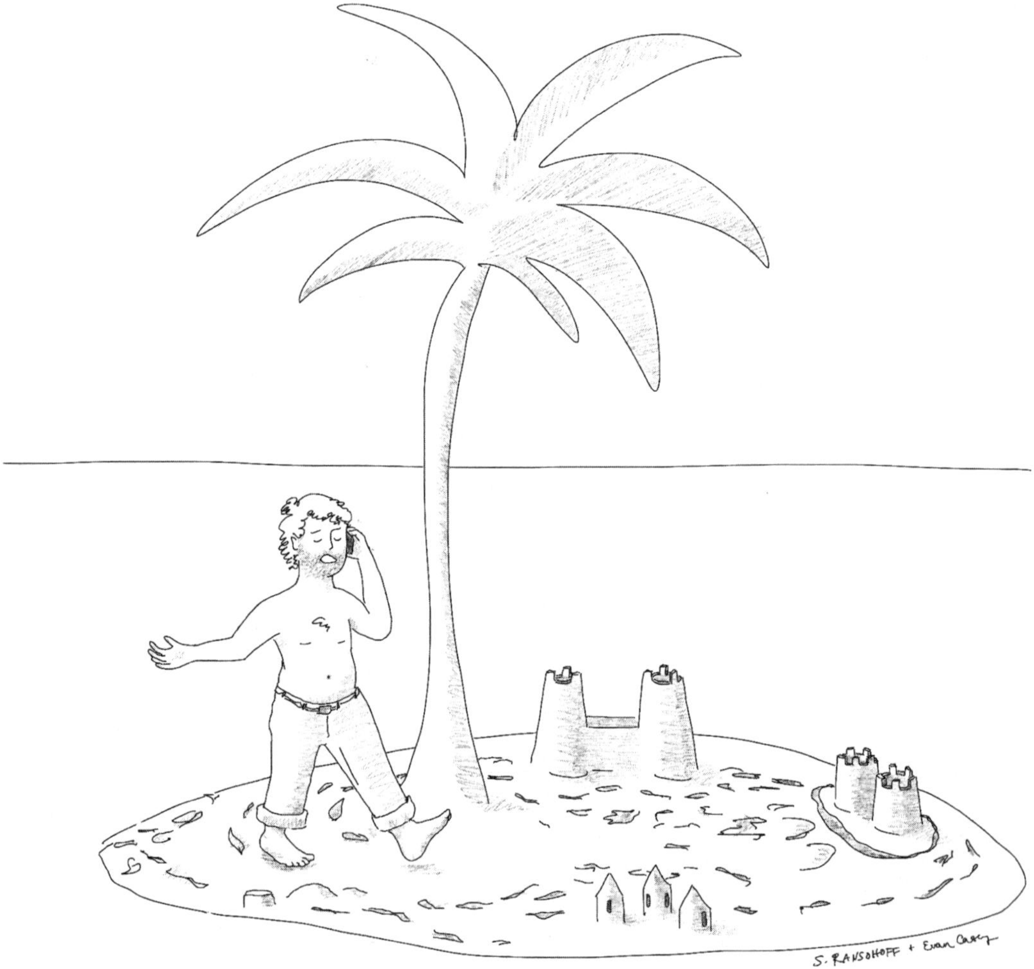
S. RANSOHOFF + Evan Casey

"It's a thinkpiece about the role of sand in society."

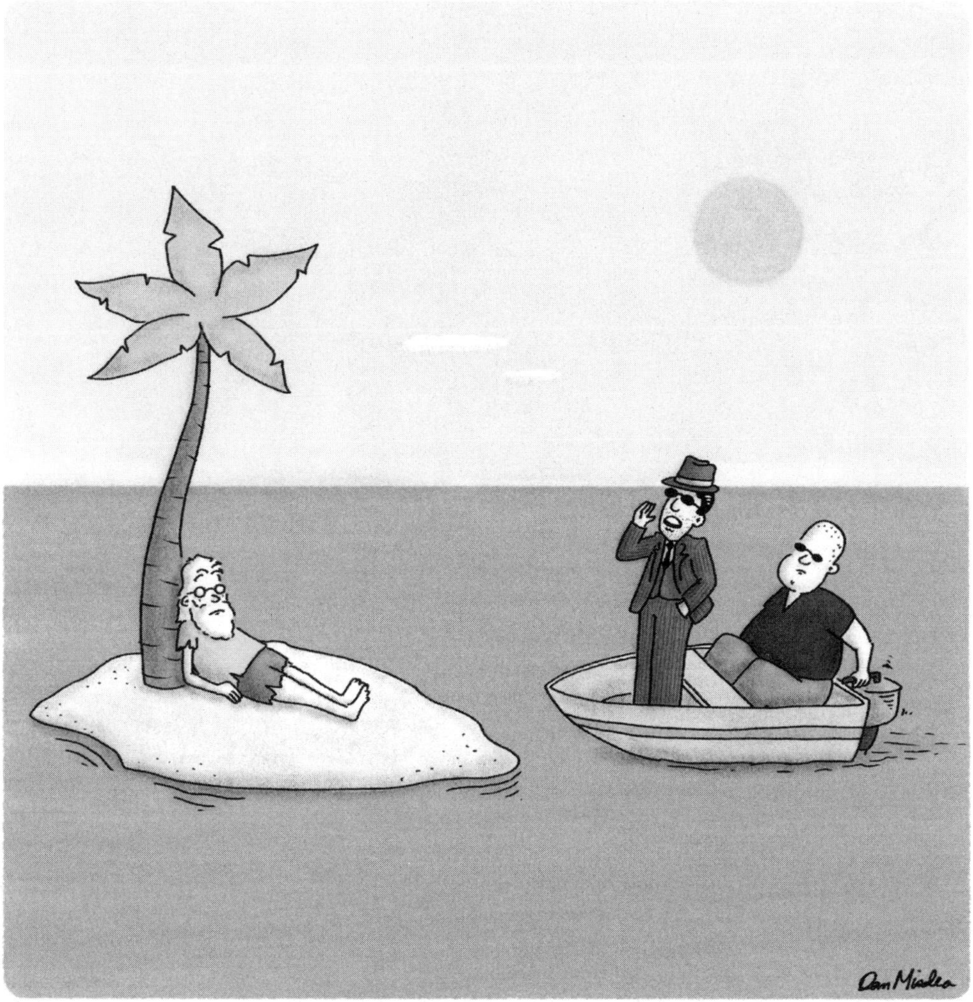
Dan Misdea

"Looks like you can use a little protection against the sun."

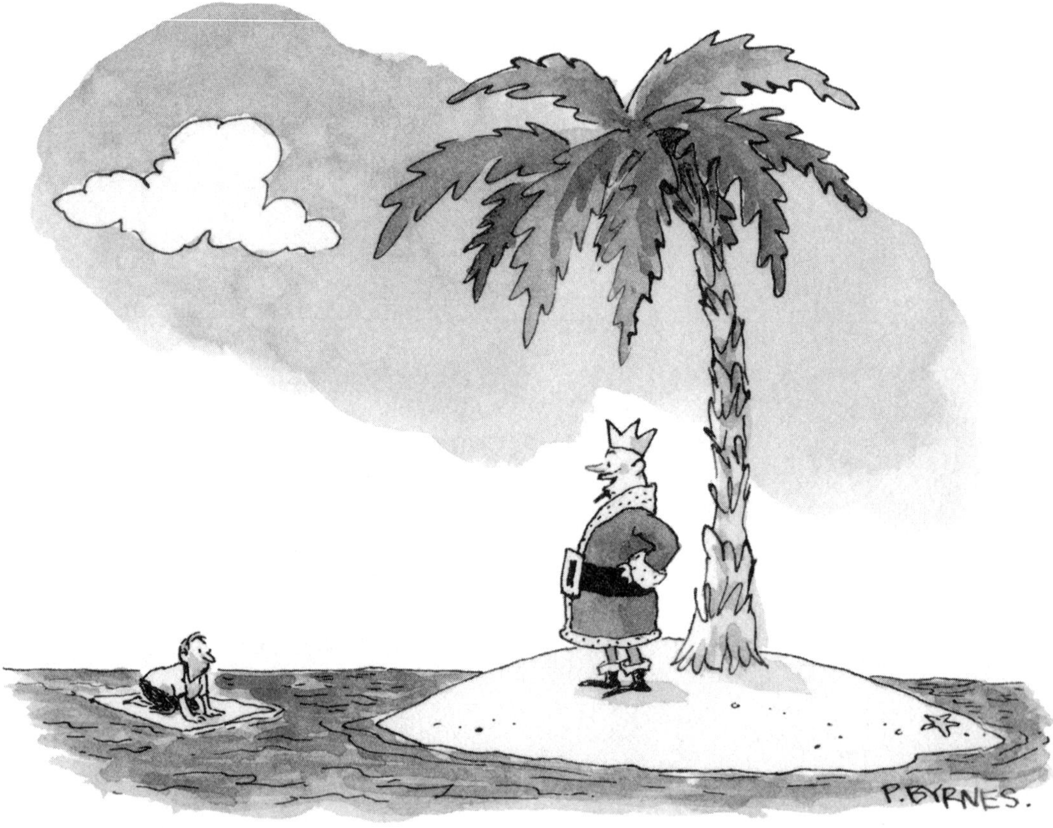
P. BYRNES.

"Finally, a peasant!"

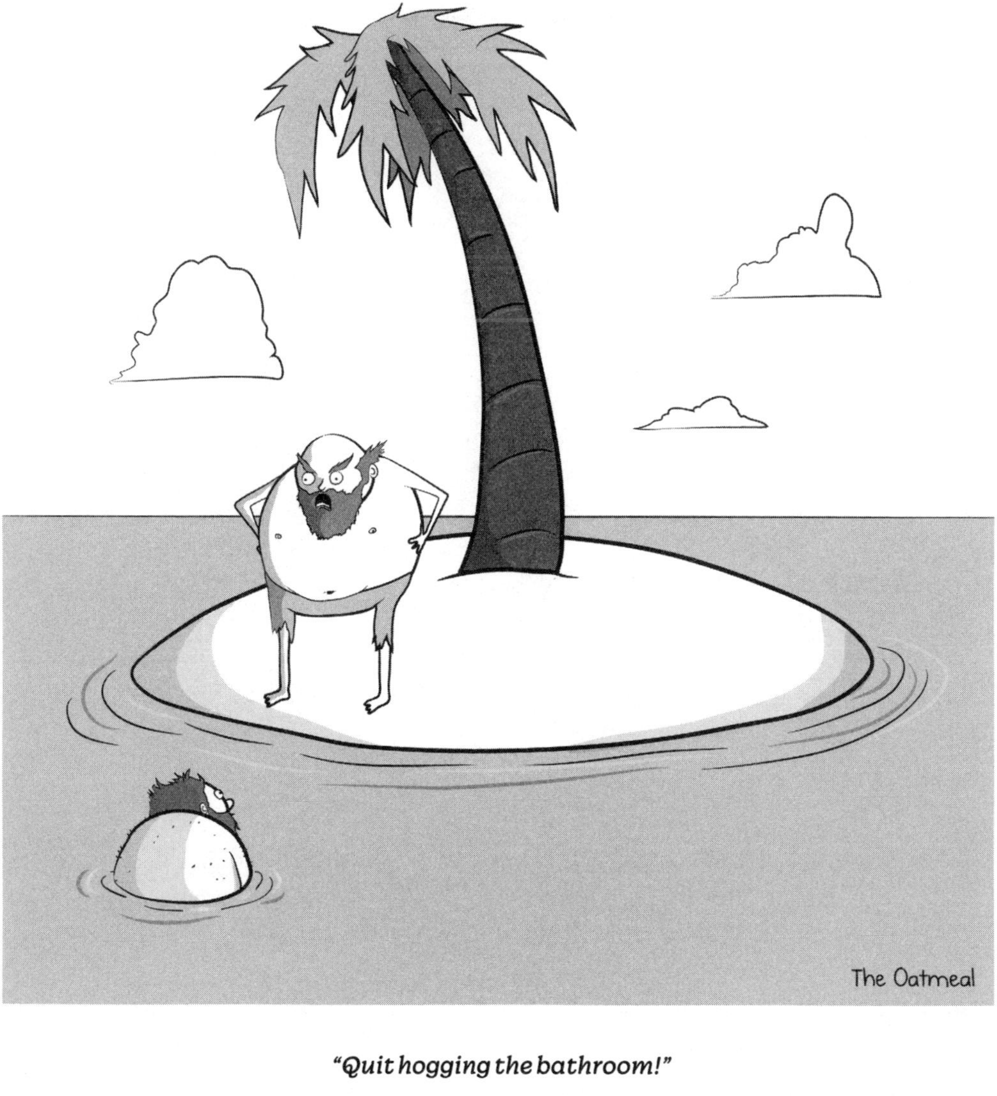
The Oatmeal

"Quit hogging the bathroom!"

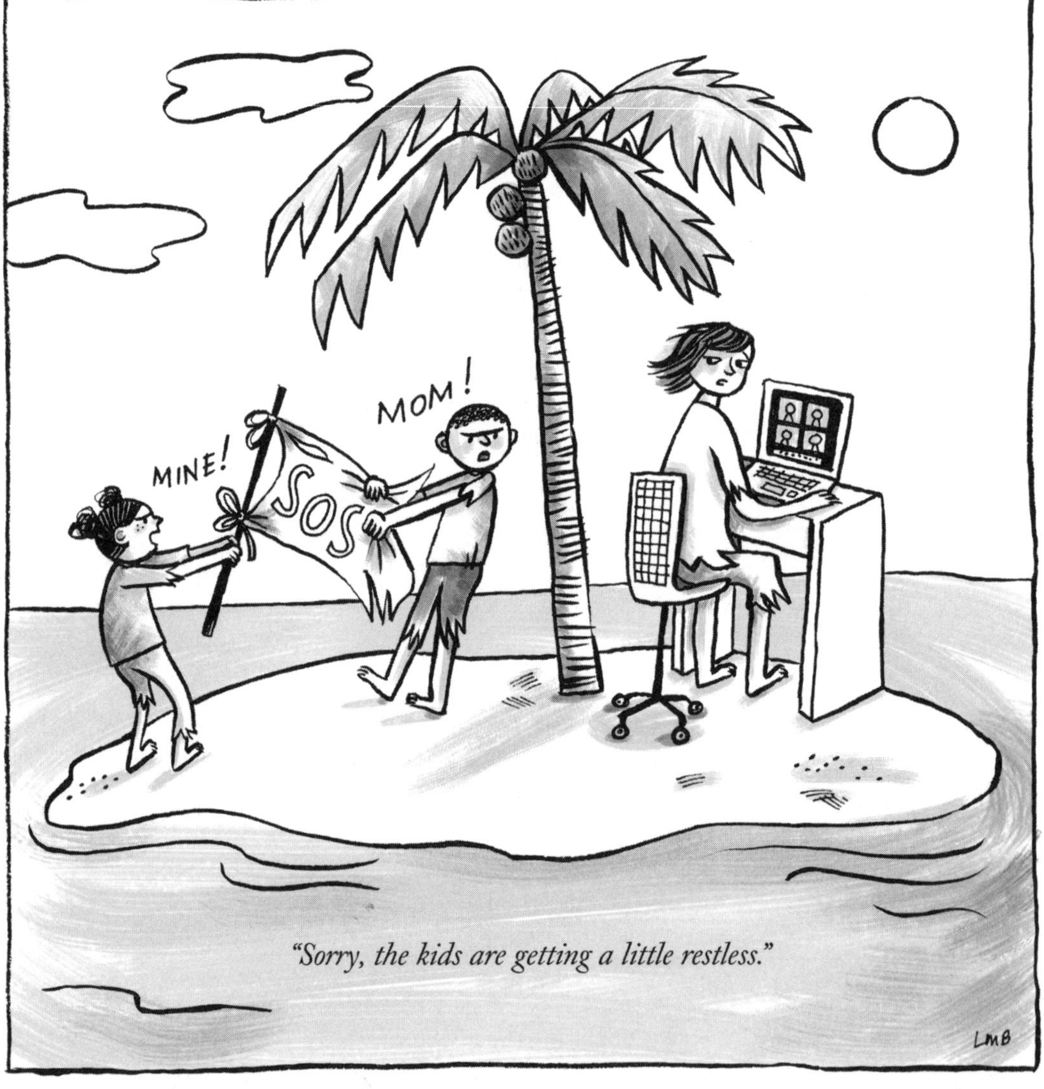
MINE!
MOM!
SOS
LMB

"Sorry, the kids are getting a little restless."

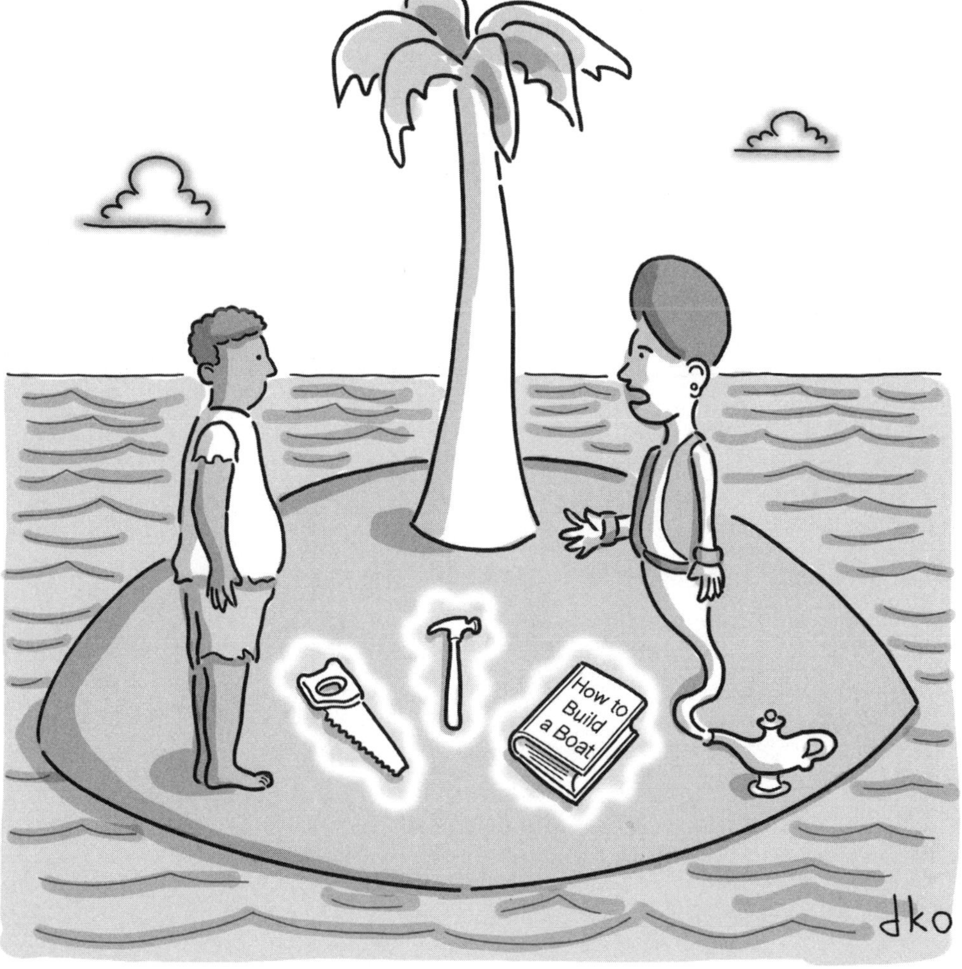
How to Build a Boat
dko

"I'm not supposed to do this, but I'll give you one do-over."

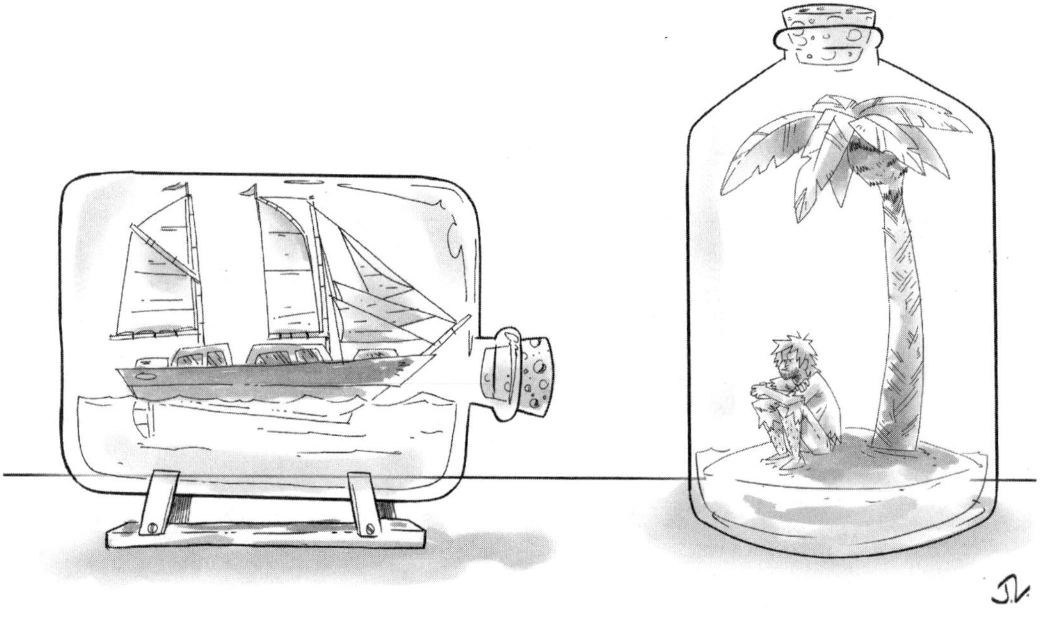
J.V.

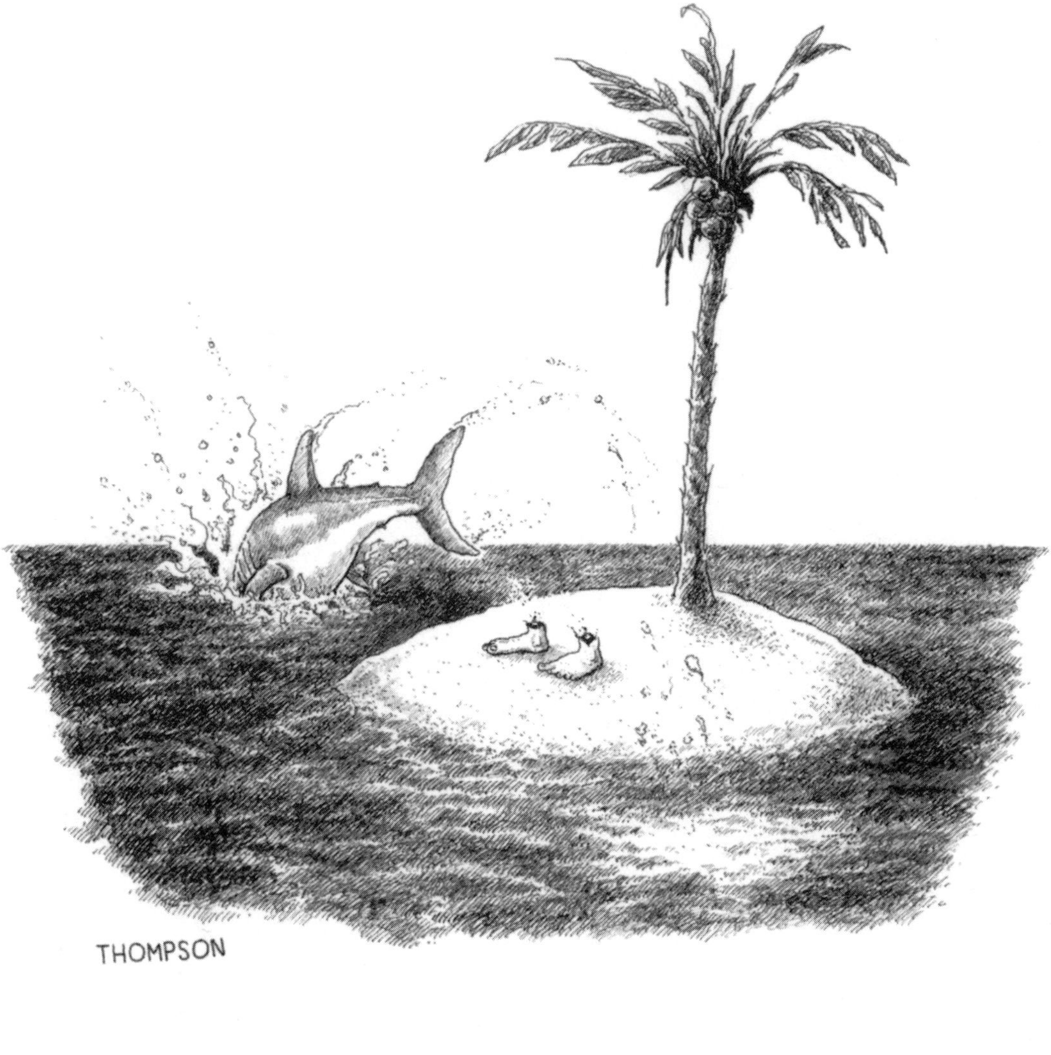
THOMPSON

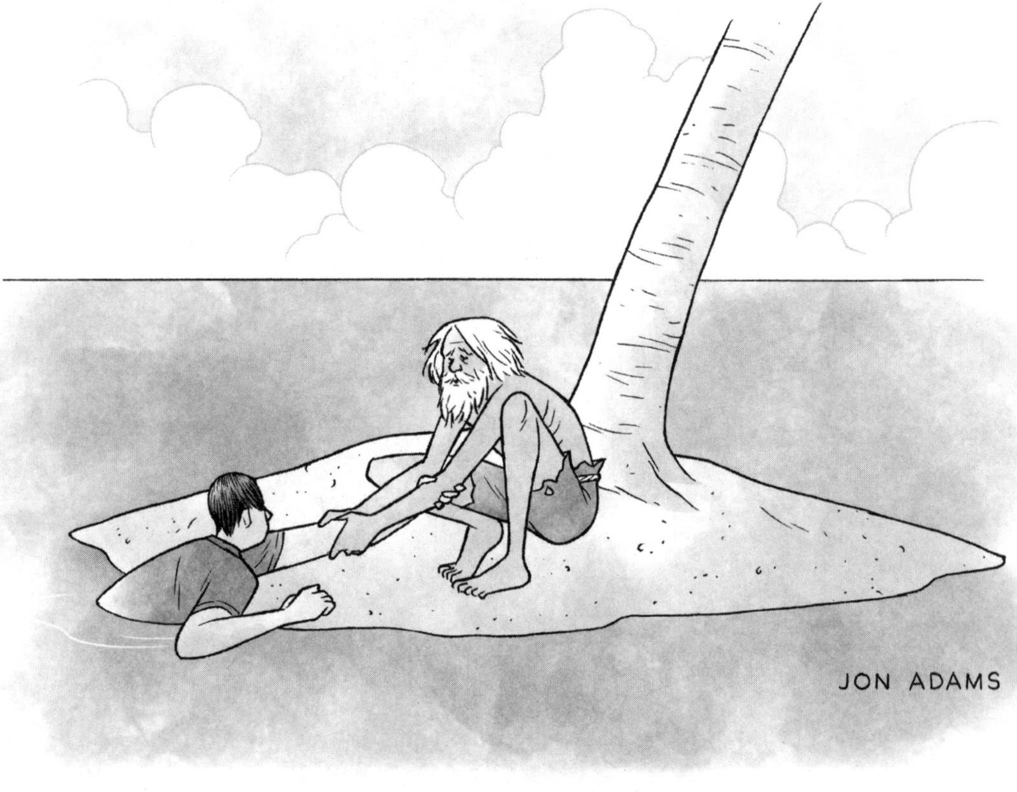
JON ADAMS

"Thank god you've arrived. I need someone to compare myself to."

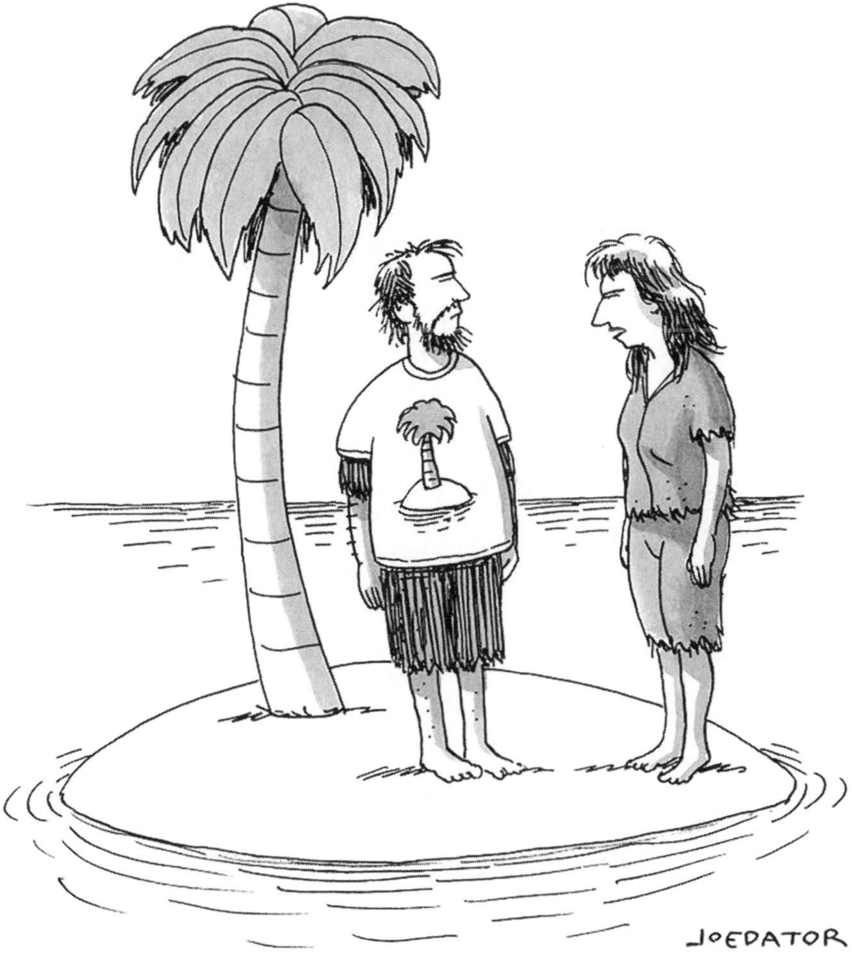
JOEDATOR

"It makes you look like a tourist."

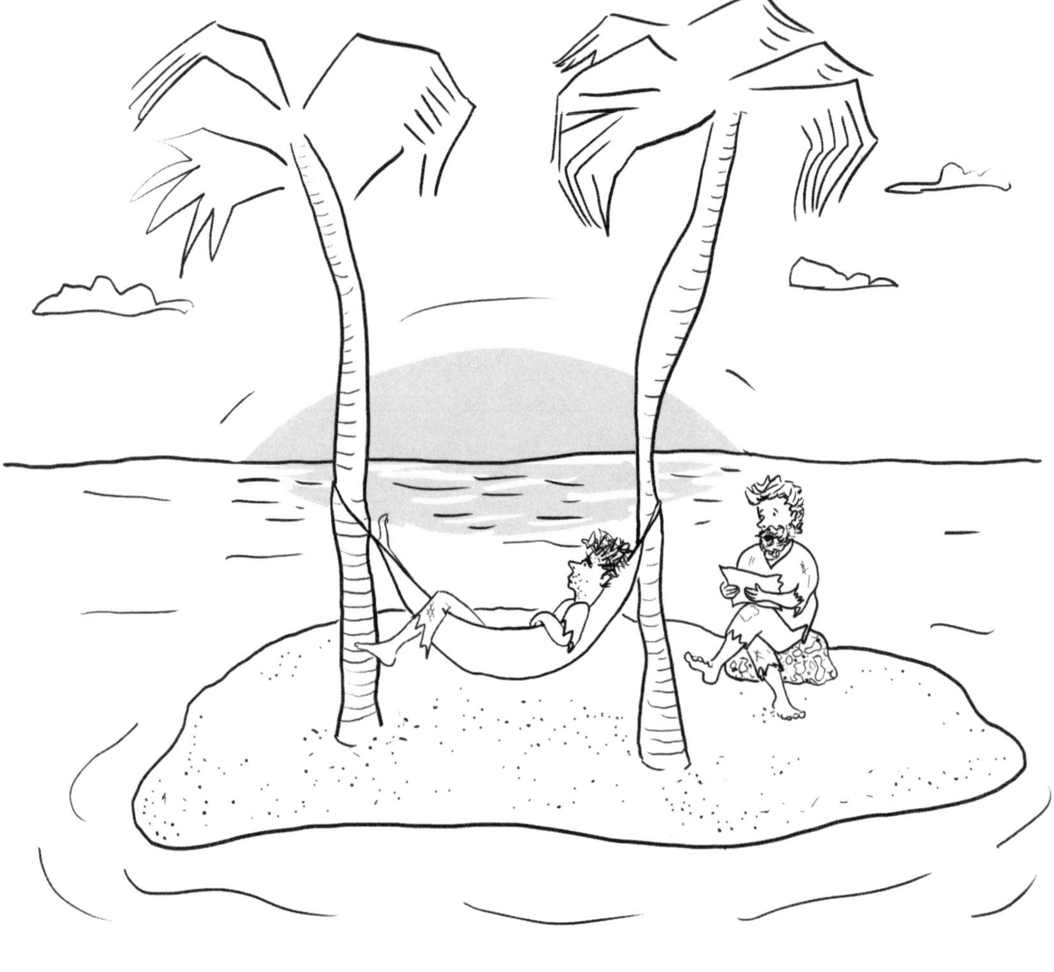

"Sorry to cut you off, but we're just about out of time for today."

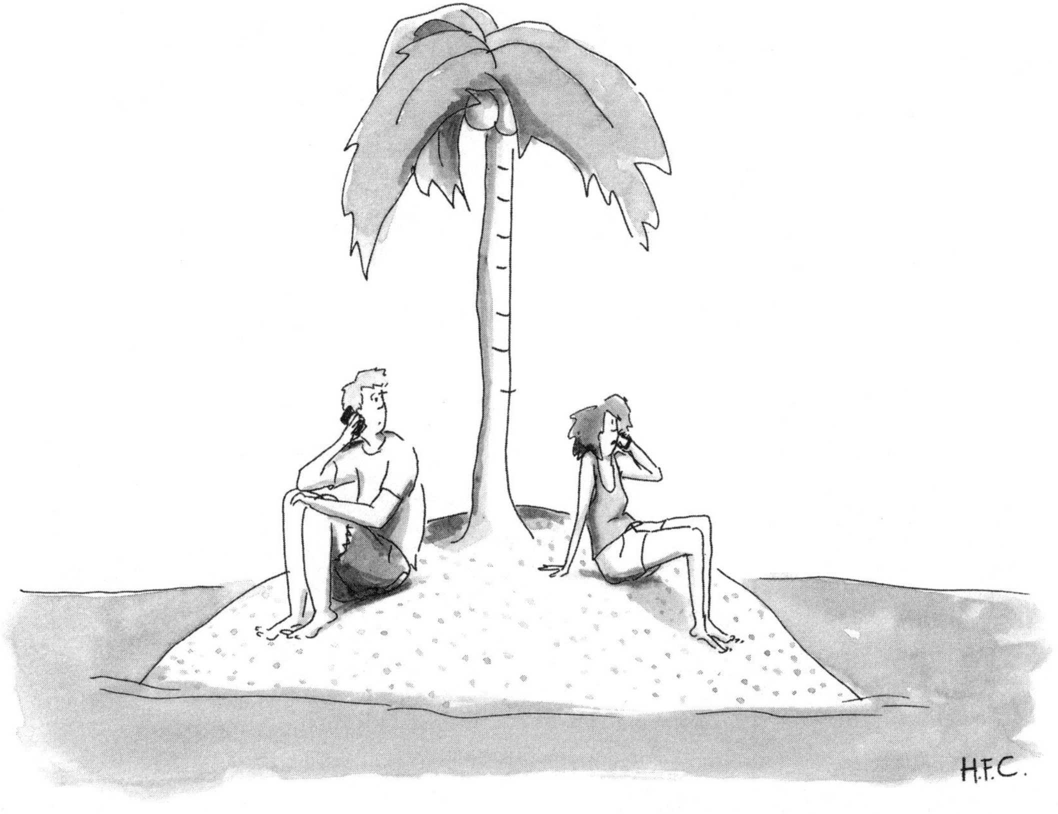
H.F.C.

"I can't tonight. I have to wash my hair."

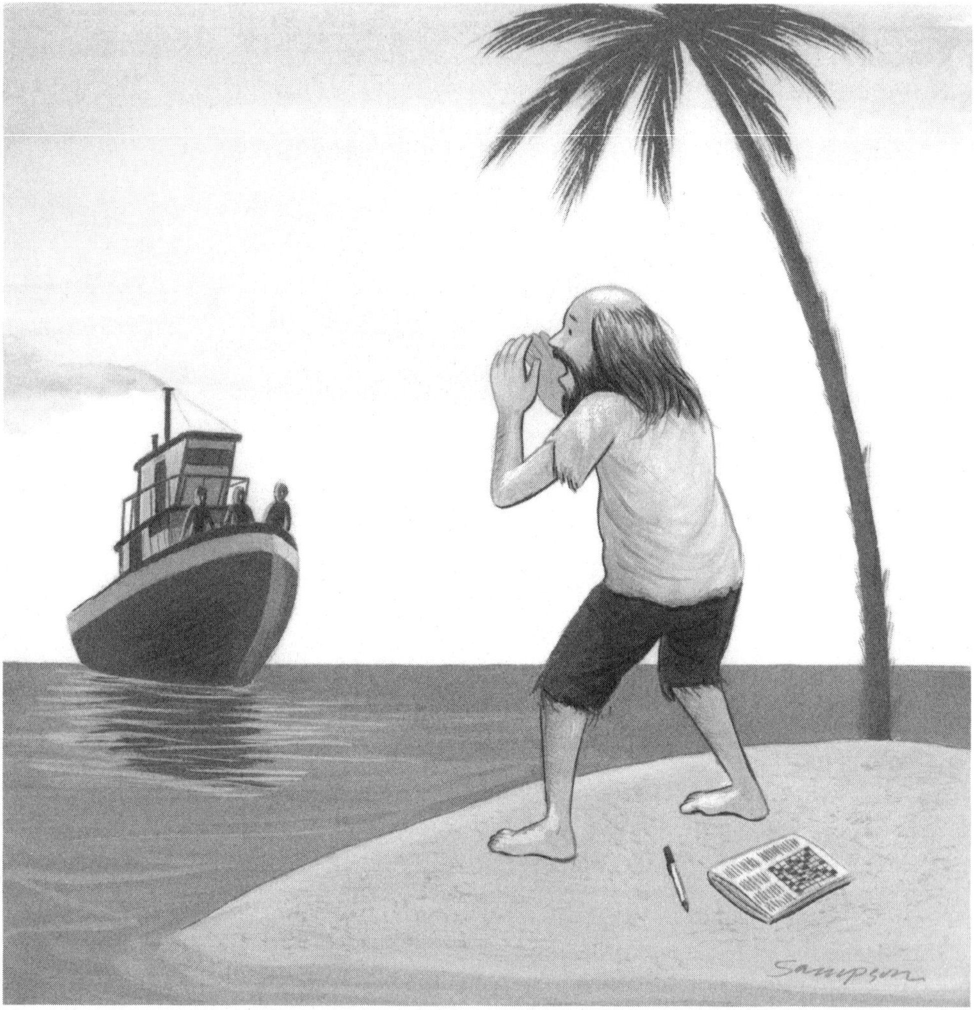
Sampson

"Thank god you're here! Do any of you know the capital of Mongolia? Eleven letters."

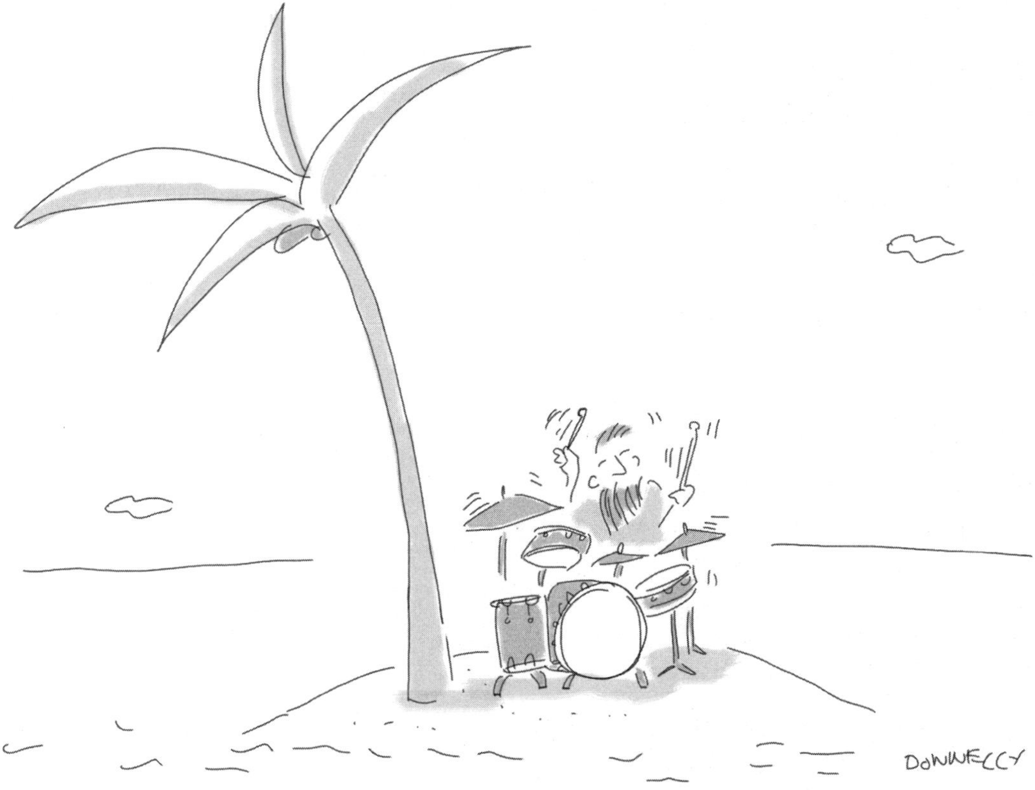
DONNELLY

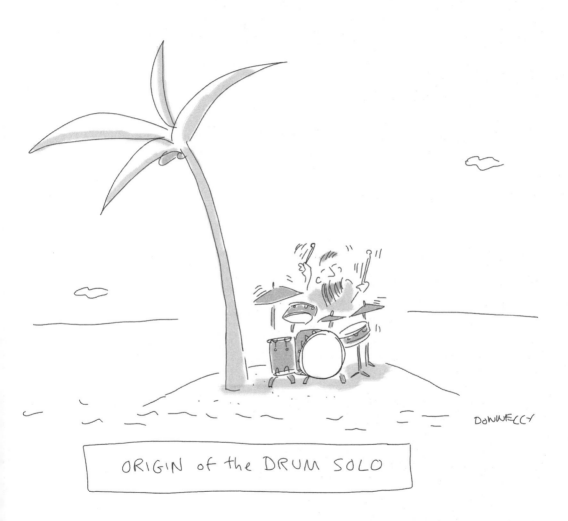

ORIGIN of the DRUM SOLO

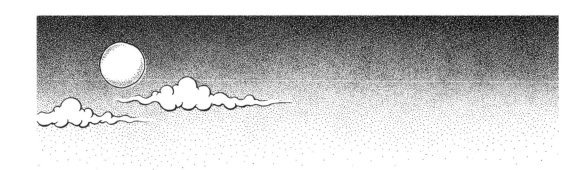

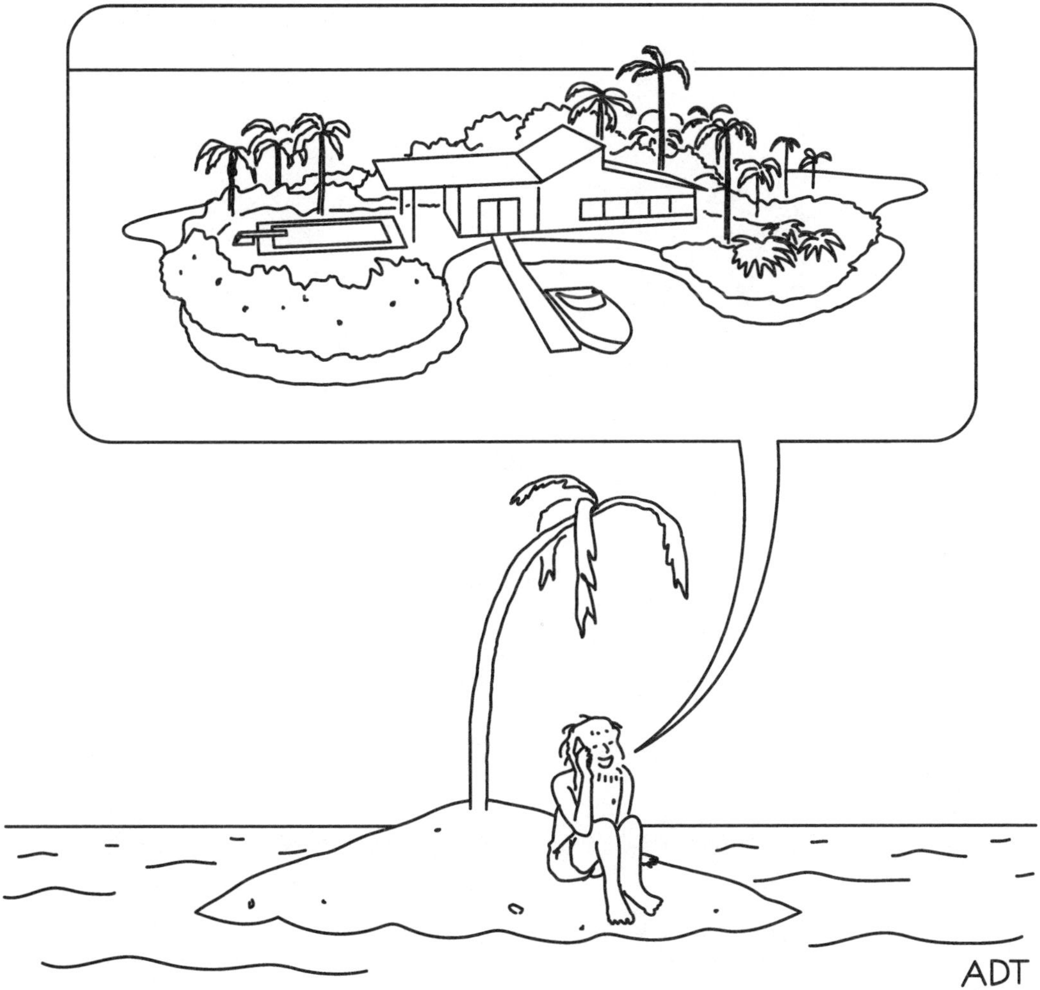
ADT

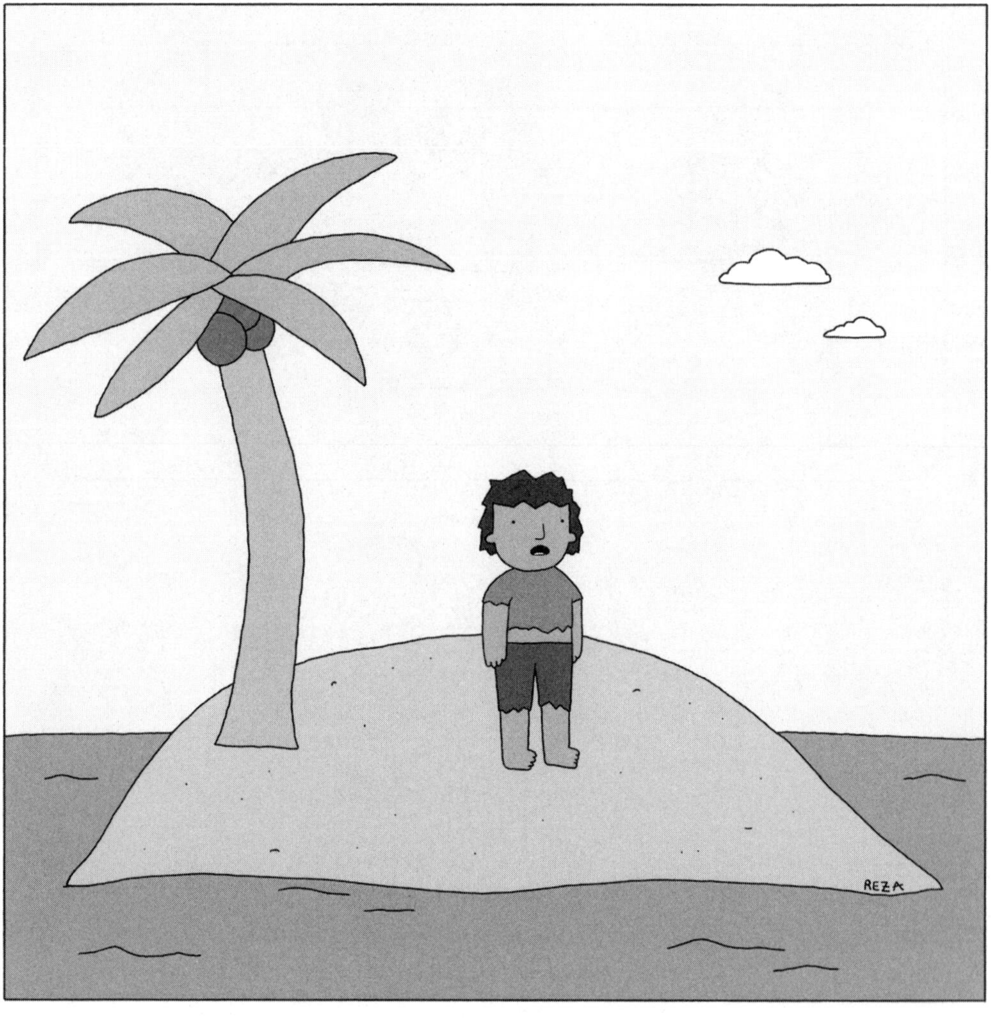
REZA

"Bad time to be a guy with no hobbies."

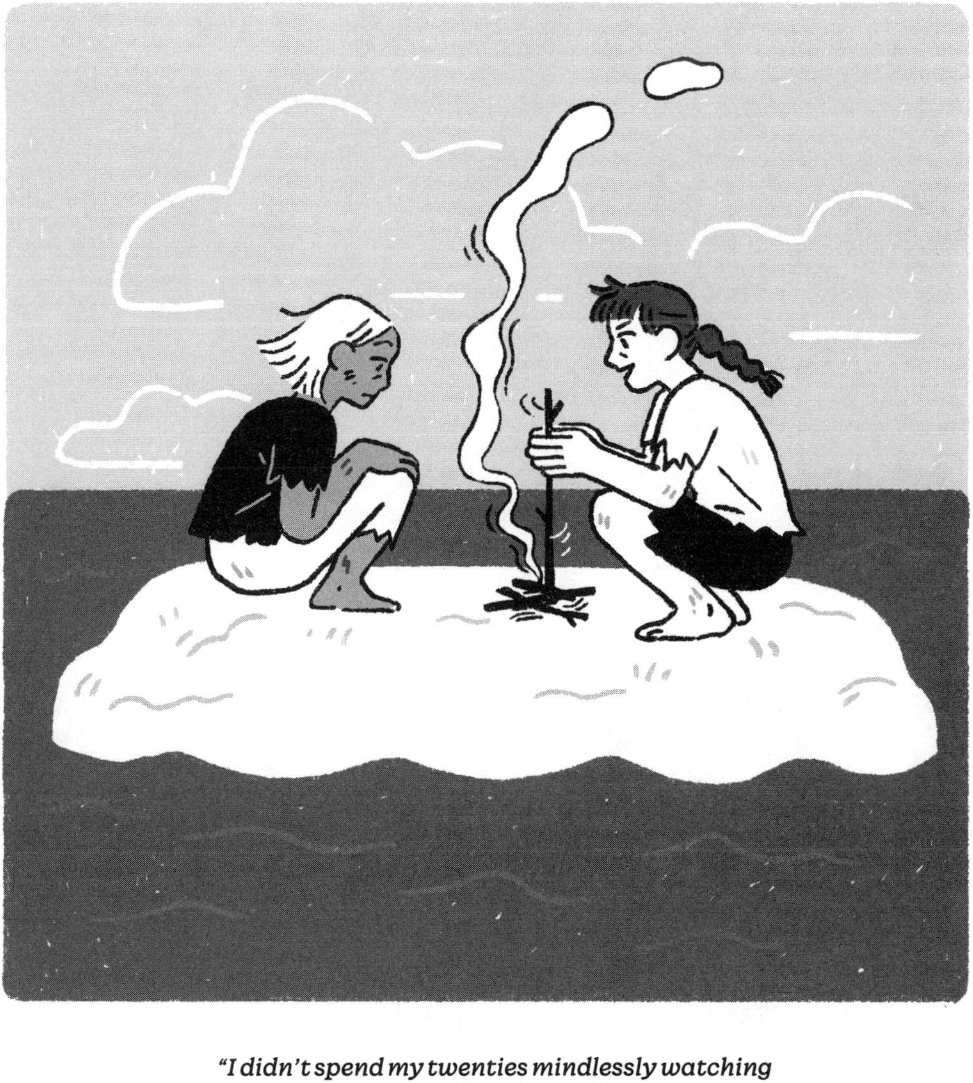

"I didn't spend my twenties mindlessly watching YouTube videos for nothing."

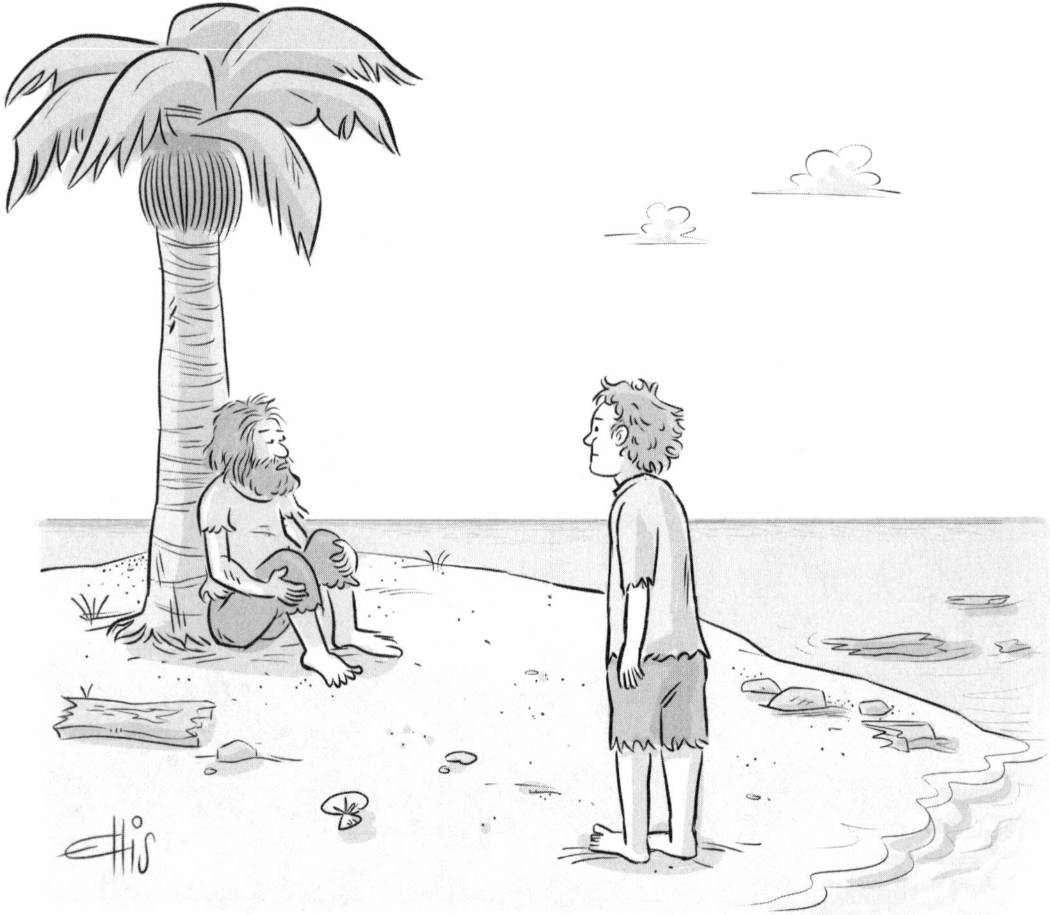
ellis

"I came here intentionally. I accidentally called my boss 'Dad.'"

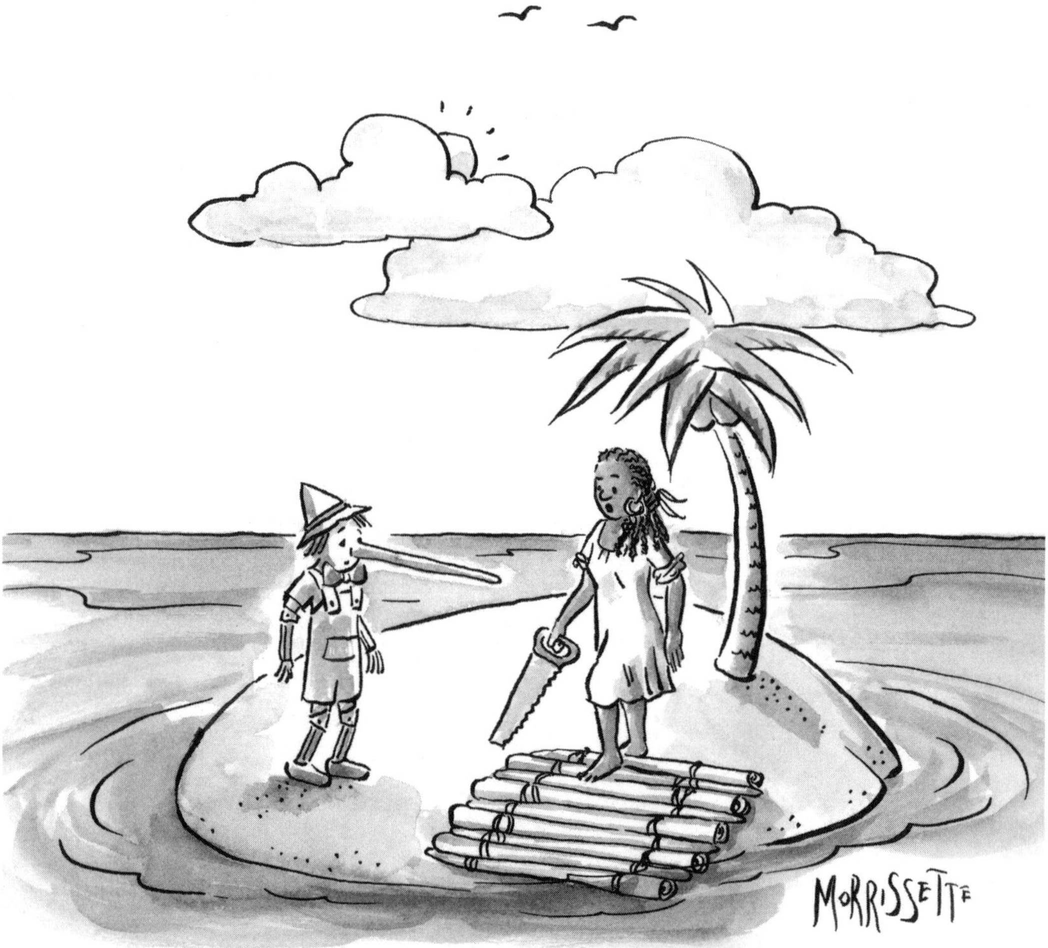
MORRISSETTE

"Okay, now tell a big one for the mast."

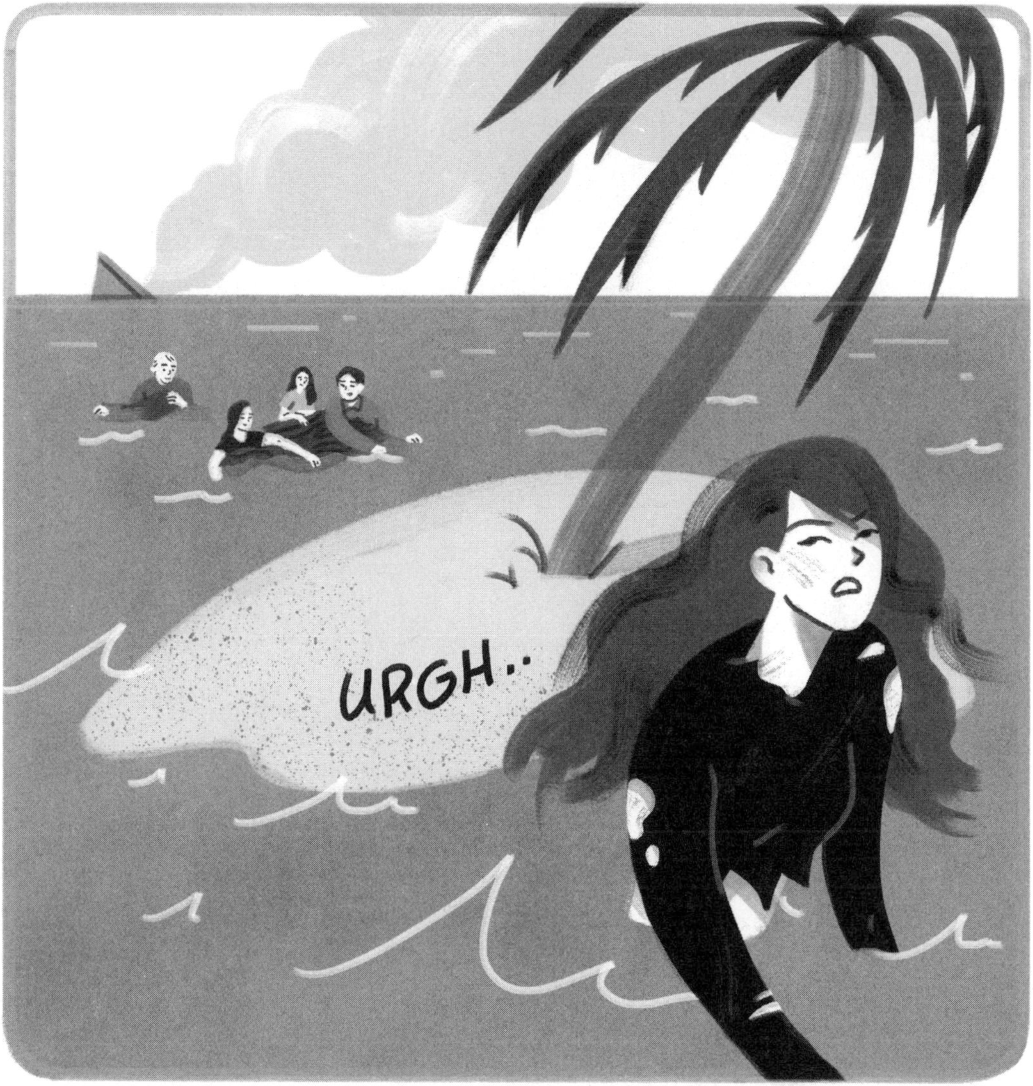
URGH..

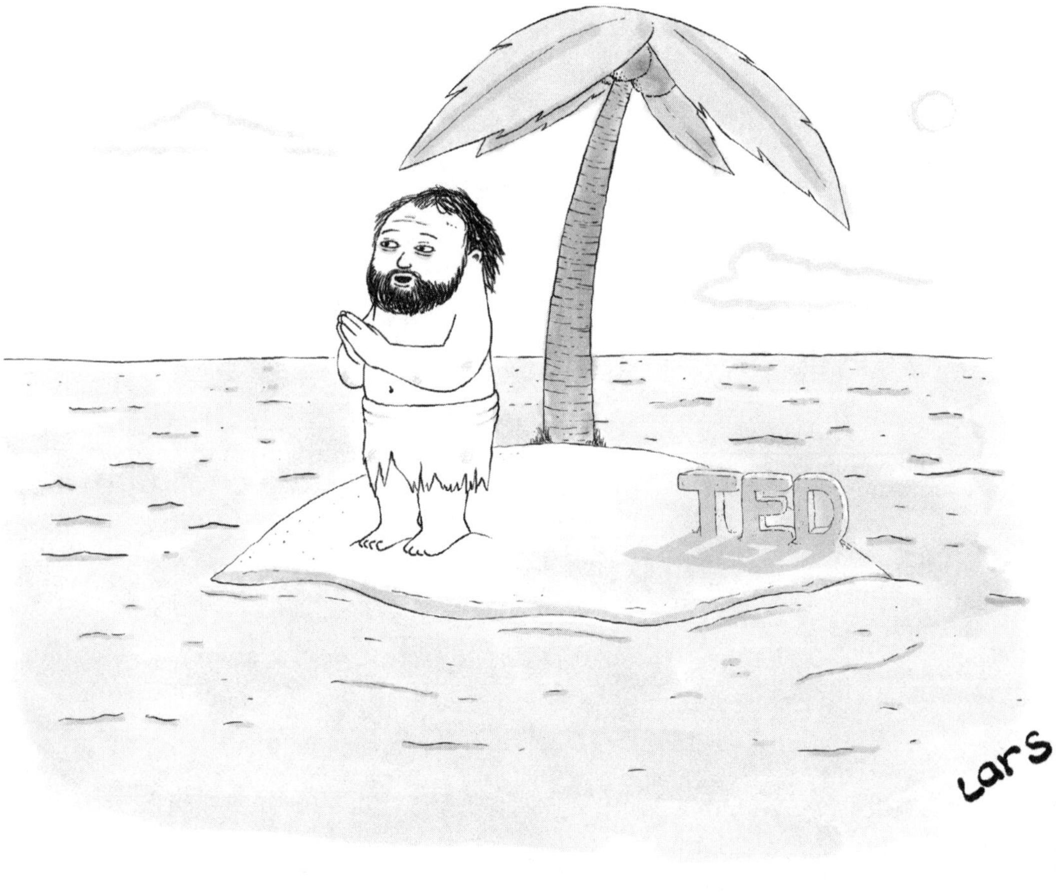
TED
Lars

"What if I told you that everything you knew about slowly going insane on a desert island was wrong."

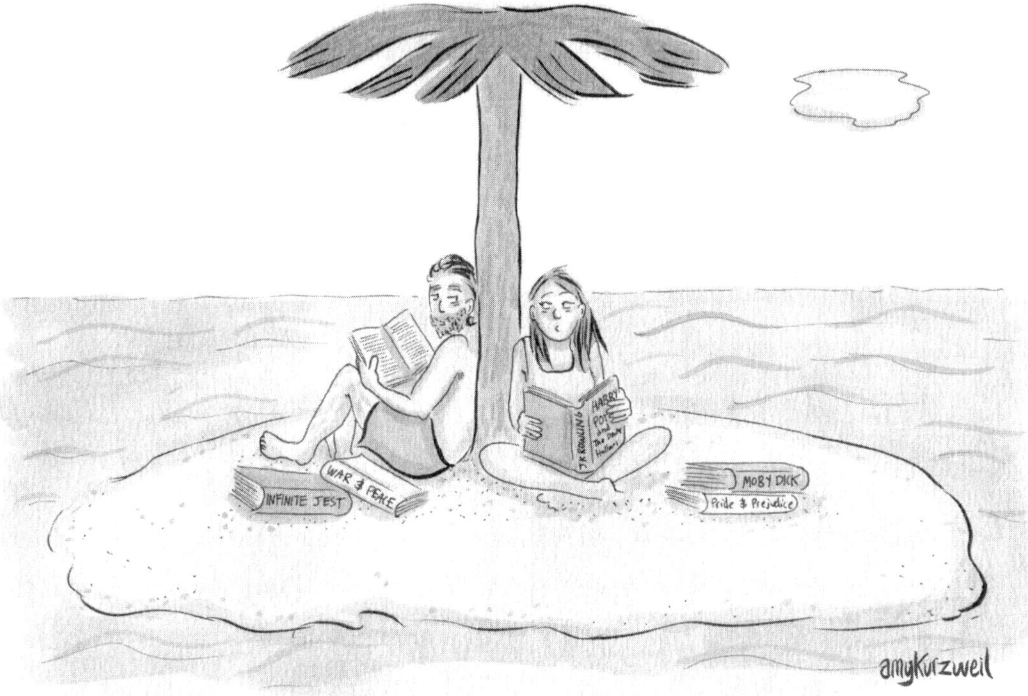
INFINITE JEST
WAR & PEACE
MOBY DICK
Pride & Prejudice
amyKurzweil

"I miss not reading."

ADT

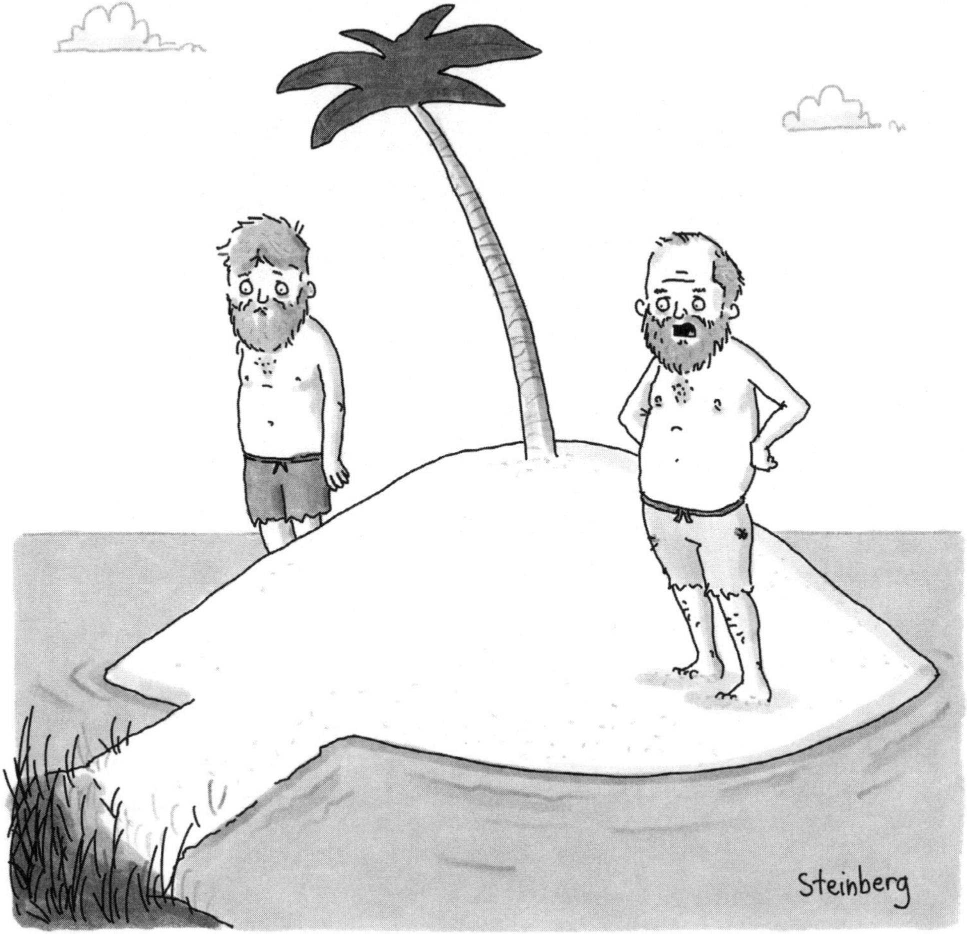
Steinberg

"I thought you walked around the whole island."

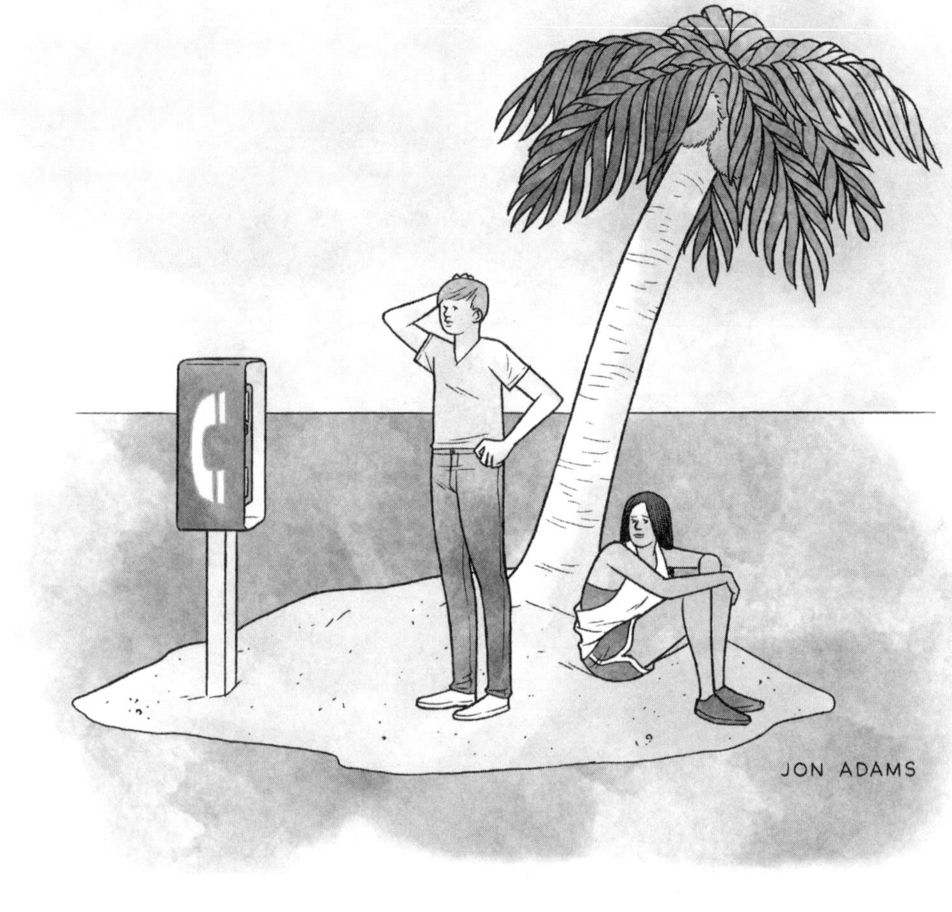
JON ADAMS

"Okay, we both agree talking on the phone is weird. Any other ideas?"

*"I can just hear my mother — 'A plane crash? You'd
make up anything to get out of visiting me.'"*

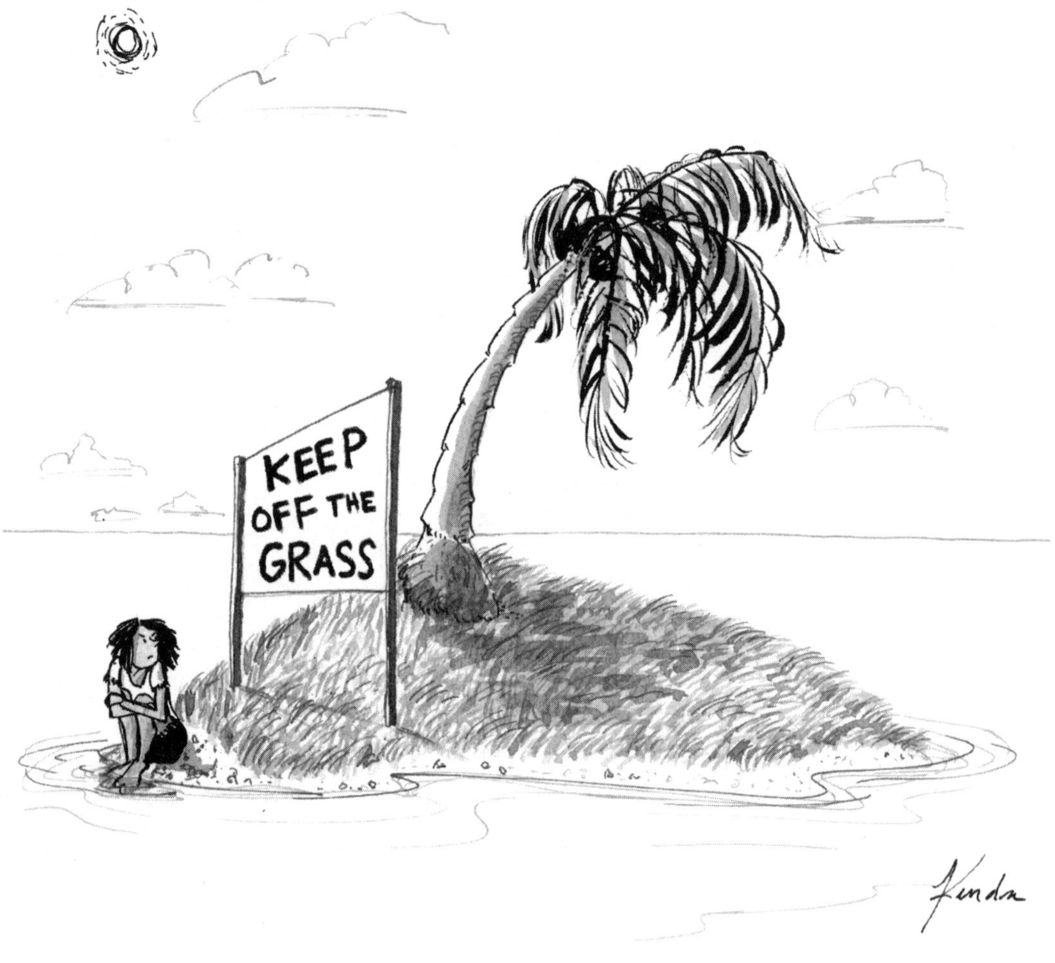
KEEP
OFF THE
GRASS

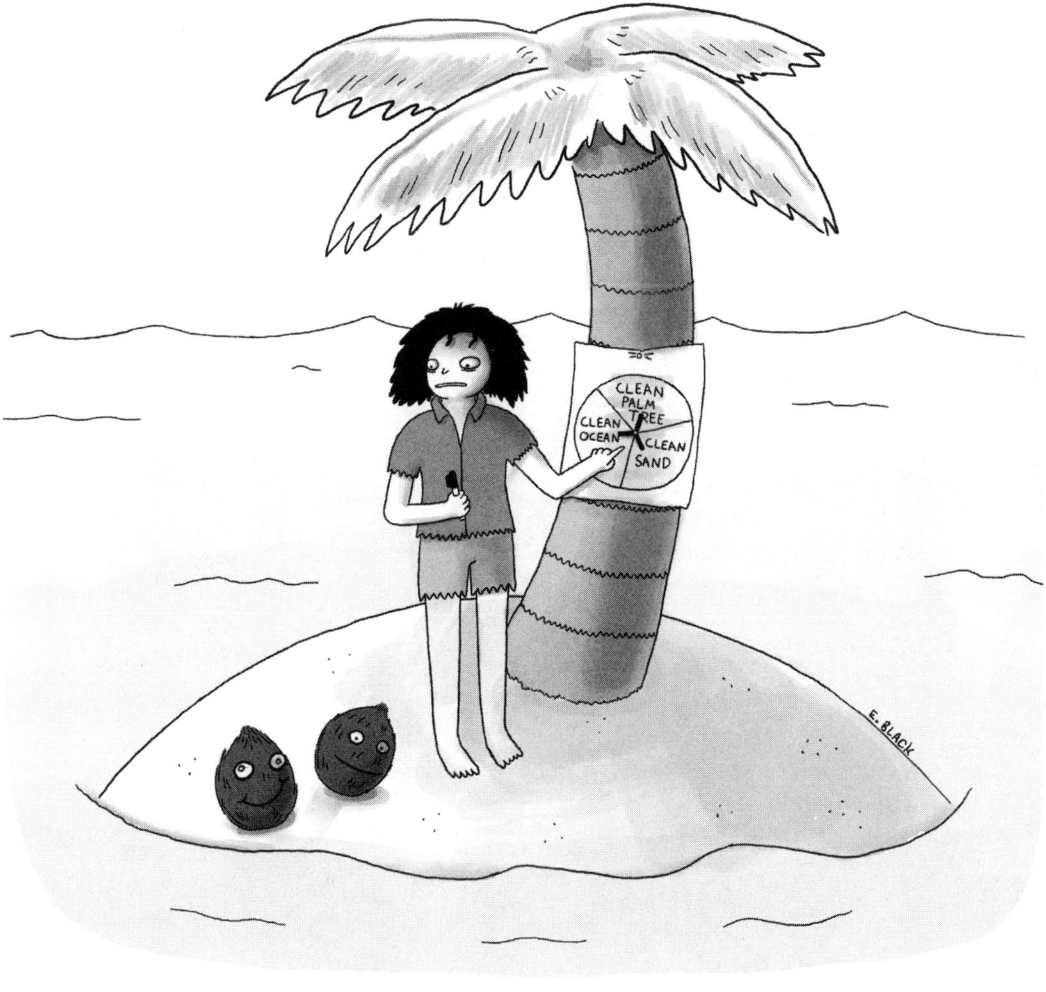
CLEAN PALM TREE
CLEAN OCEAN
CLEAN SAND
E. BLACK

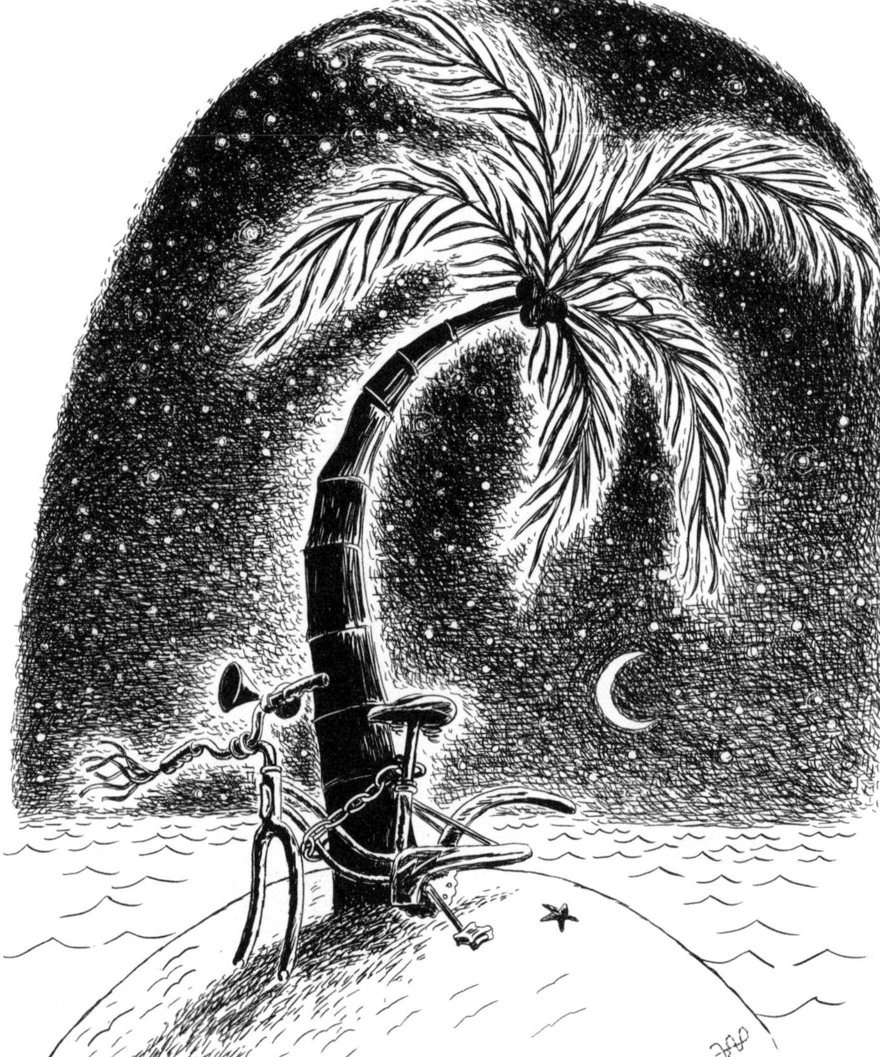

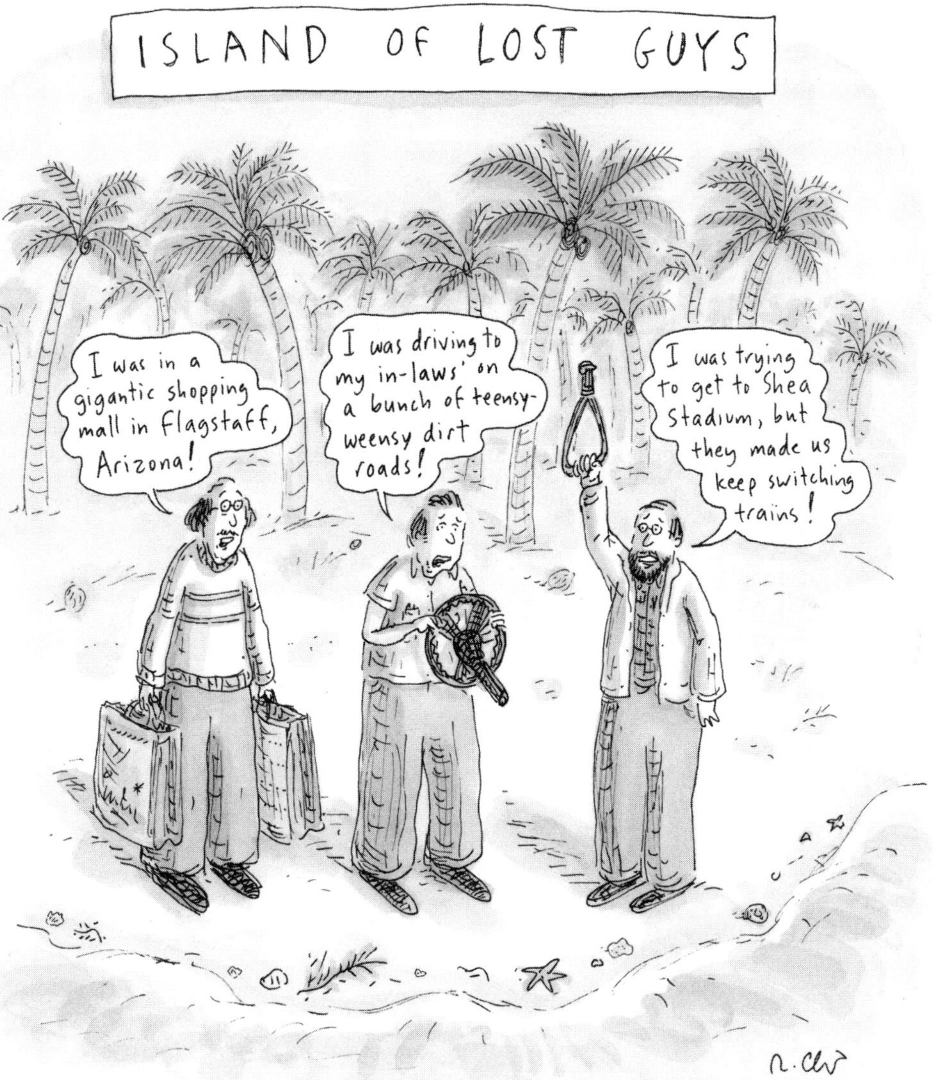
ISLAND OF LOST GUYS
I was in a gigantic shopping mall in Flagstaff, Arizona!
I was driving to my in-laws' on a bunch of teensy-weensy dirt roads!
I was trying to get to Shea Stadium, but they made us keep switching trains!

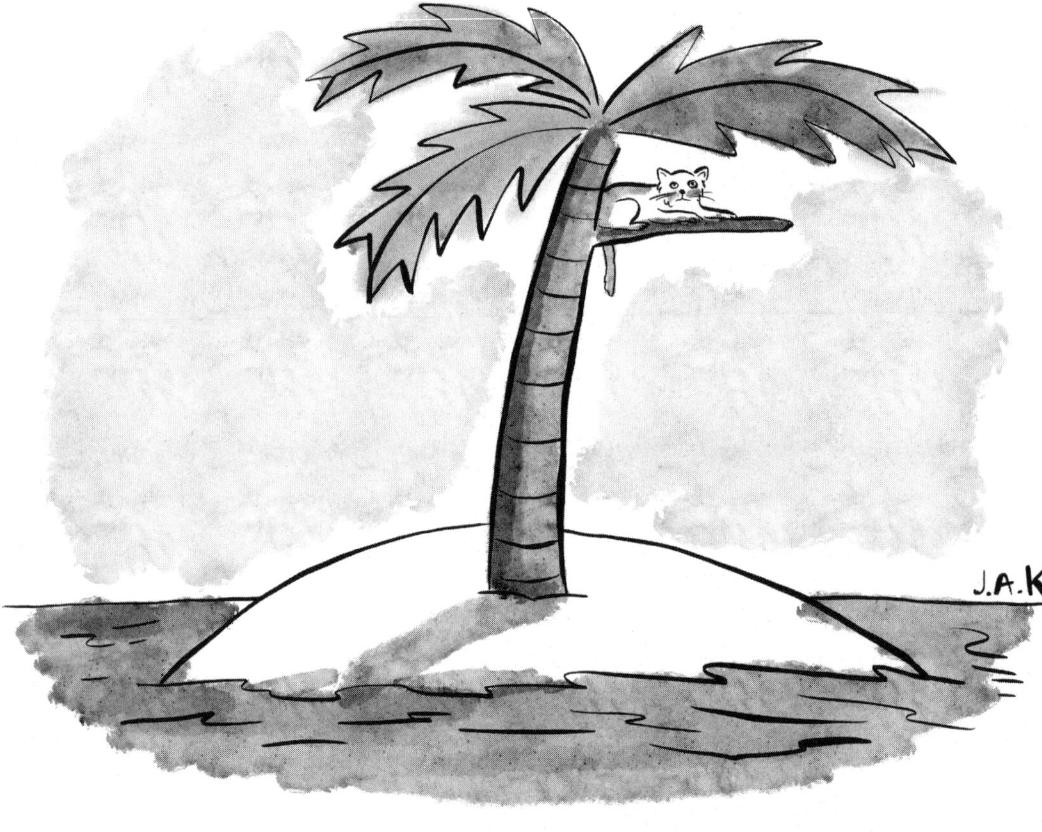
J.A.K.

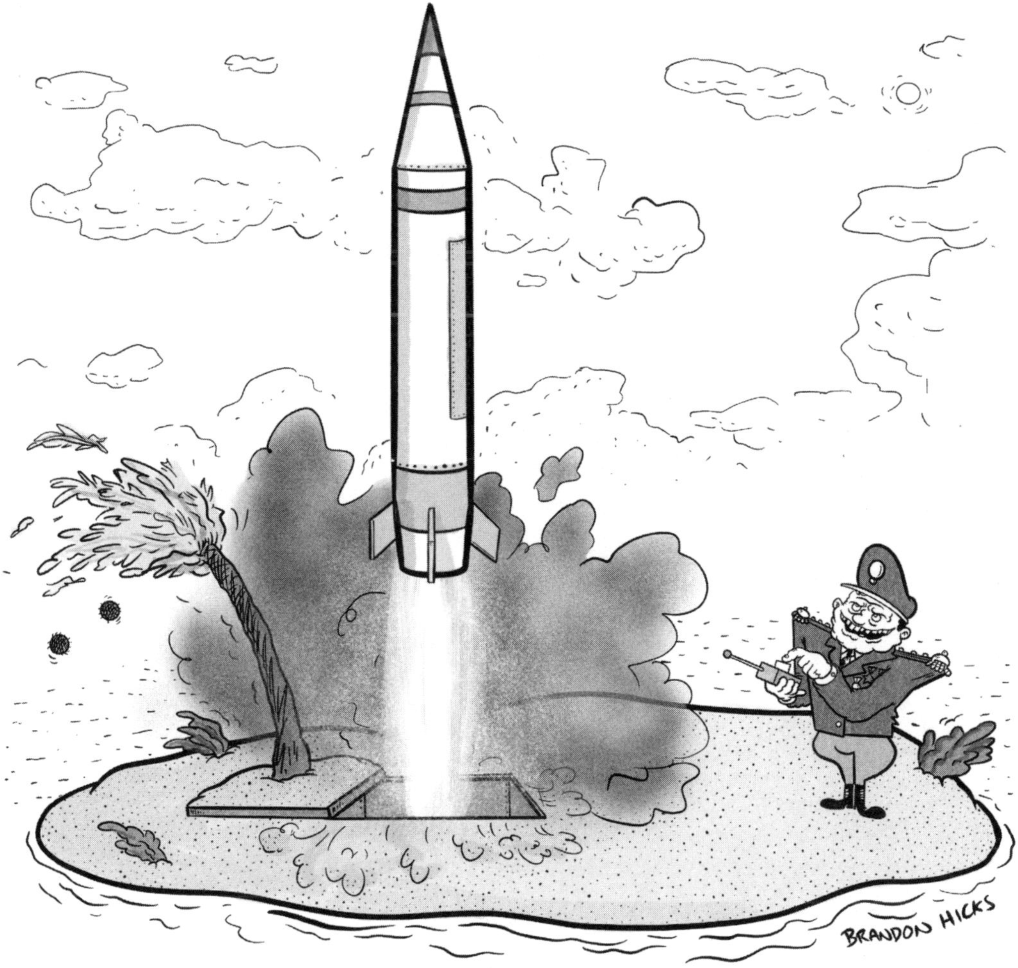
BRANDON HICKS

"We'll see who is 'just a small desert island' now!"

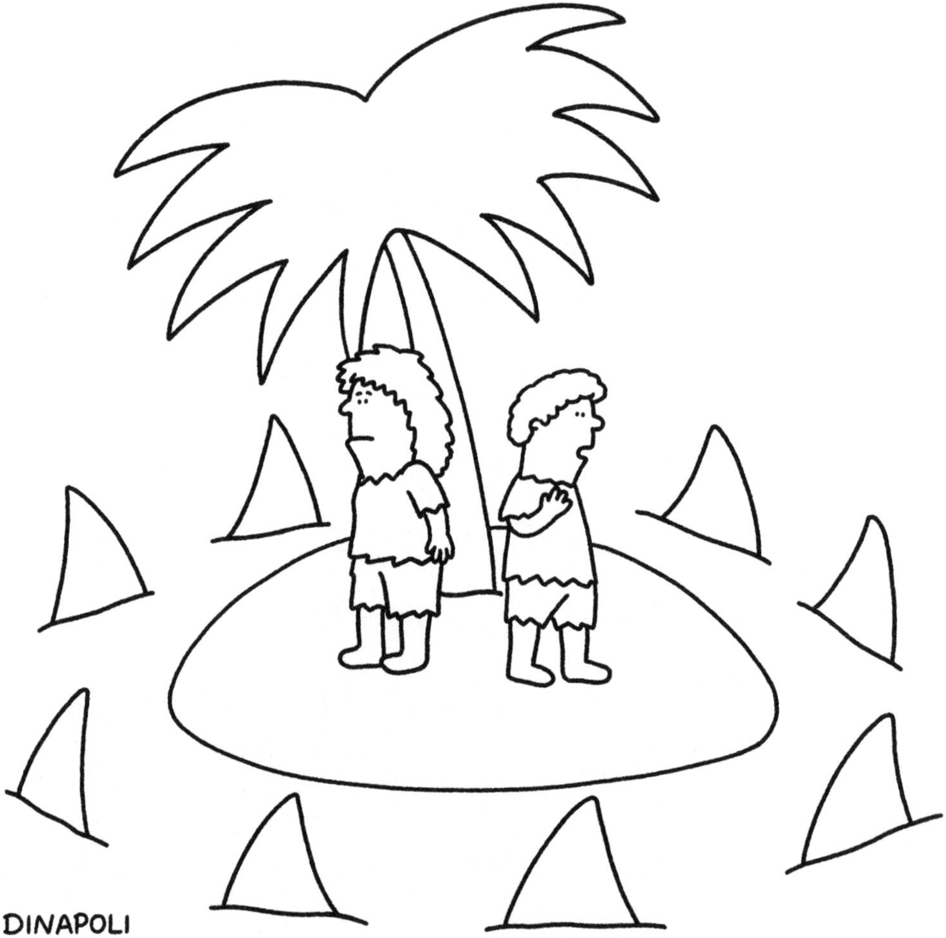
DINAPOLI

"As a human, I'm terrified. As a synchronized swimmer, I'm delighted and entranced."

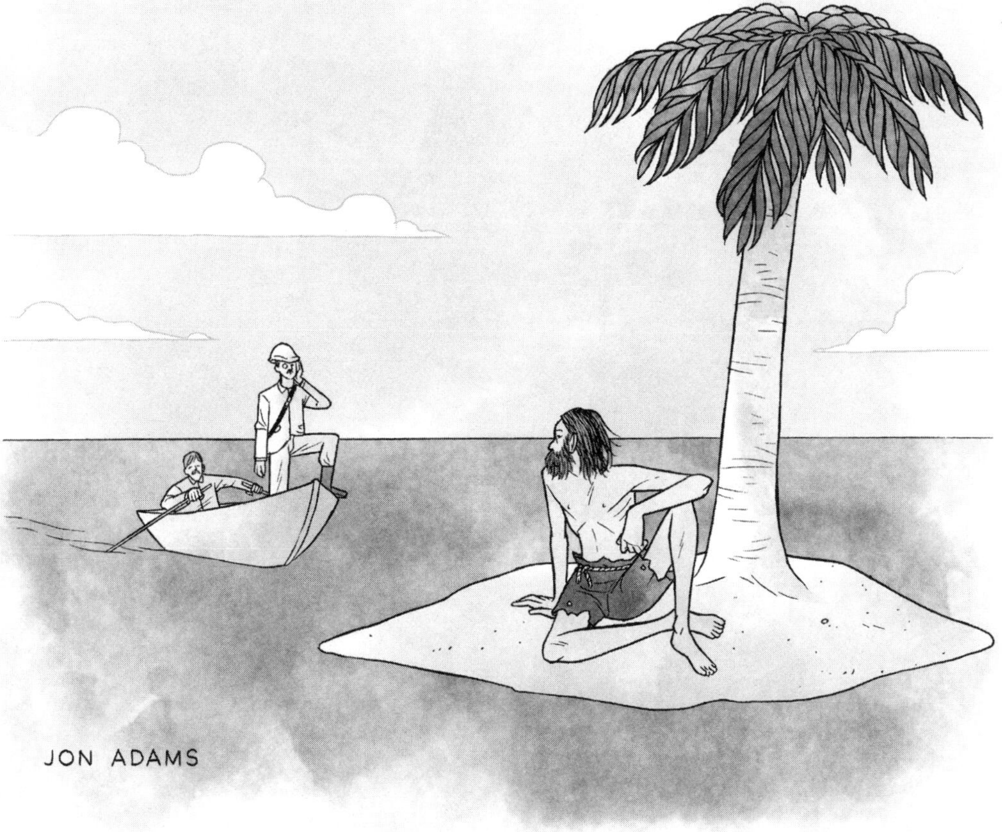
JON ADAMS

"Don't get too excited. We're here to colonize you."

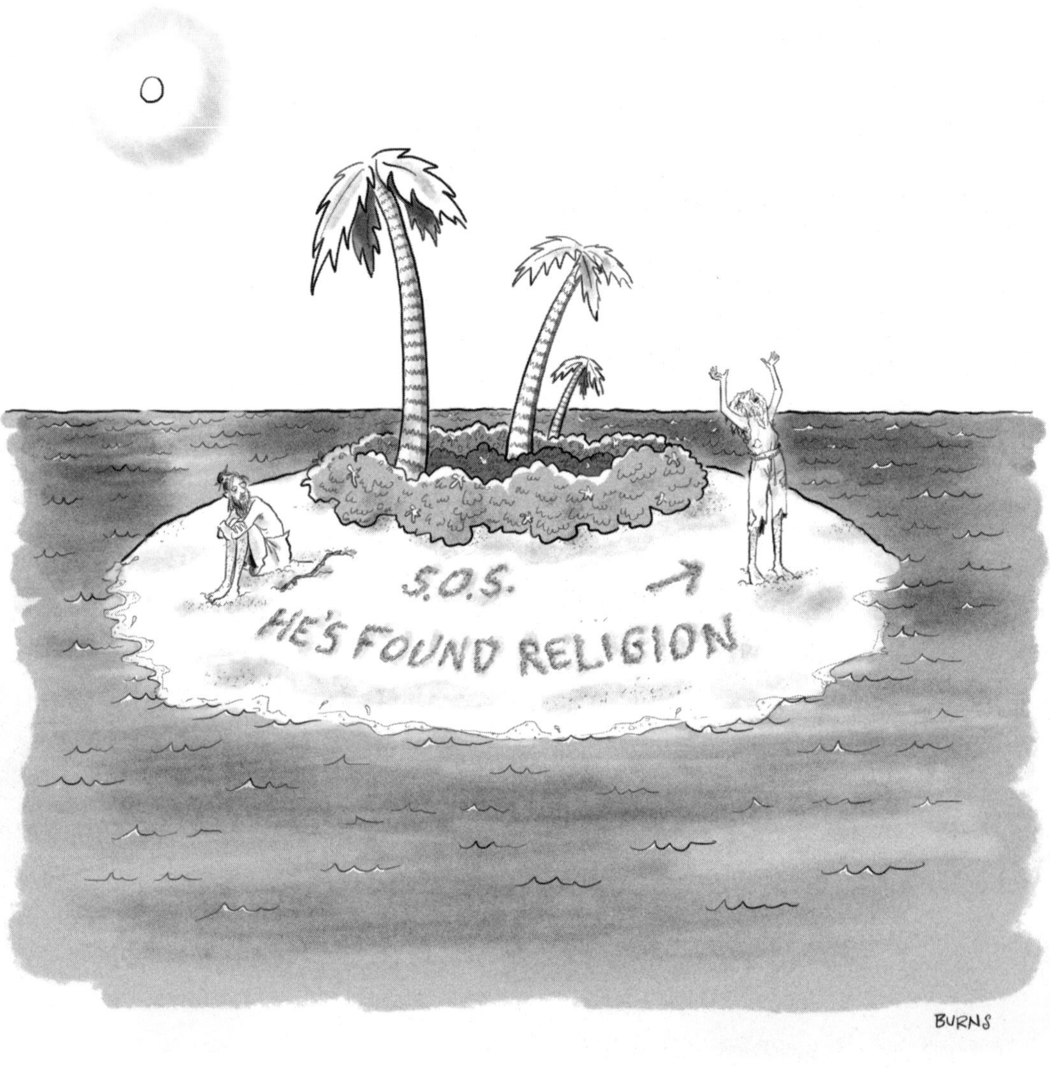
S.O.S.
HE'S FOUND RELIGION
BURNS

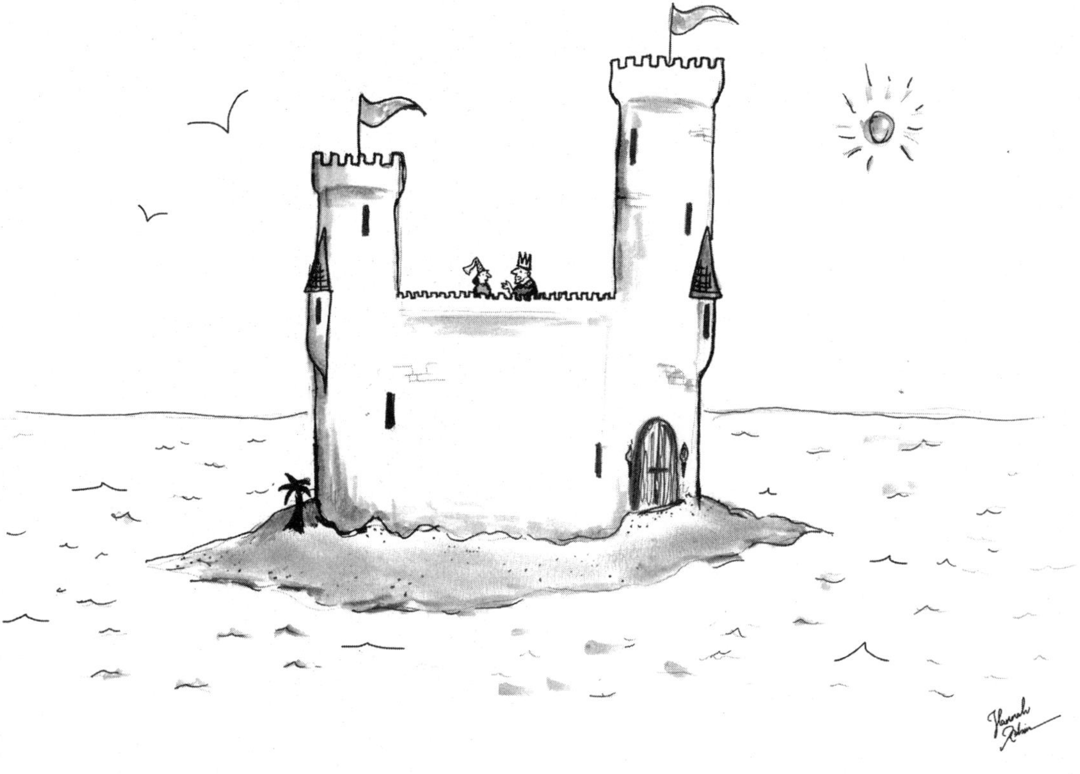

"Do you think I overdid it with the moat?"

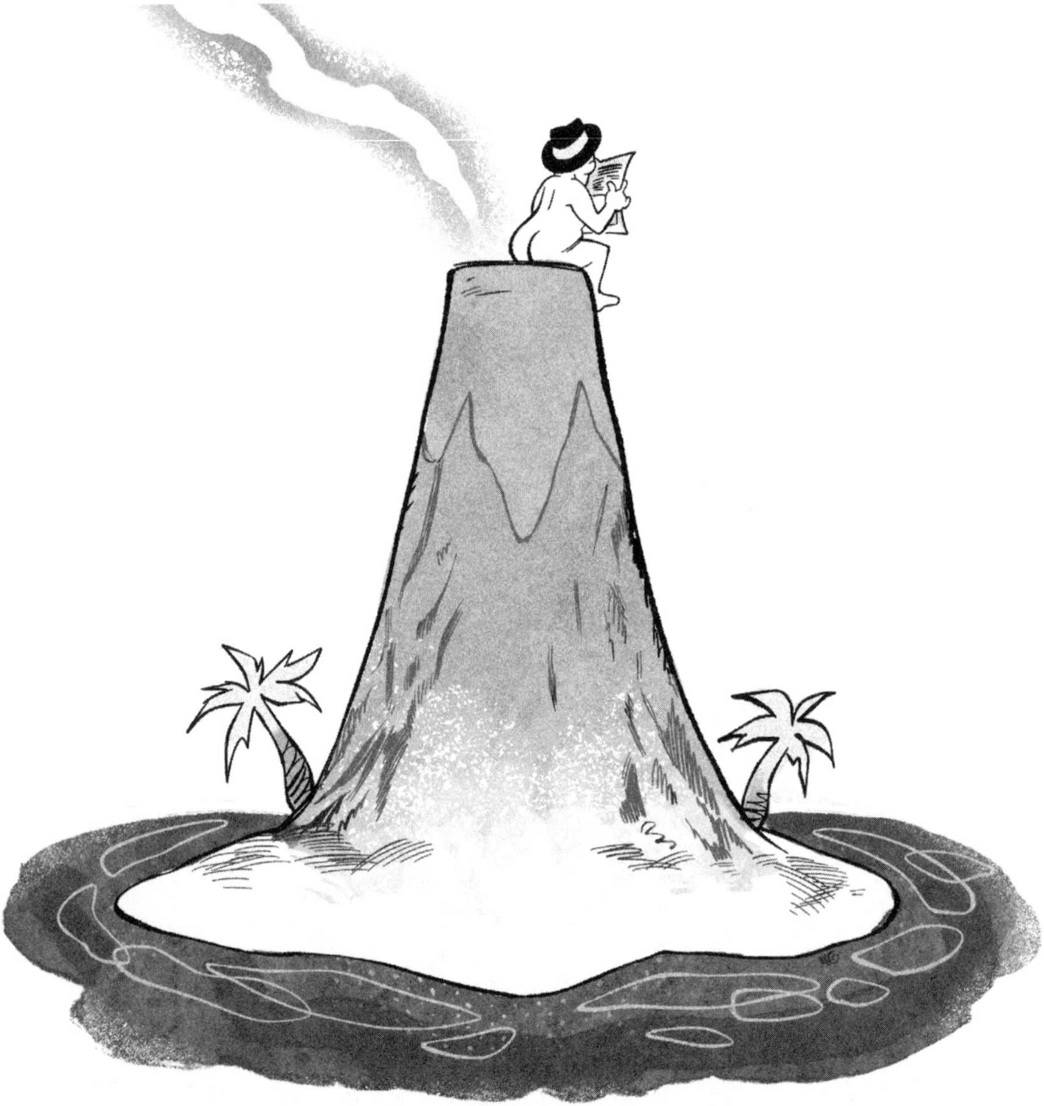

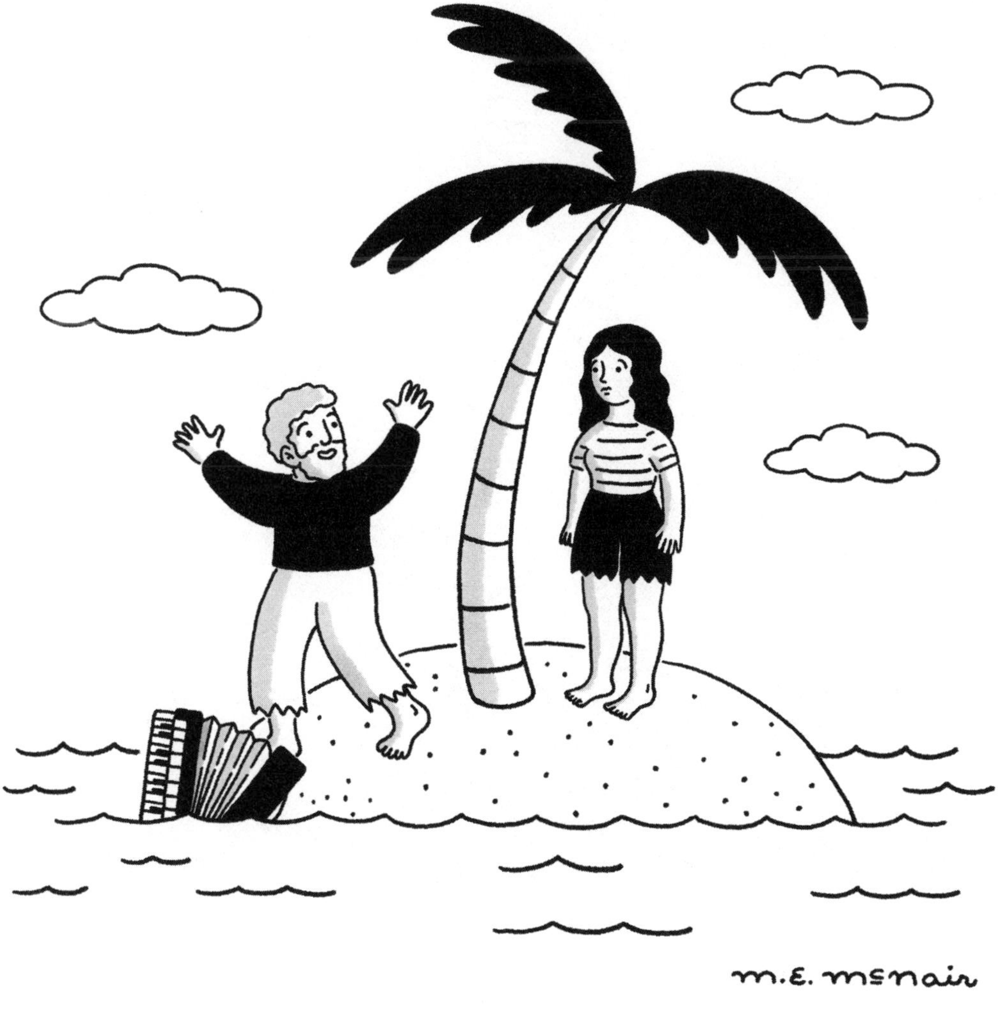
m.E. mcnair

"Great news! My accordion just washed up to shore."

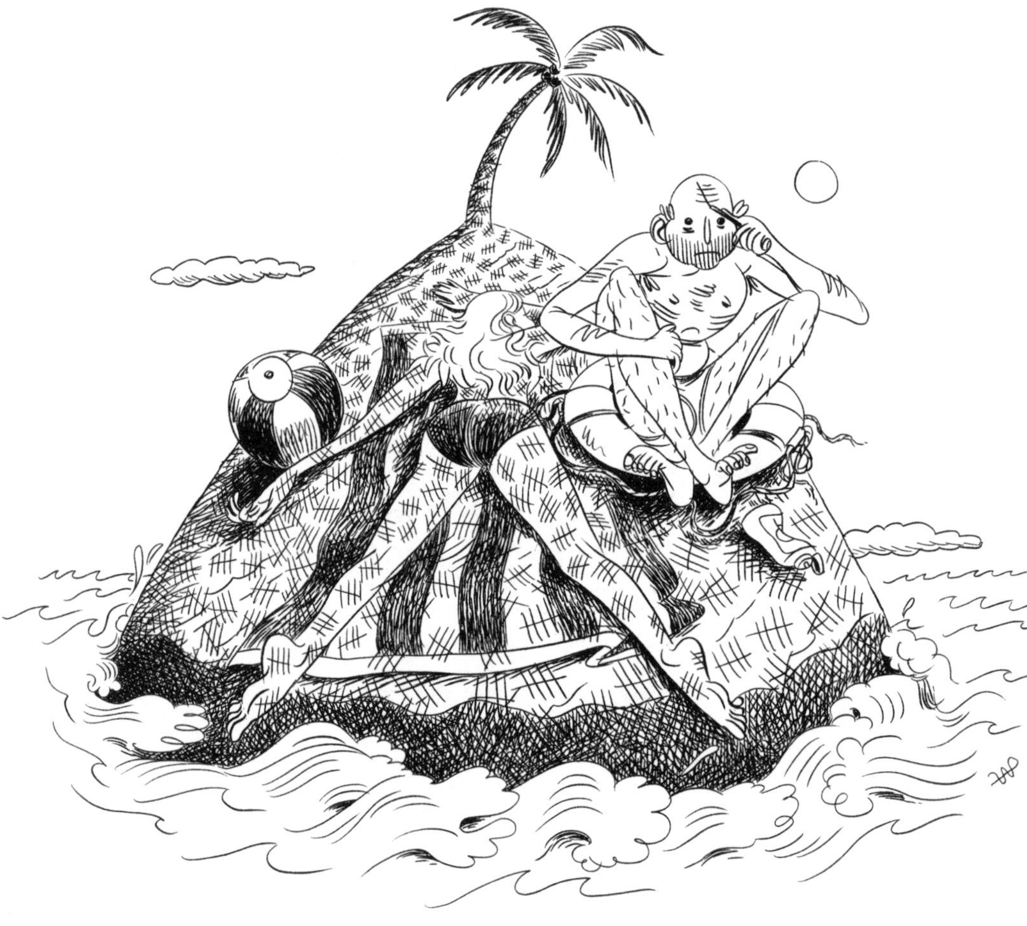

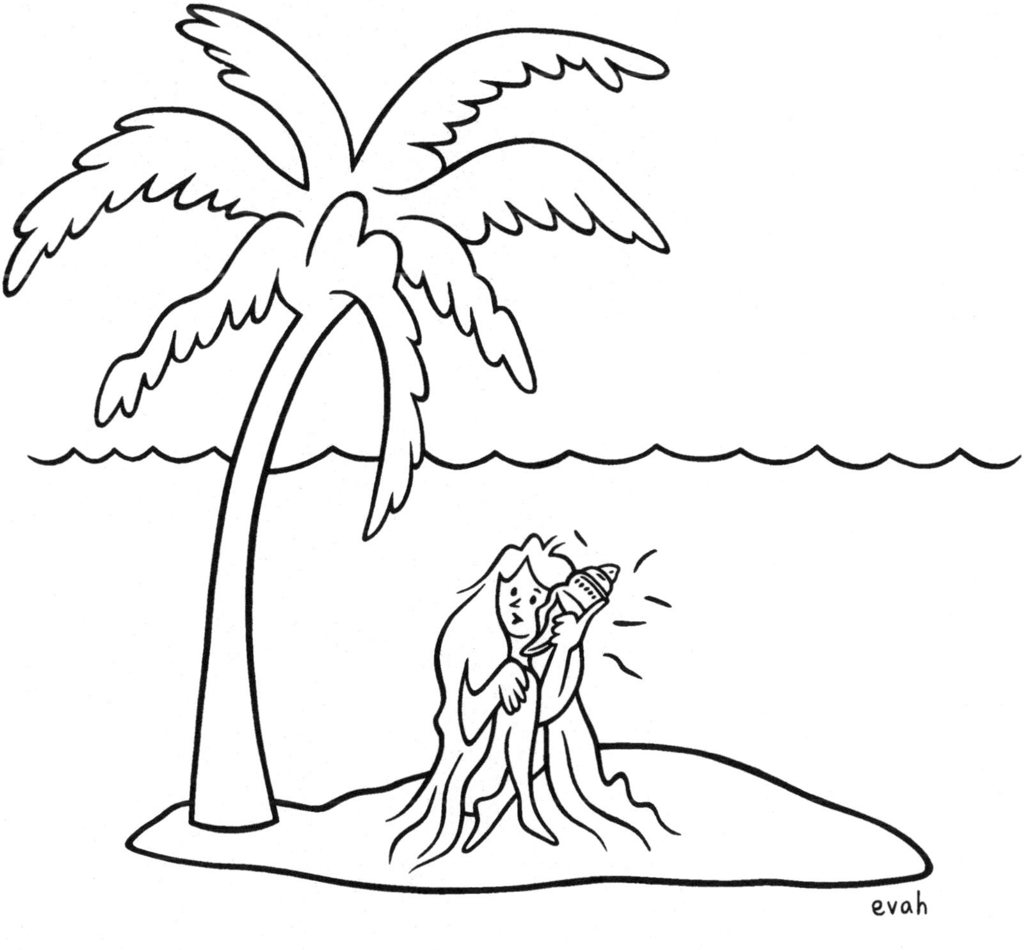
evah

"Sorry, there's no Shelly here. I'm Sally, S-A-L-L-Y."

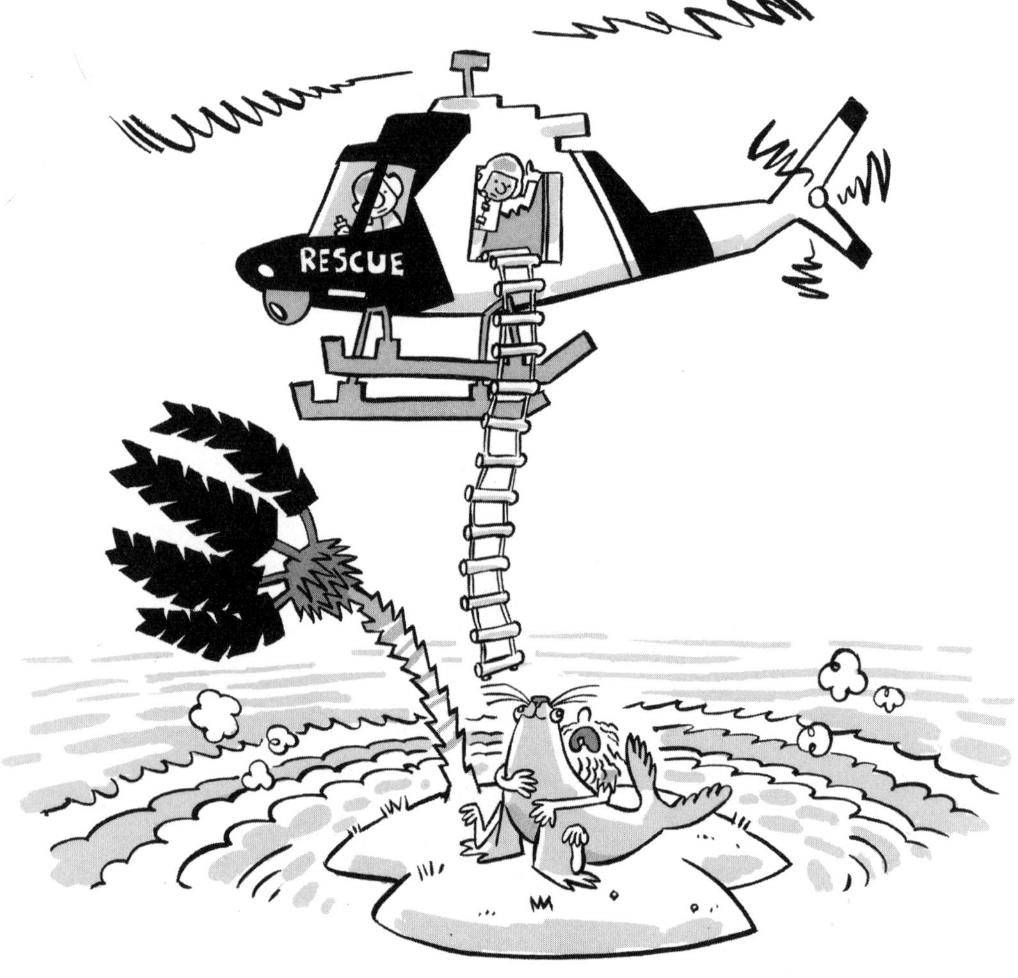
RESCUE

"Not without the mermaid!"

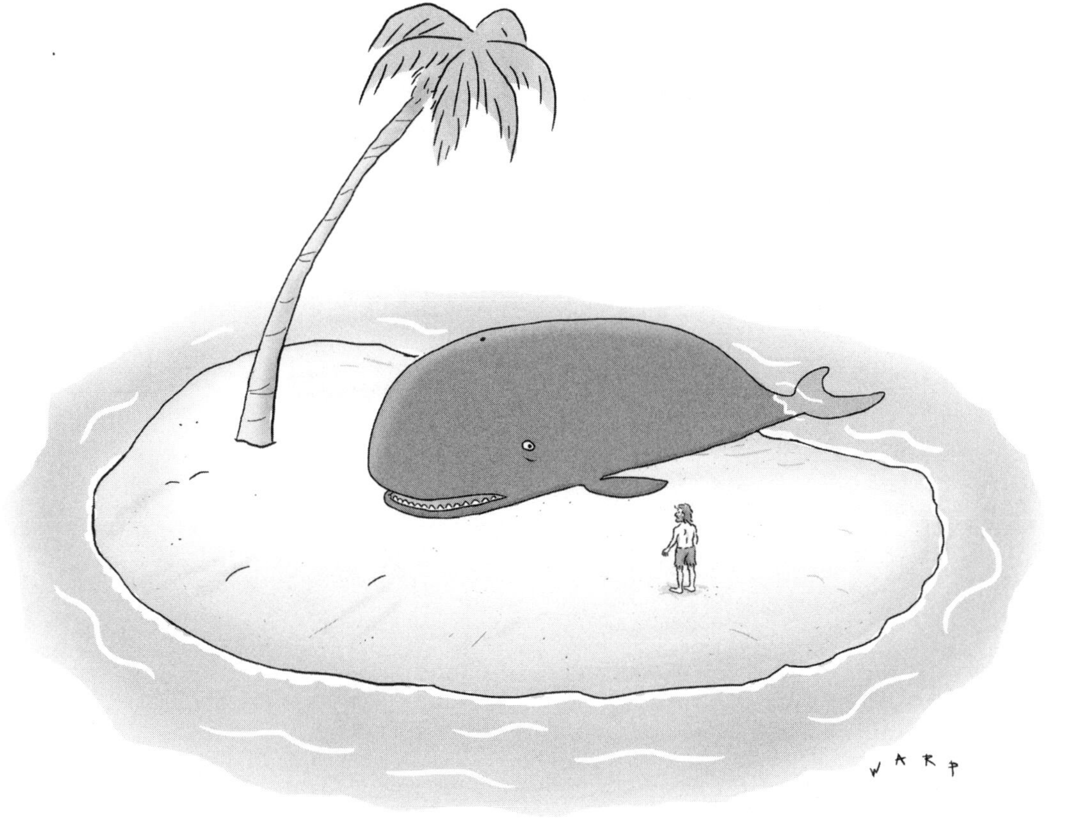
WARP

"I'll get you off this island if you'll get me off this beach."

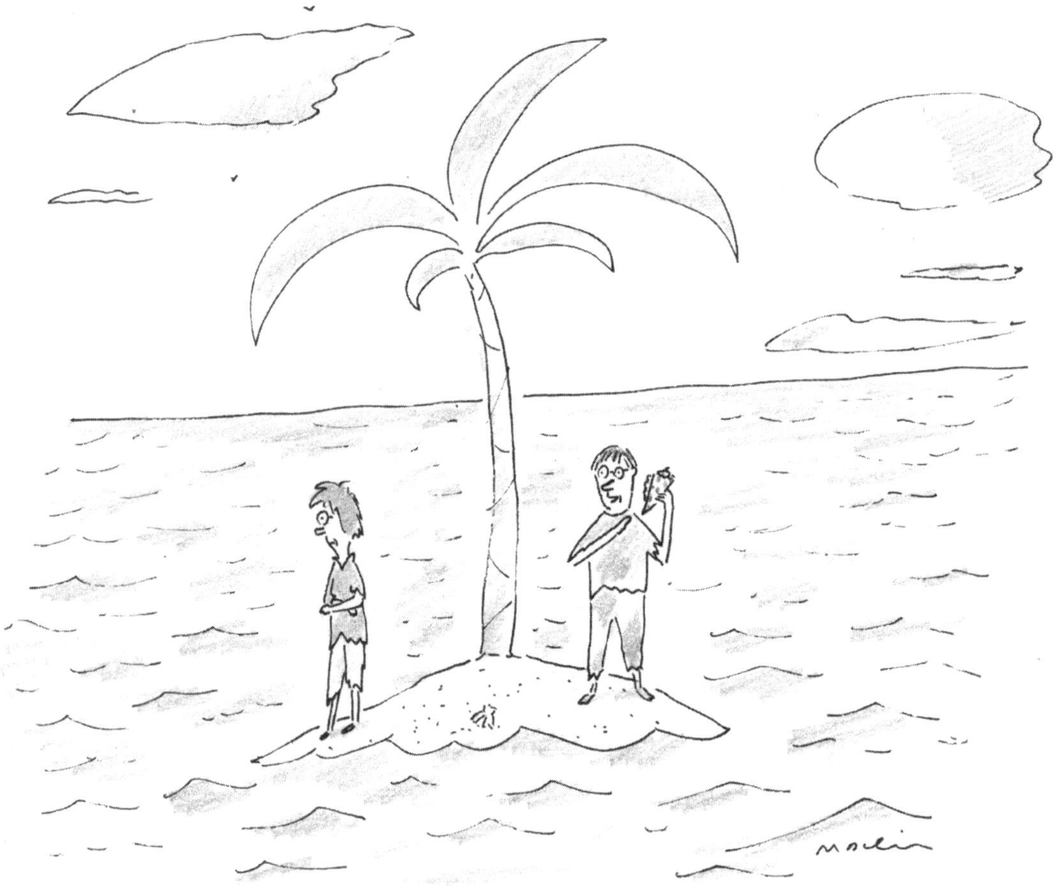

"Hey, Mavis – you want to hear the ocean?"

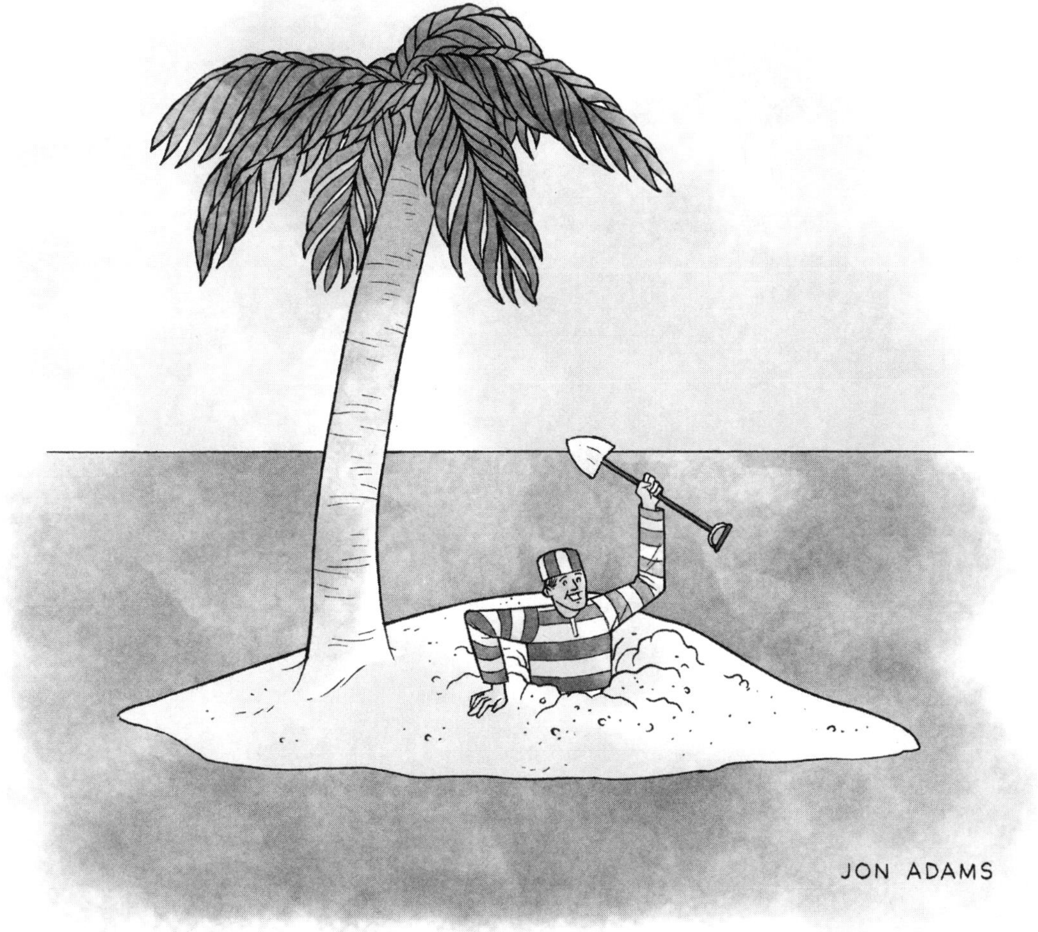
JON ADAMS

"I'm free!"

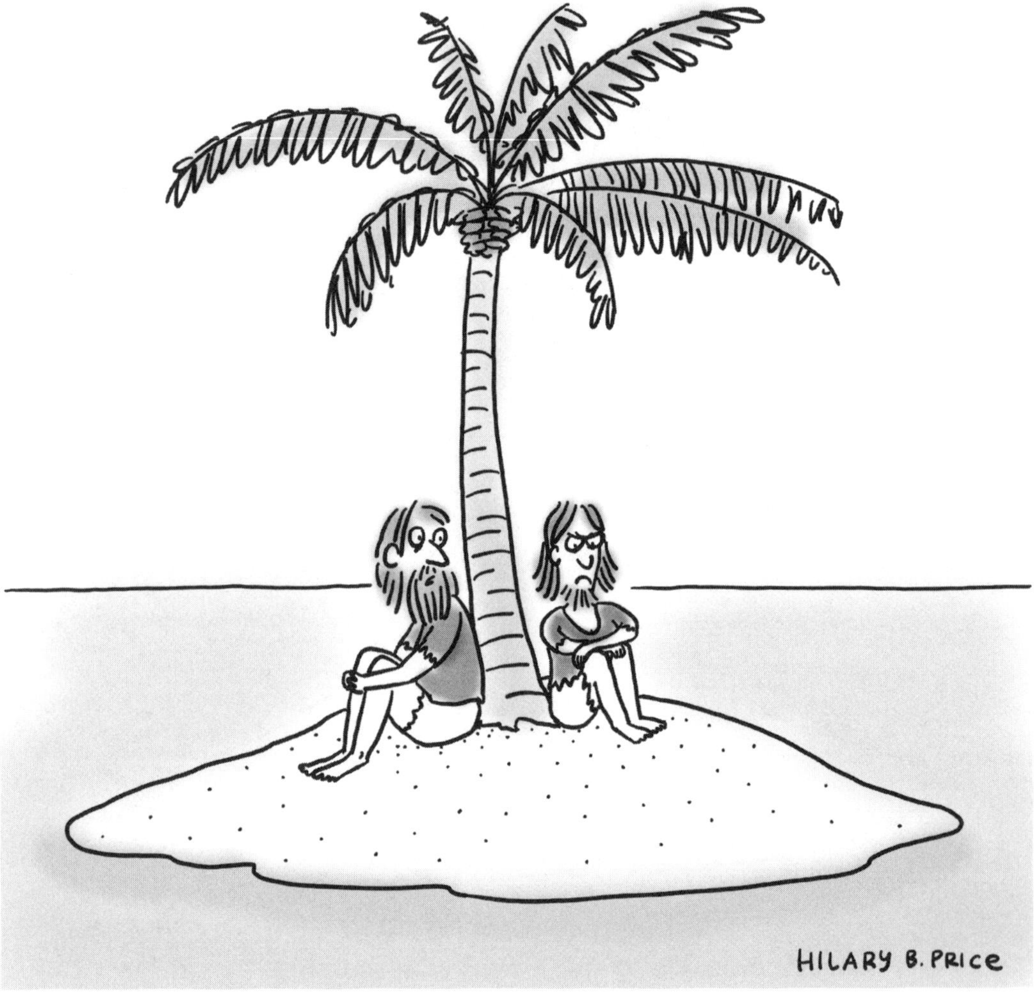
HILARY B. PRICE

"It's a fact of being stranded. We all grow beards, Helen."

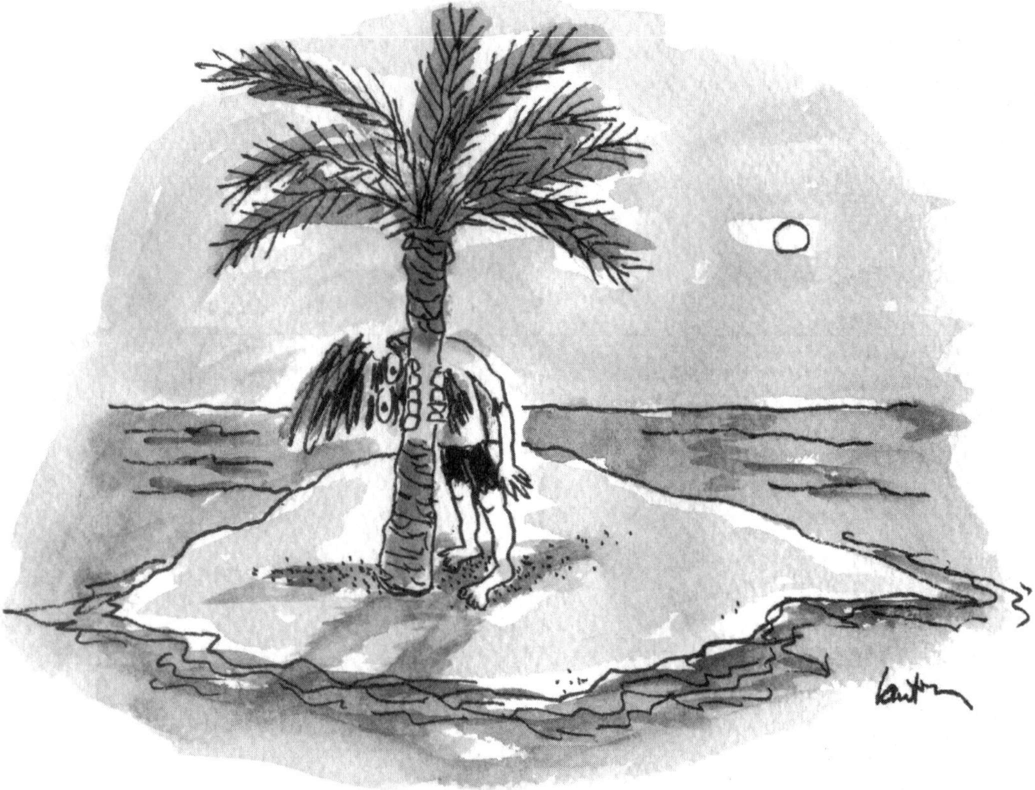

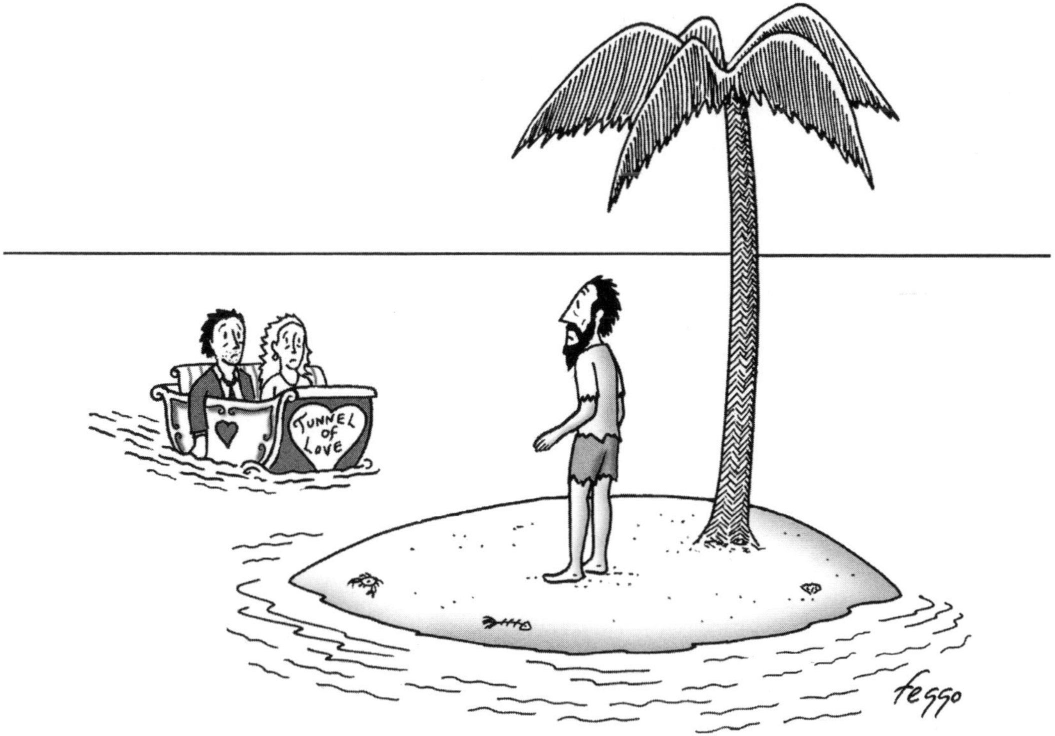
TUNNEL OF LOVE
feggo

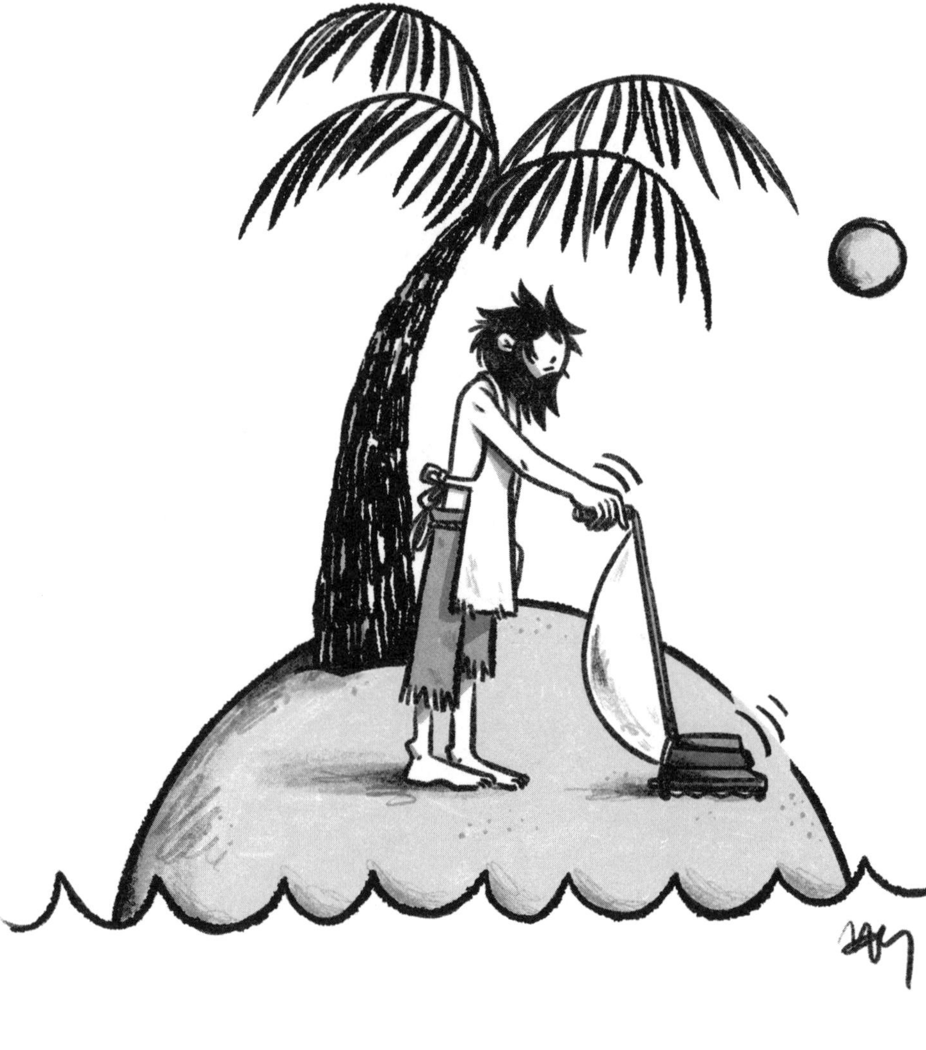

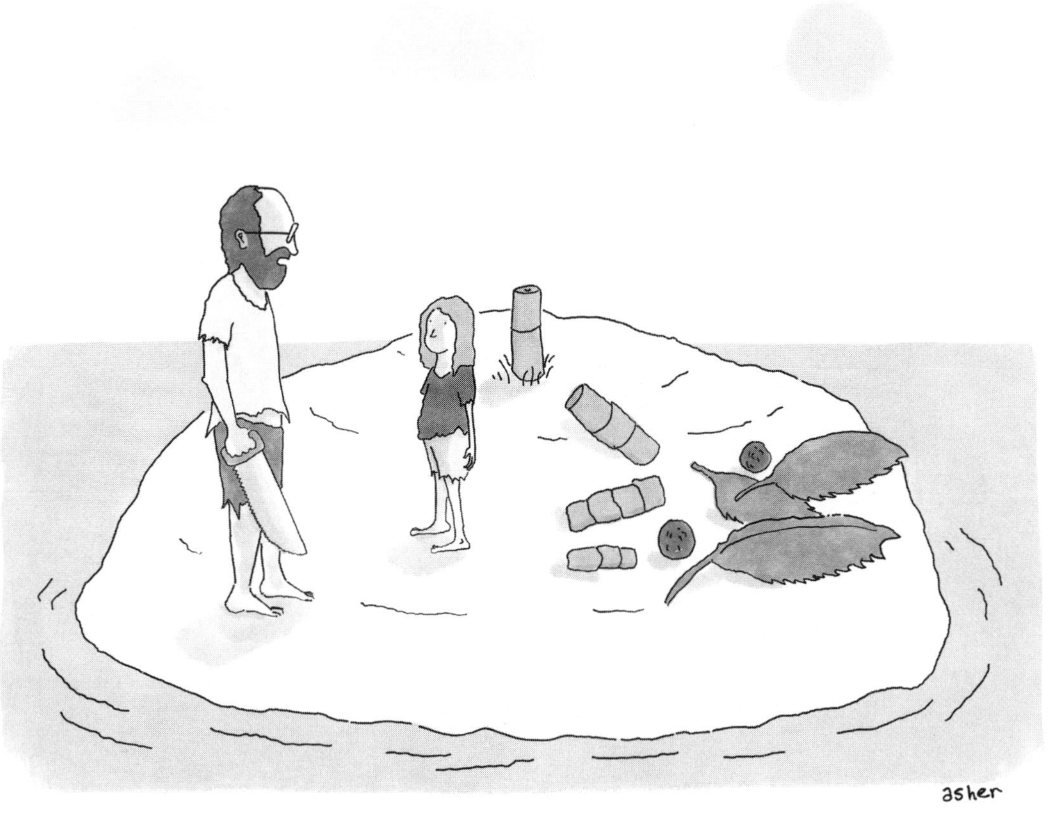
asher

"Sorry, kid. Your old man didn't totally think through this tree house."

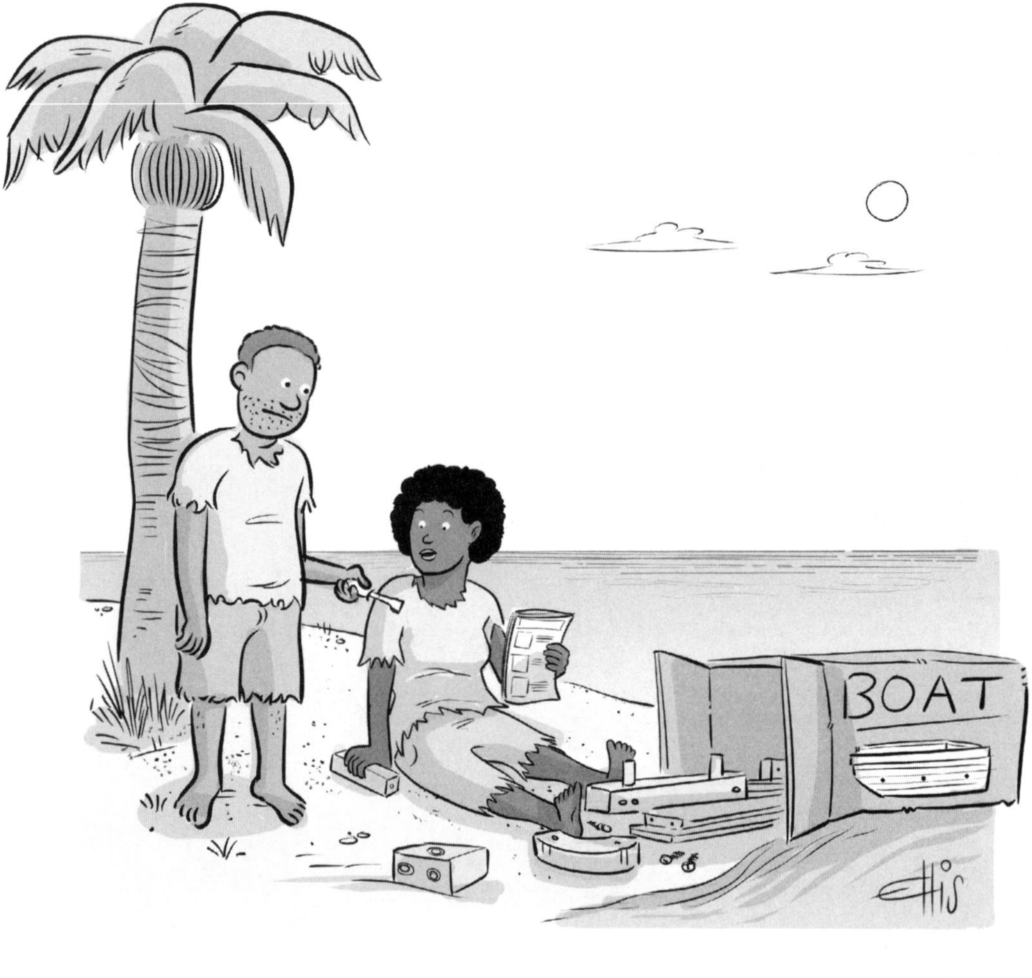
BOAT

"That's a flathead. We need a Phillips."

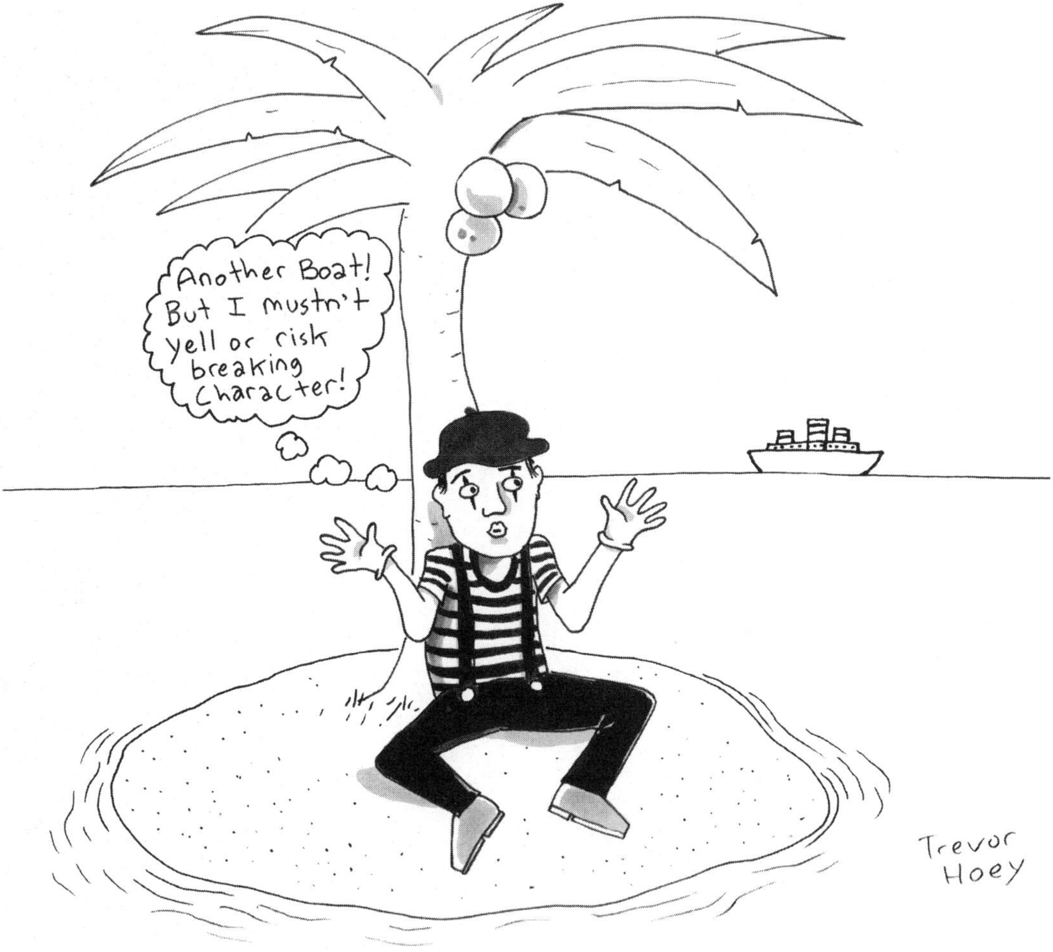
Another Boat! But I mustn't yell or risk breaking Character!
Trevor Hoey

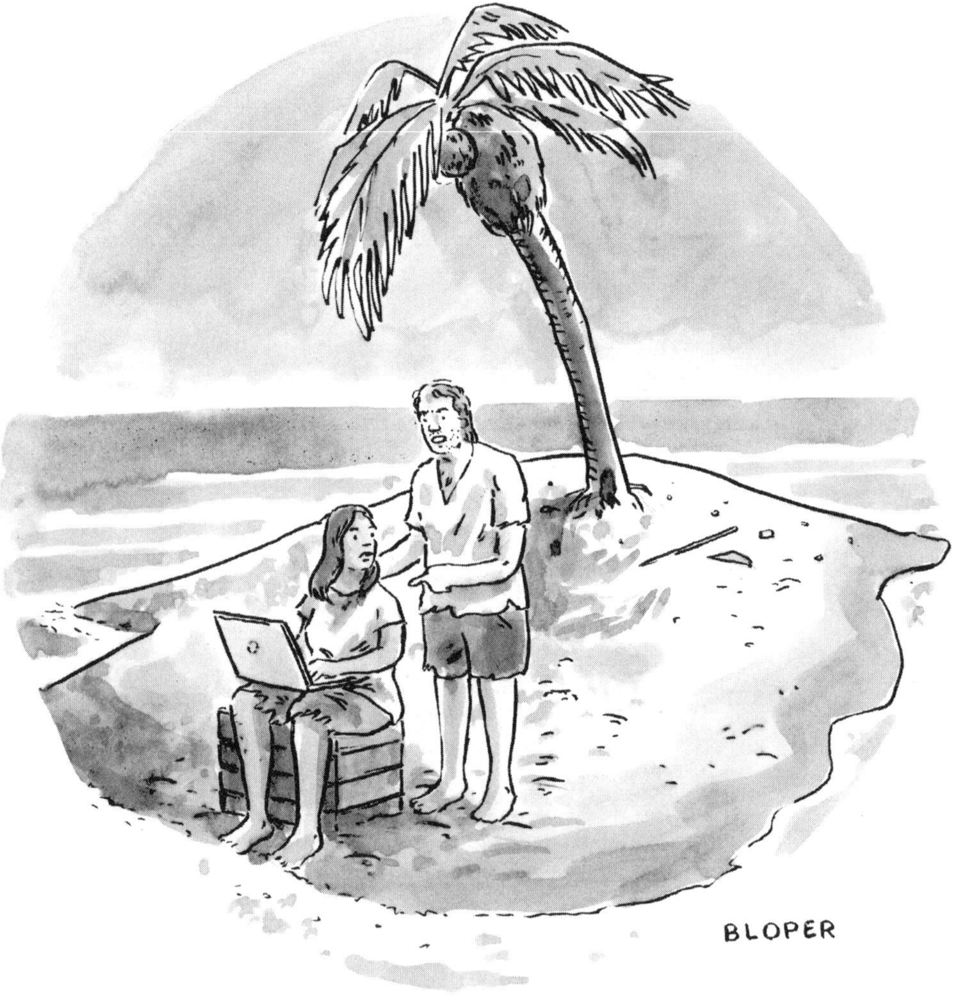
BLOPER

"Try clicking 'Help.'"

Steinberg

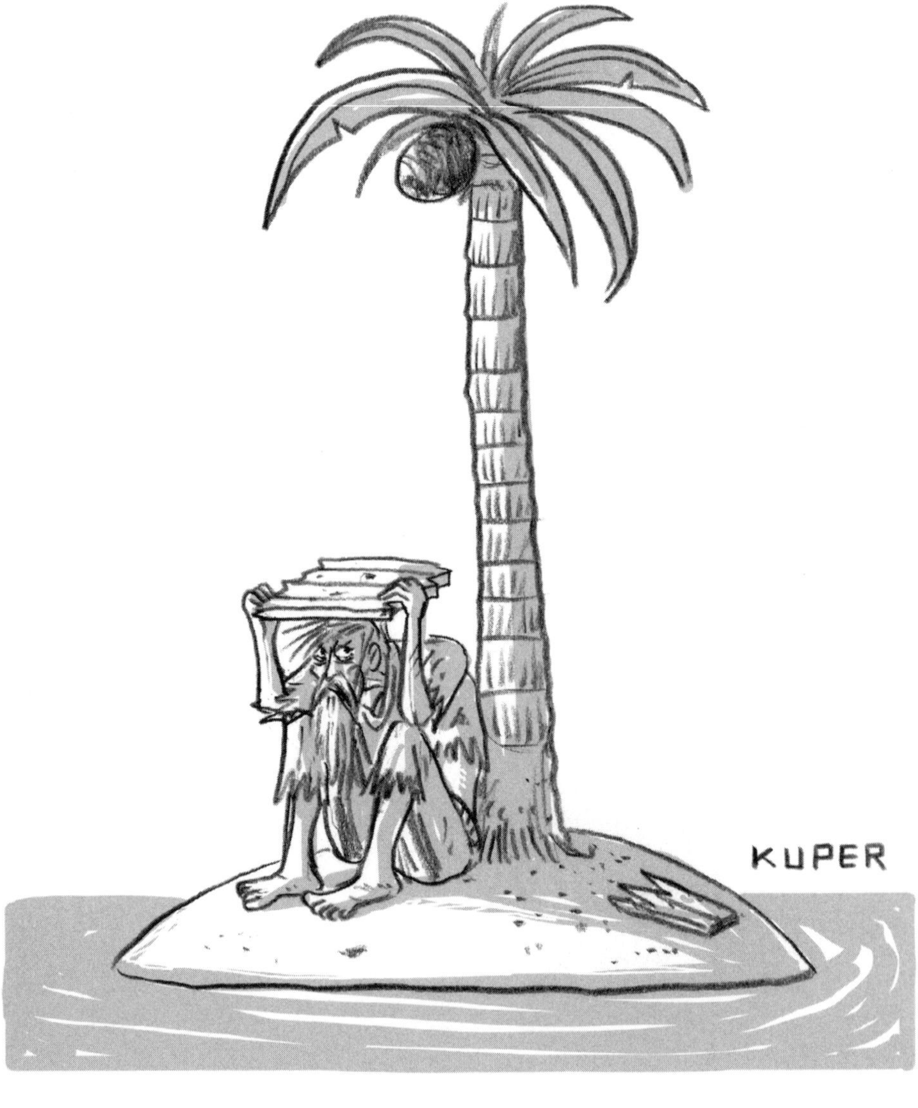
KUPER

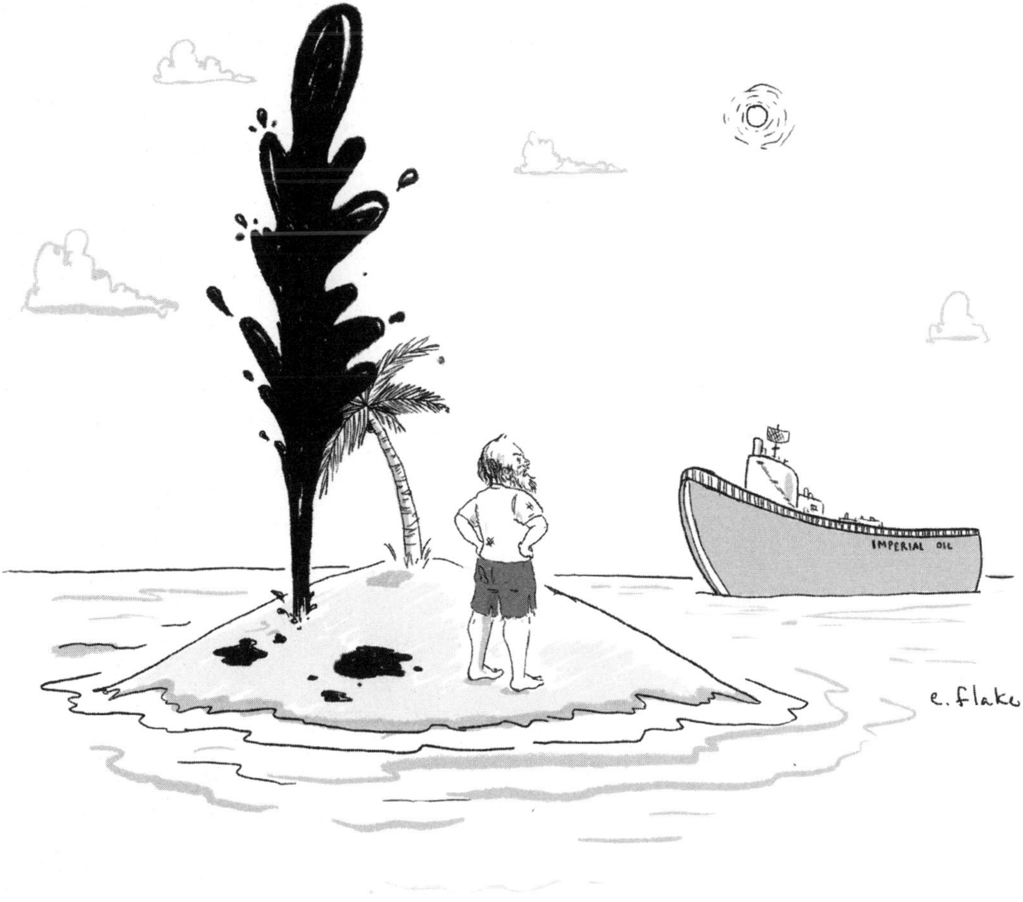
IMPERIAL OIL
e. flake

"Oh, sure, now you know where the island is."

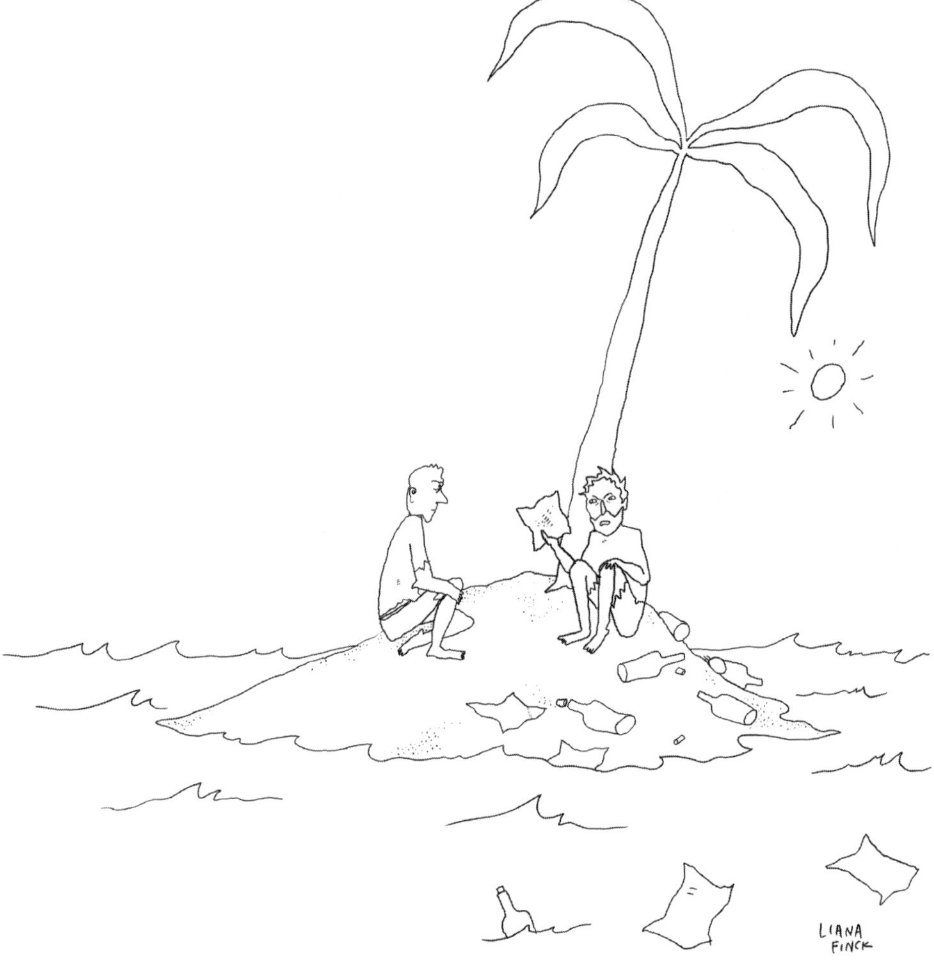
LIANA
FINCK

"Another desert island cartoon clipping from my uncle."

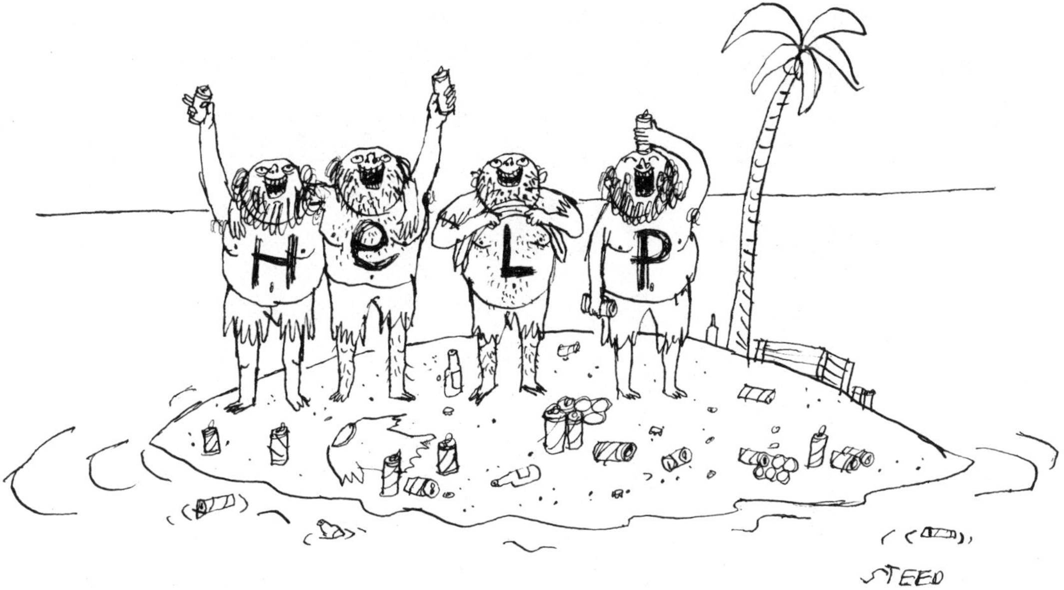
HeLP
STEED

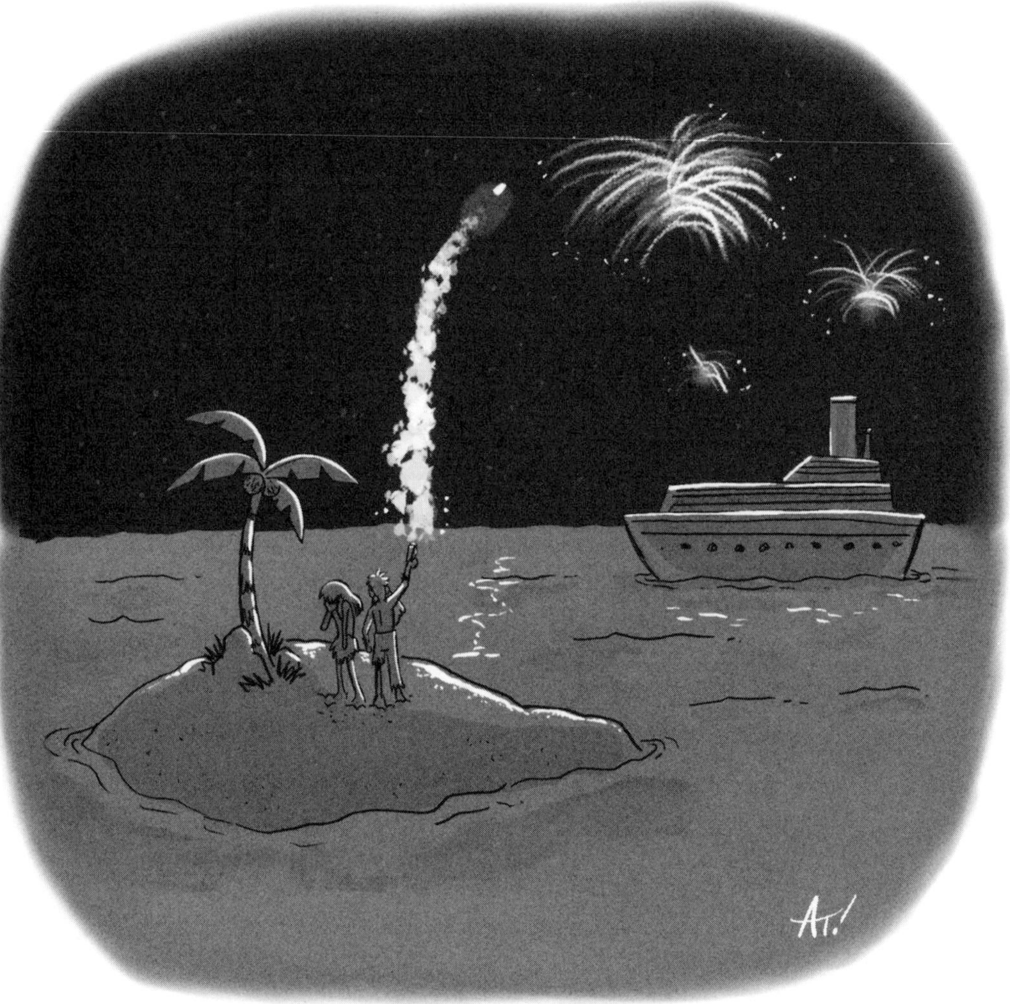

"Oops."

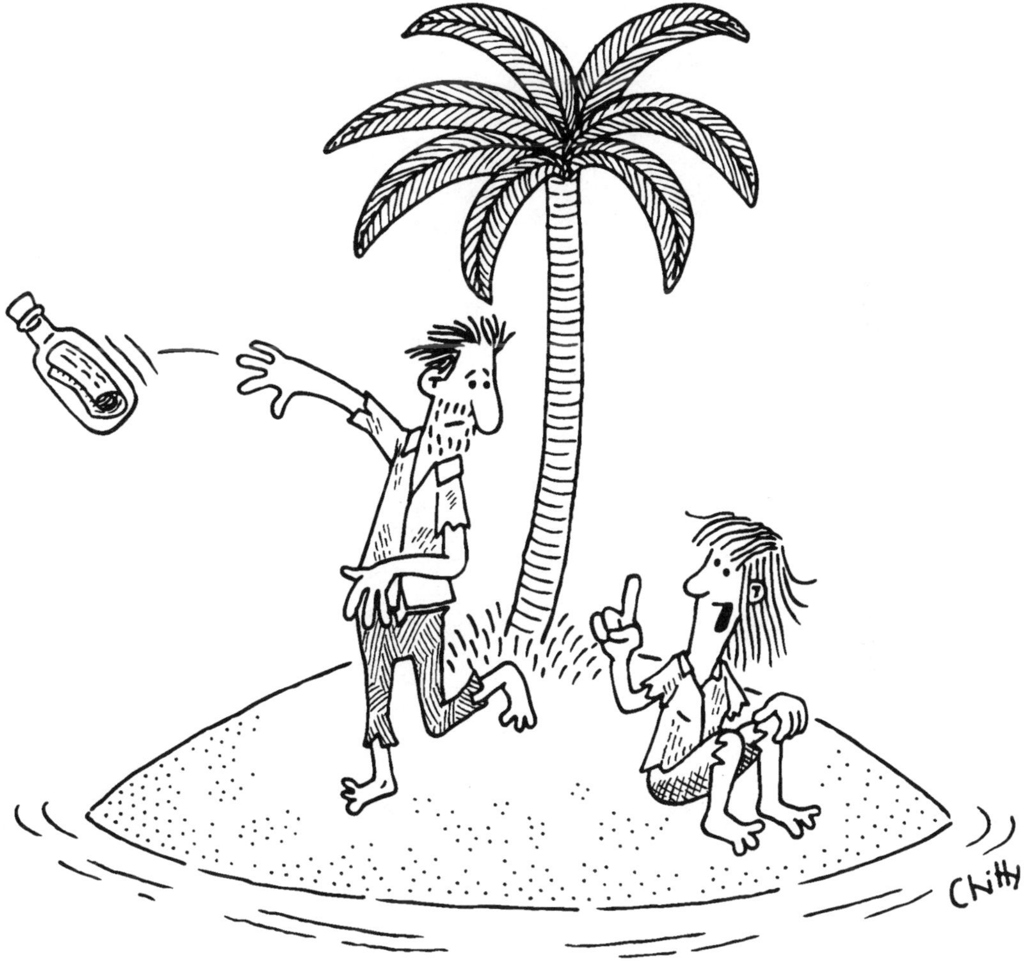
CHitty

"No, wait—thin crust!"

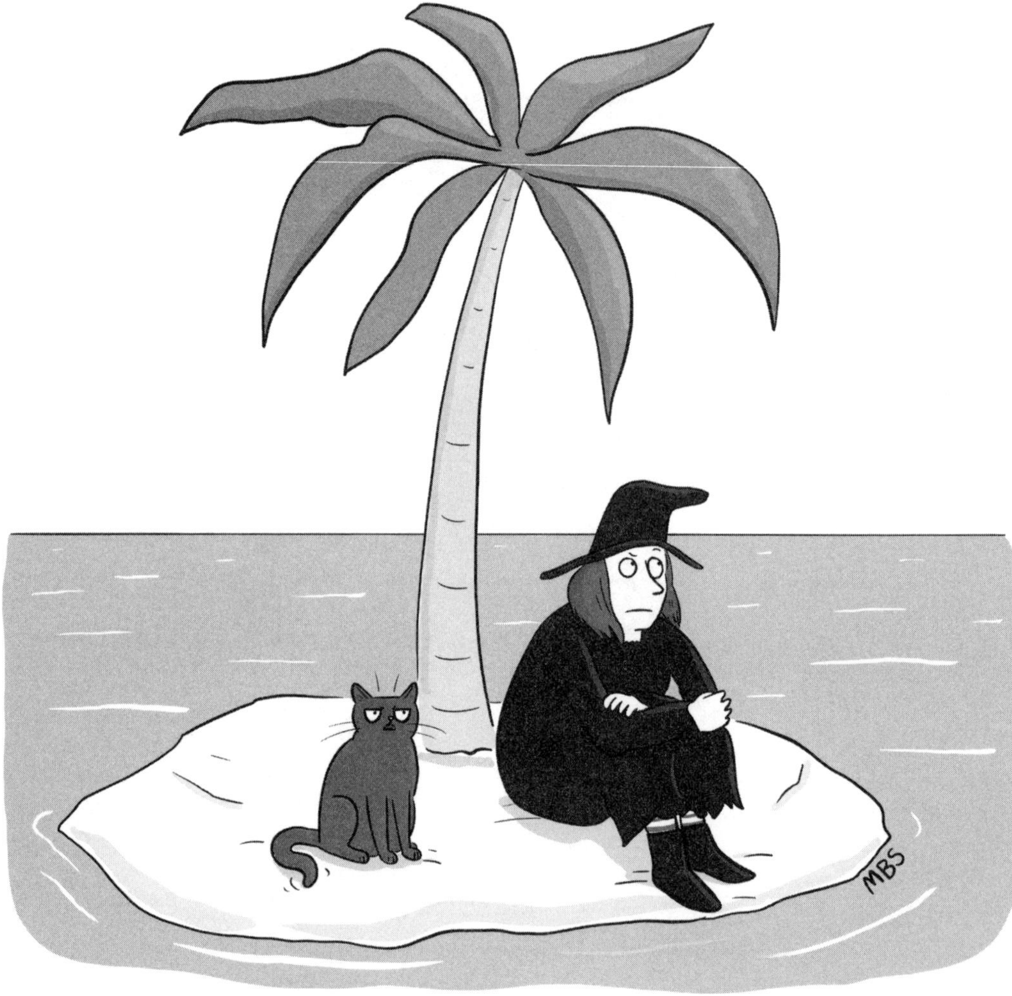
MBS

"'Bring the broom,' I said. 'Nah, we won't need it,' you said."

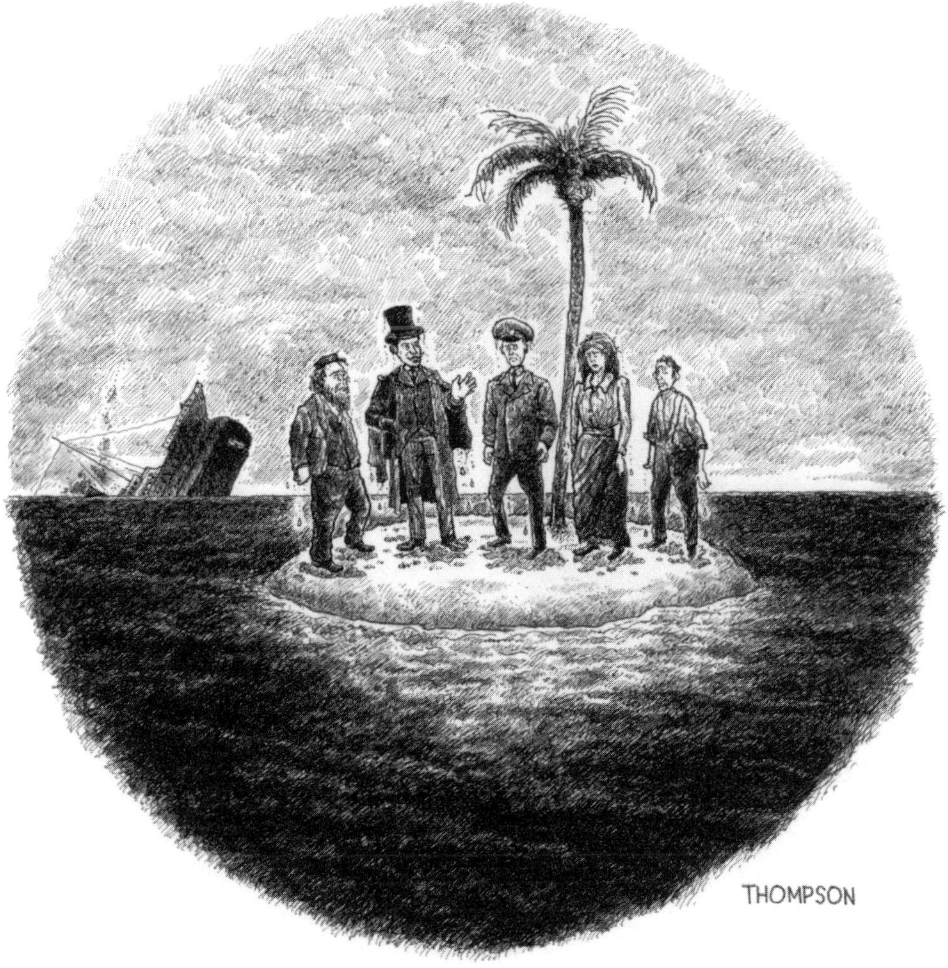
THOMPSON

"Look — if we can just find a way to maintain the permanent stratification of classes that existed on the ship, we should be able to get through this."

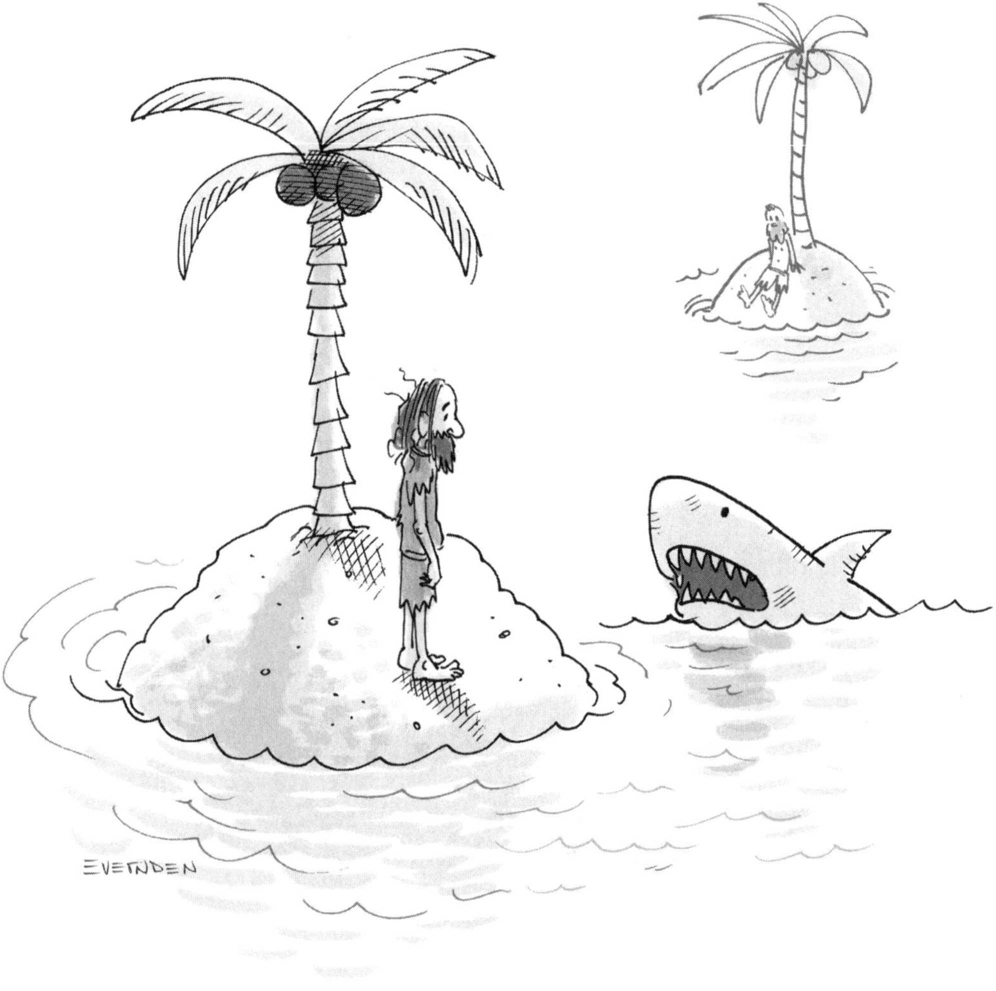
EVENDEN

"If you convince him to swim over, I'll share him with you."

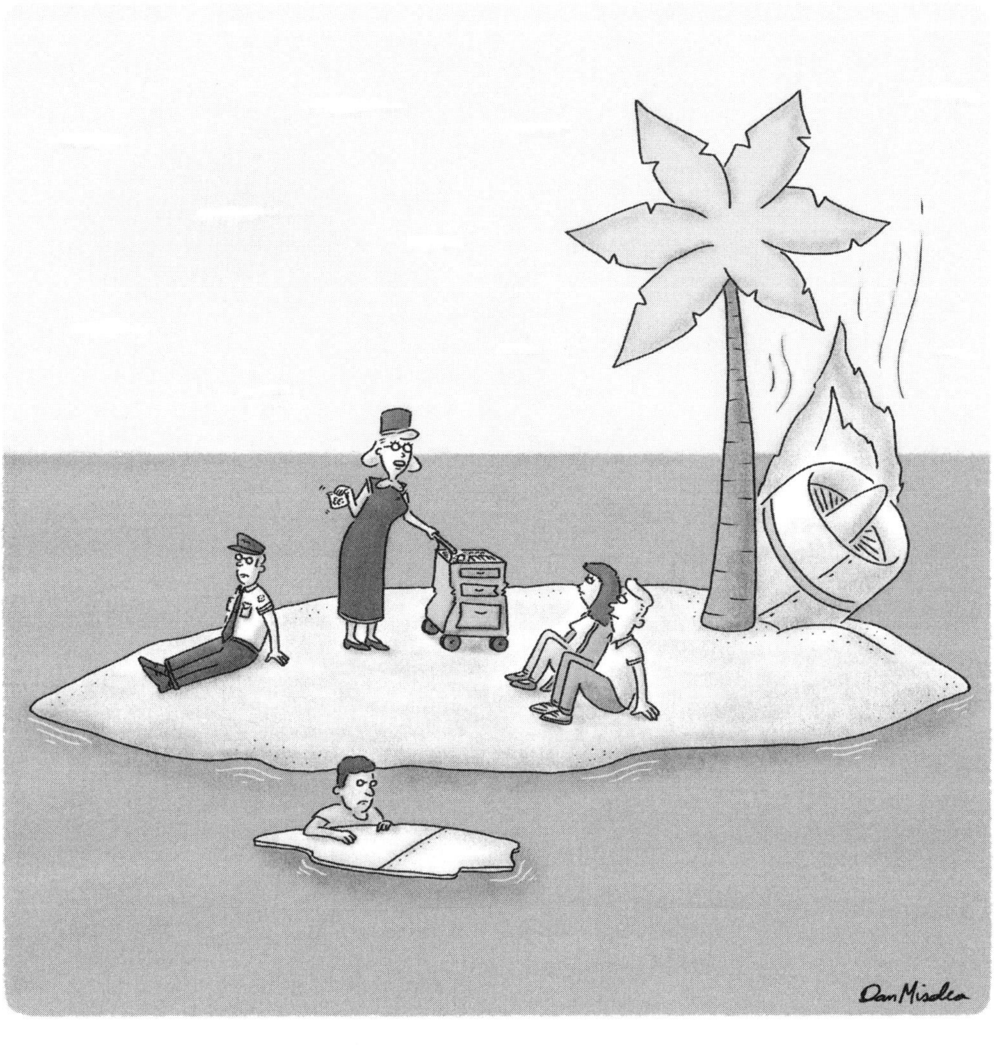
Dan Misdea

"Complimentary peanuts?"

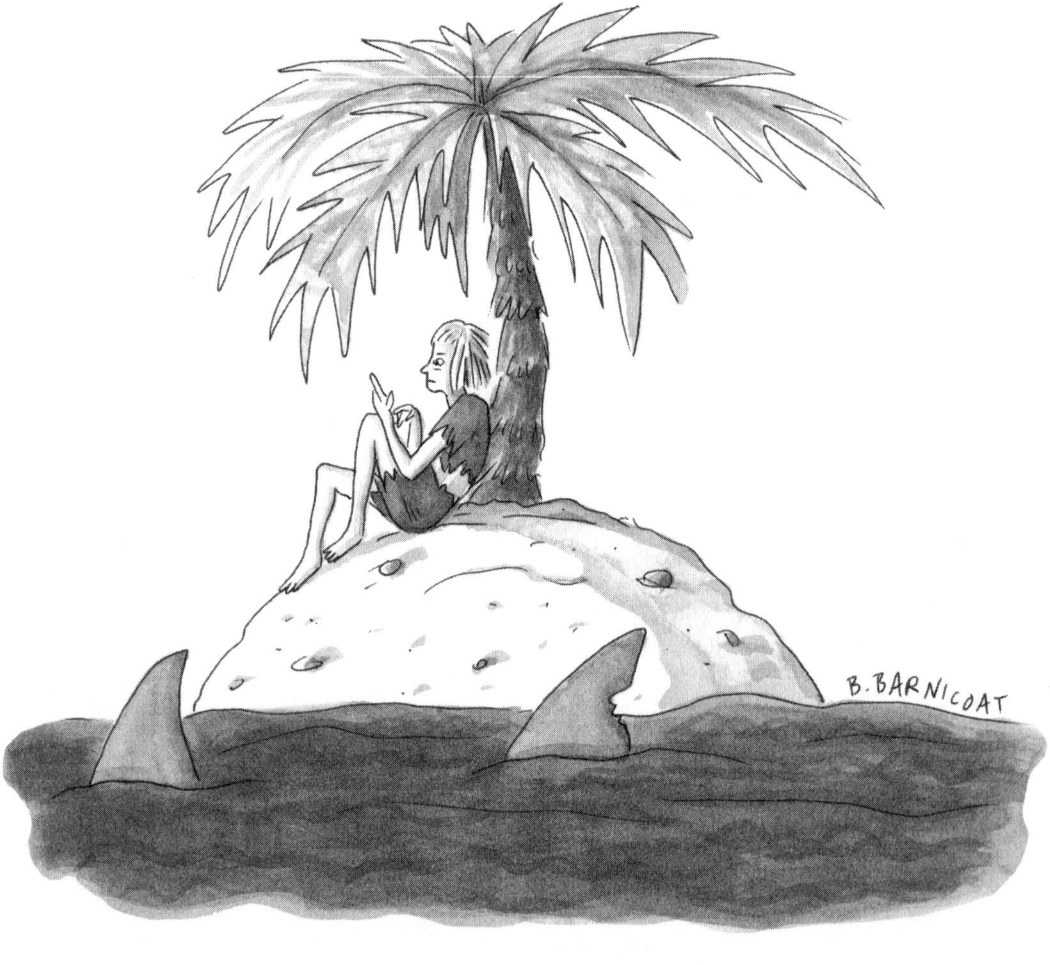
B. BARNICOAT

"#DesertIsland #Paradise #Blessed"

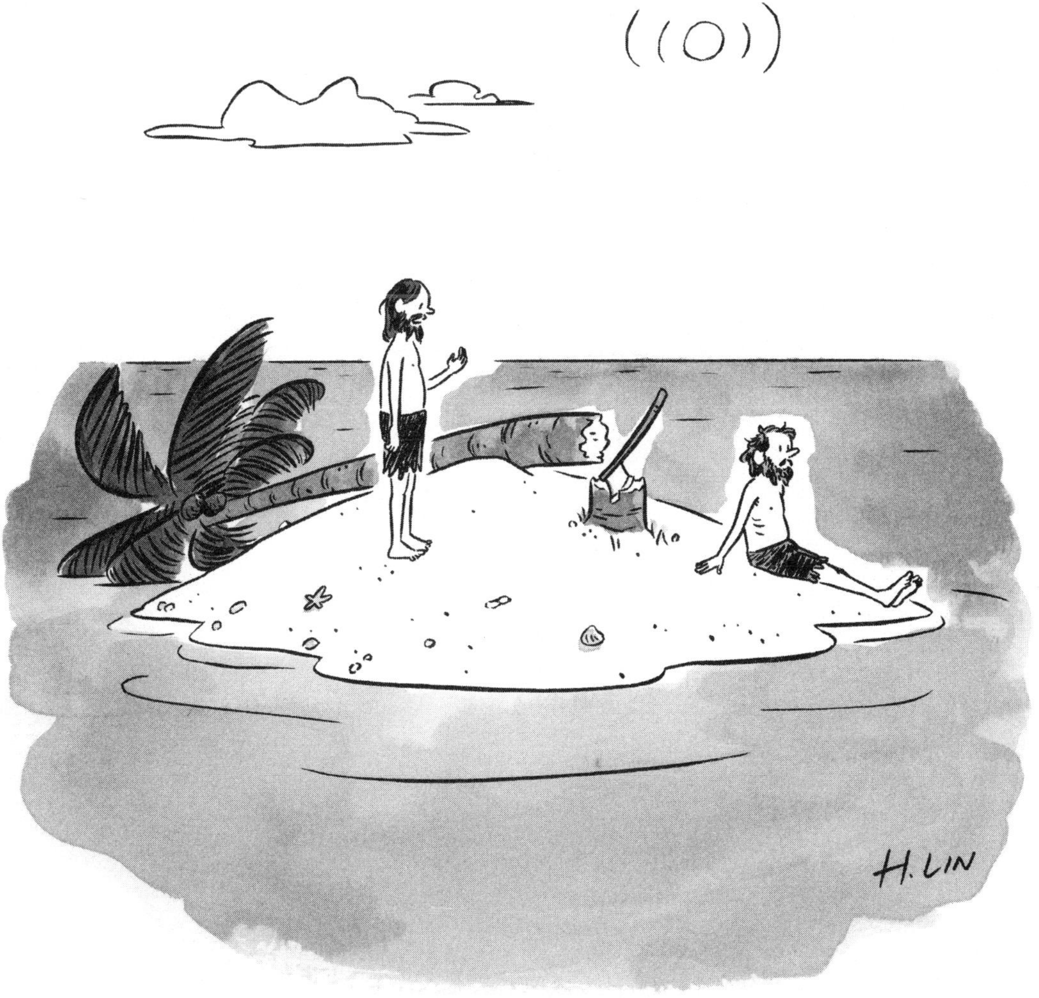
H. LIN

"Do you want me to schedule another Raft Progress meeting?"

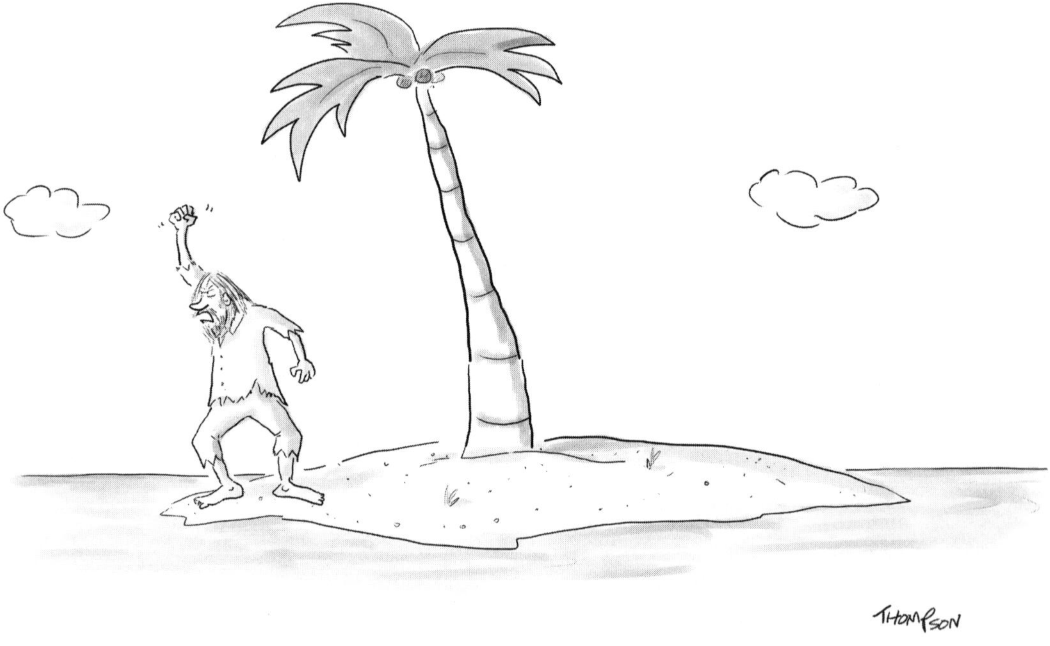
THOMPSON

"Debate me!"

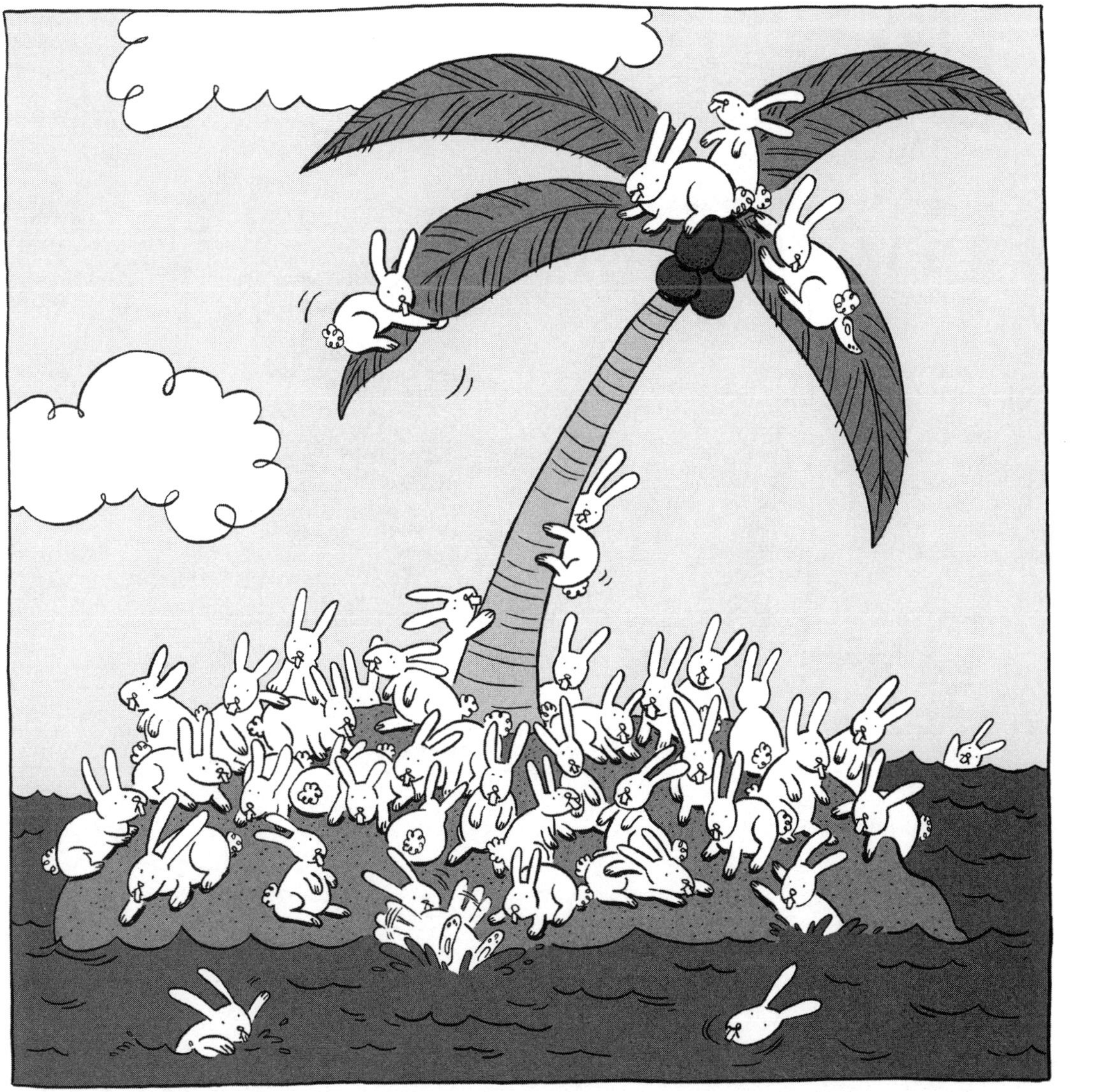

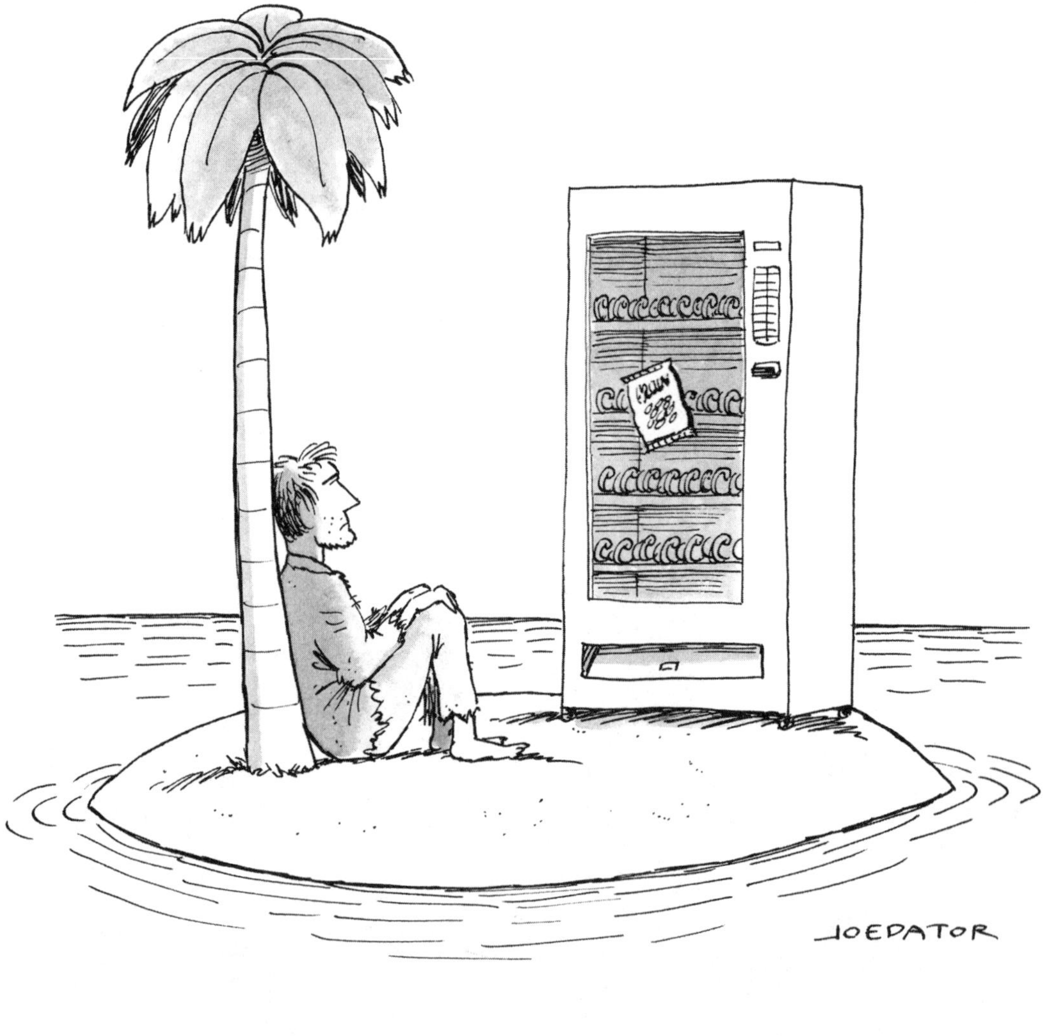
JOEDATOR

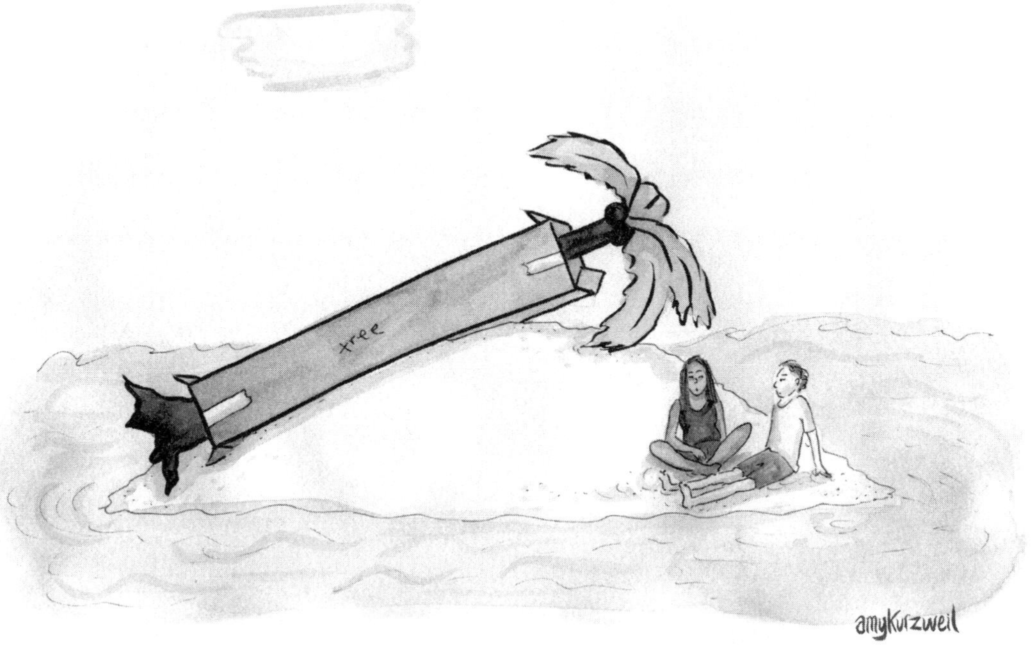
tree
amyKurzweil

"I hate unpacking."

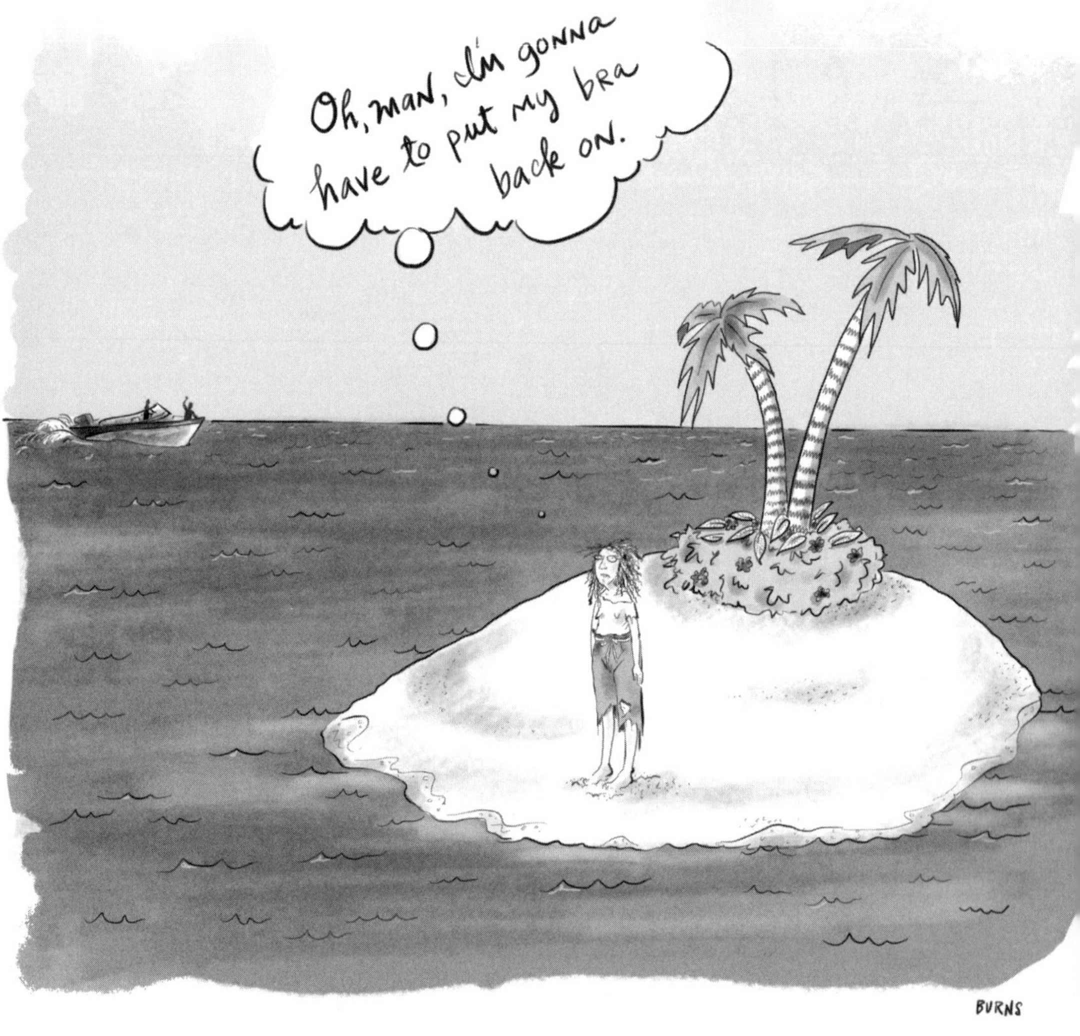
Oh, man, I'm gonna have to put my bra back on.
BURNS

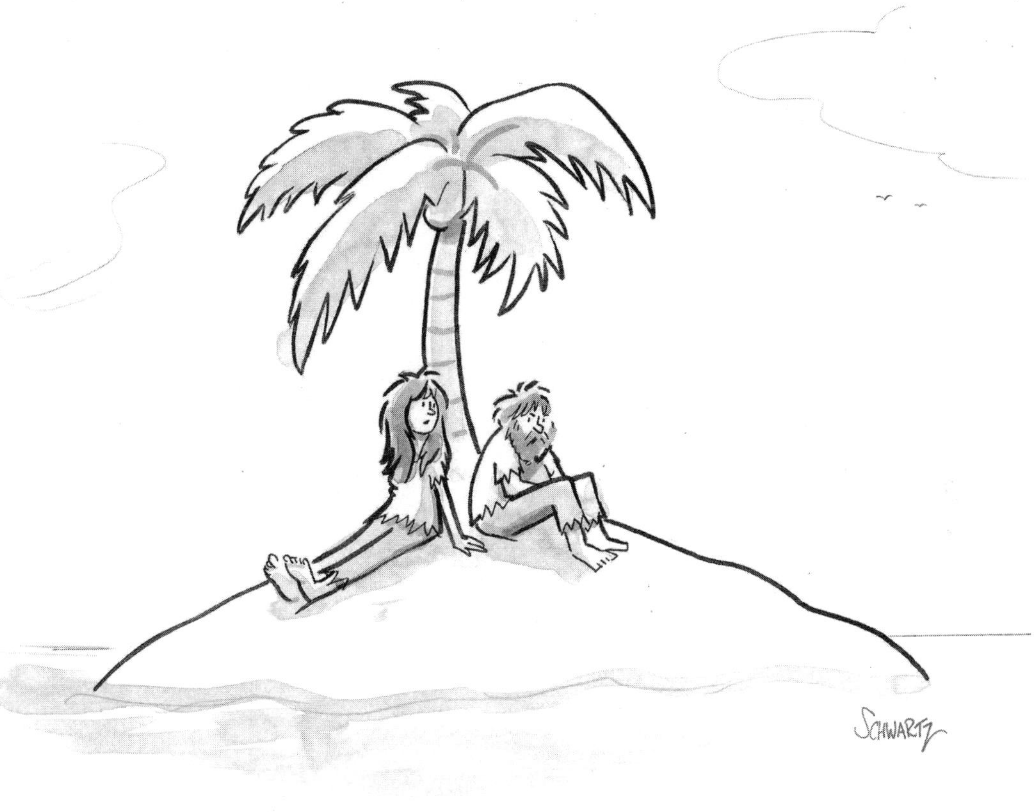
SCHWARTZ

"Any advice on dealing with a creepy roommate? Asking for a friend."

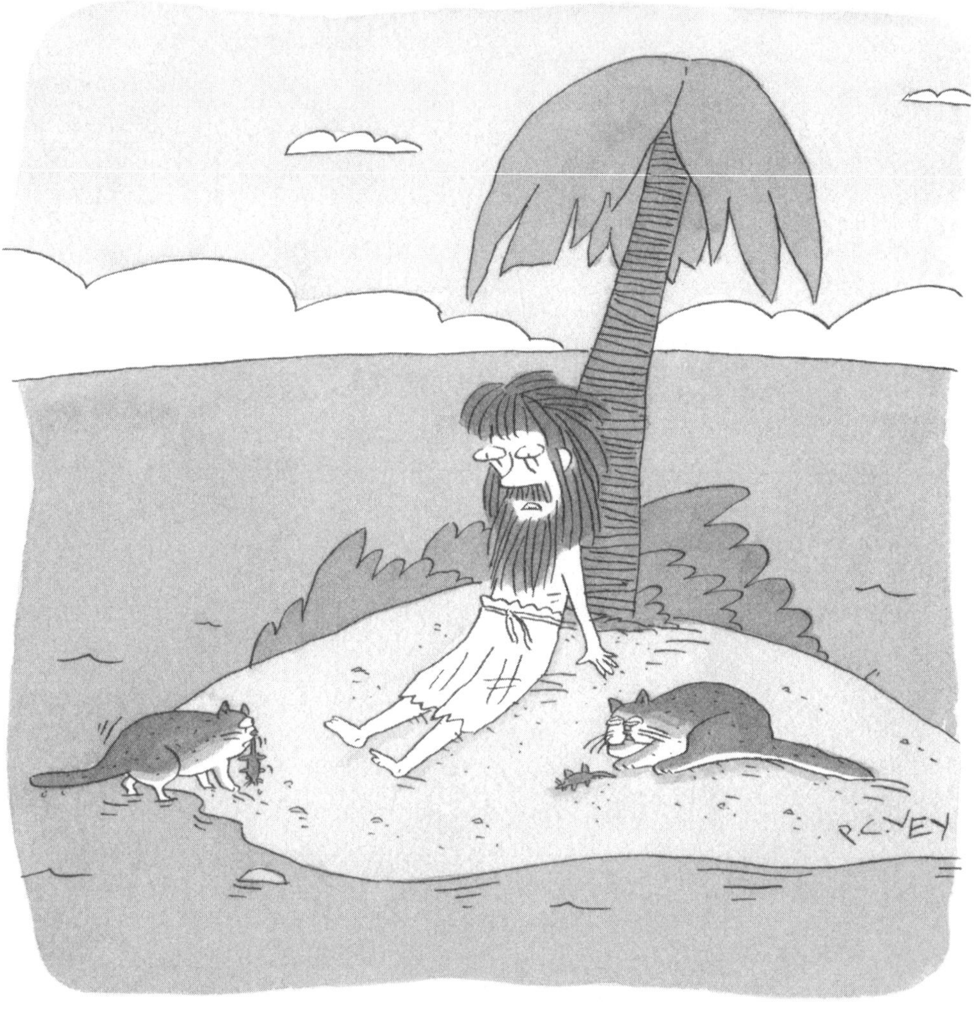
P.C.VEY

"It took you long enough. Muffin got here a week ago."

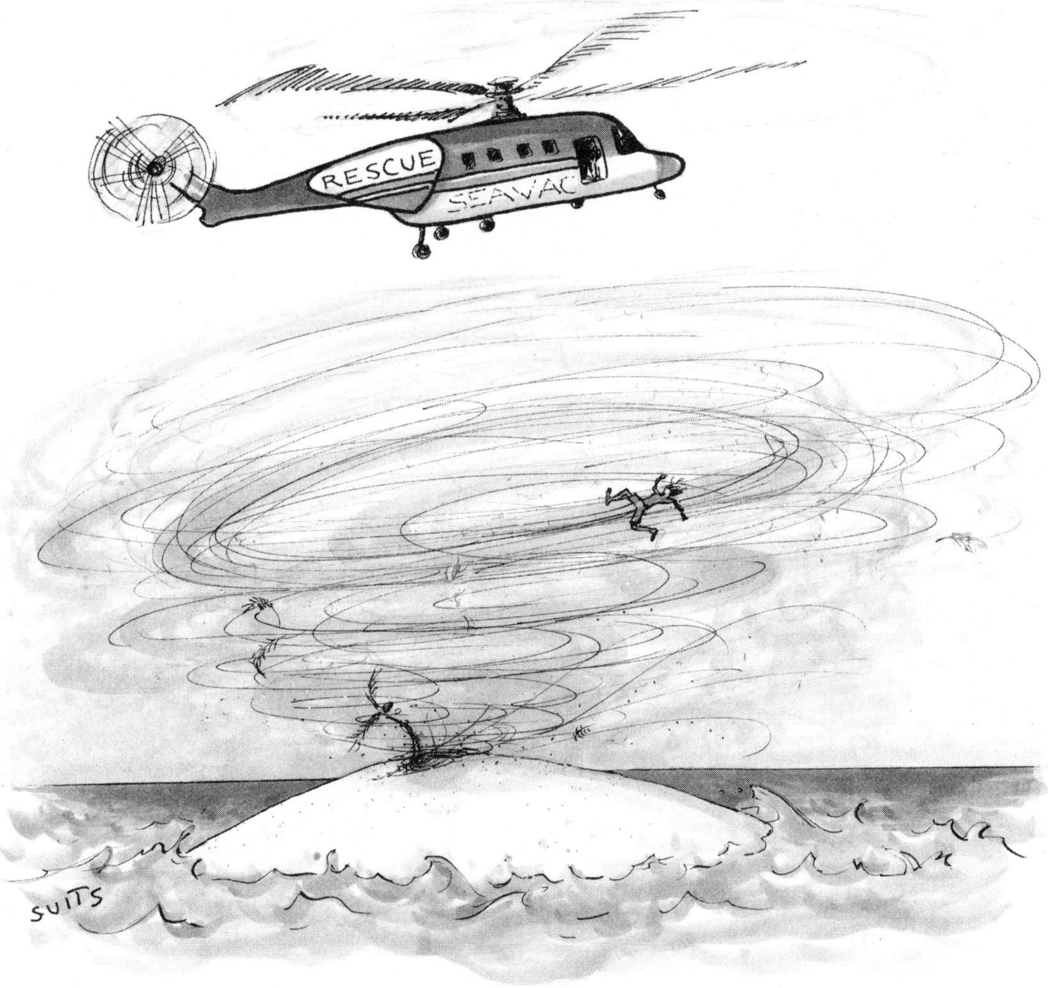
RESCUE
SEAVAC
SUITS

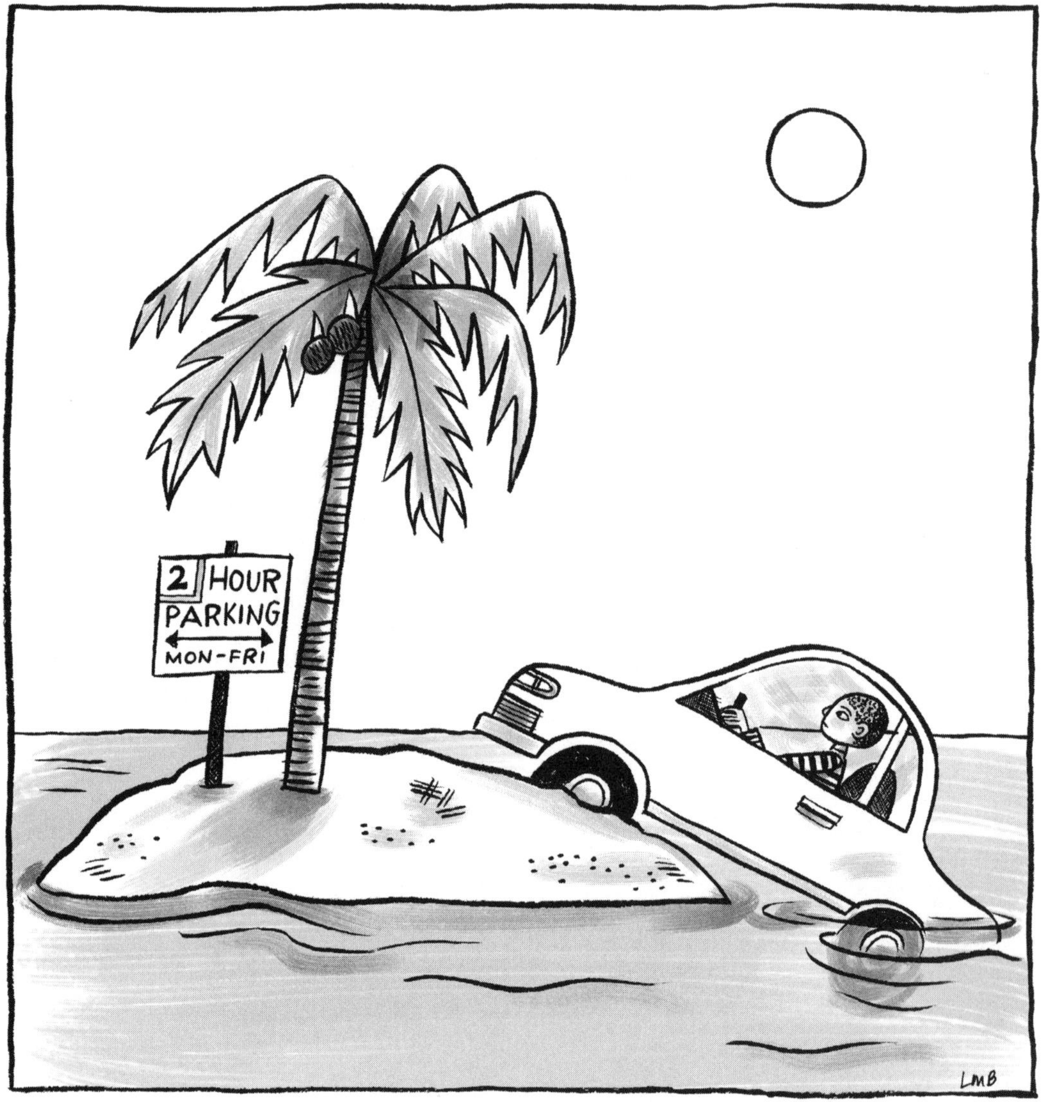
2 HOUR
PARKING
MON-FRI
LMB

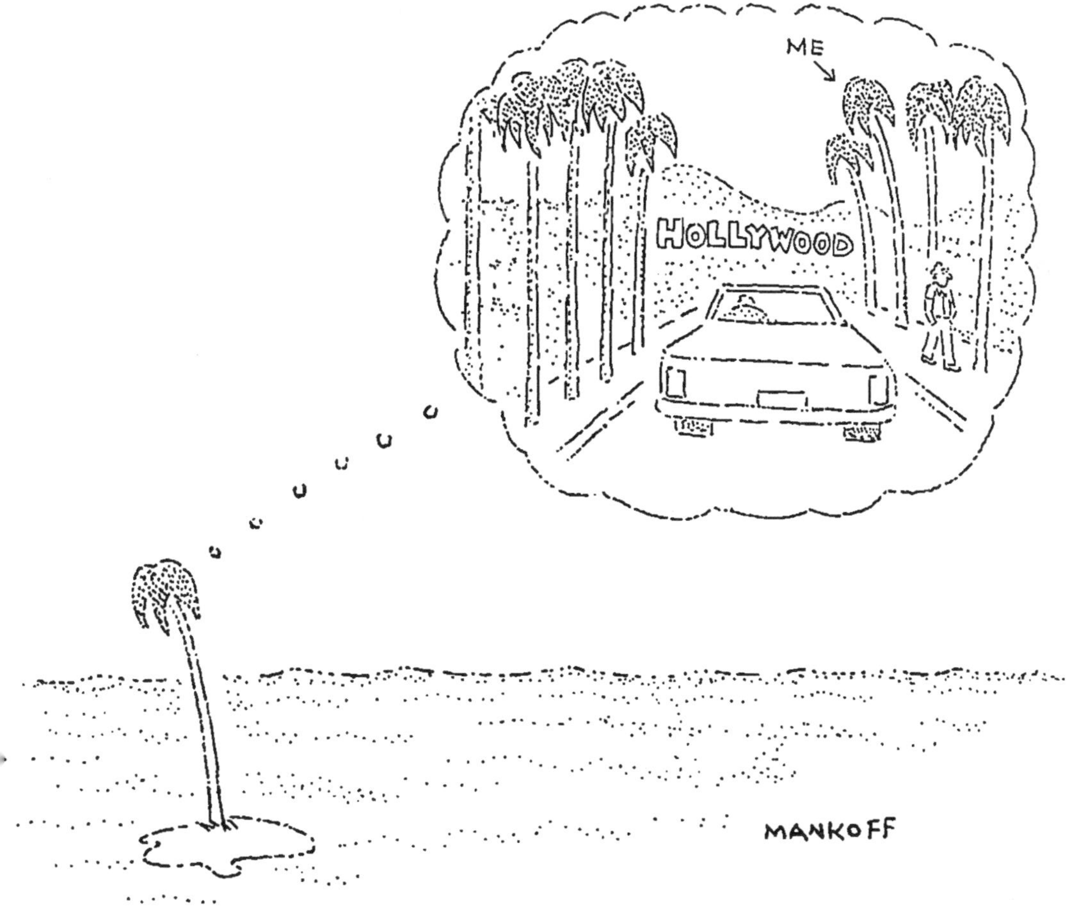
ME
HOLLYWOOD
MANKOFF

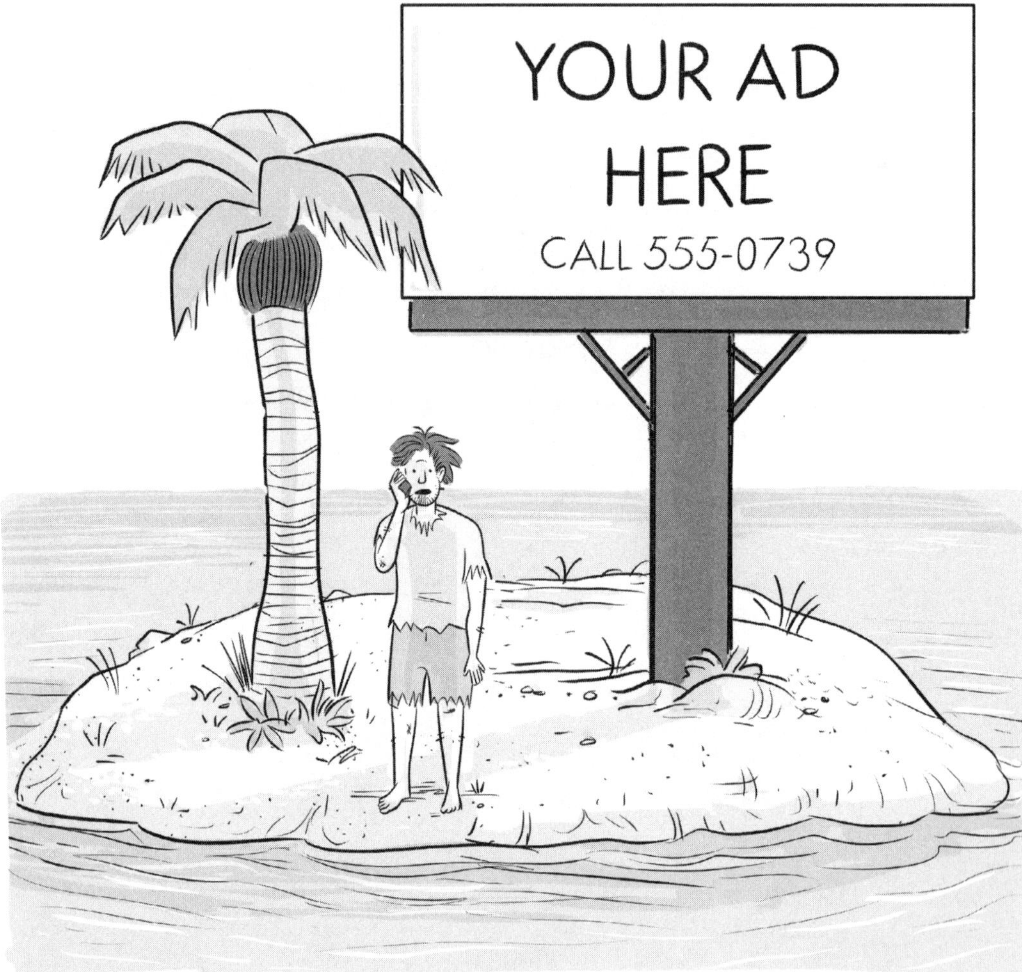
YOUR AD
HERE
CALL 555-0739

"That's Help with an 'H.'"

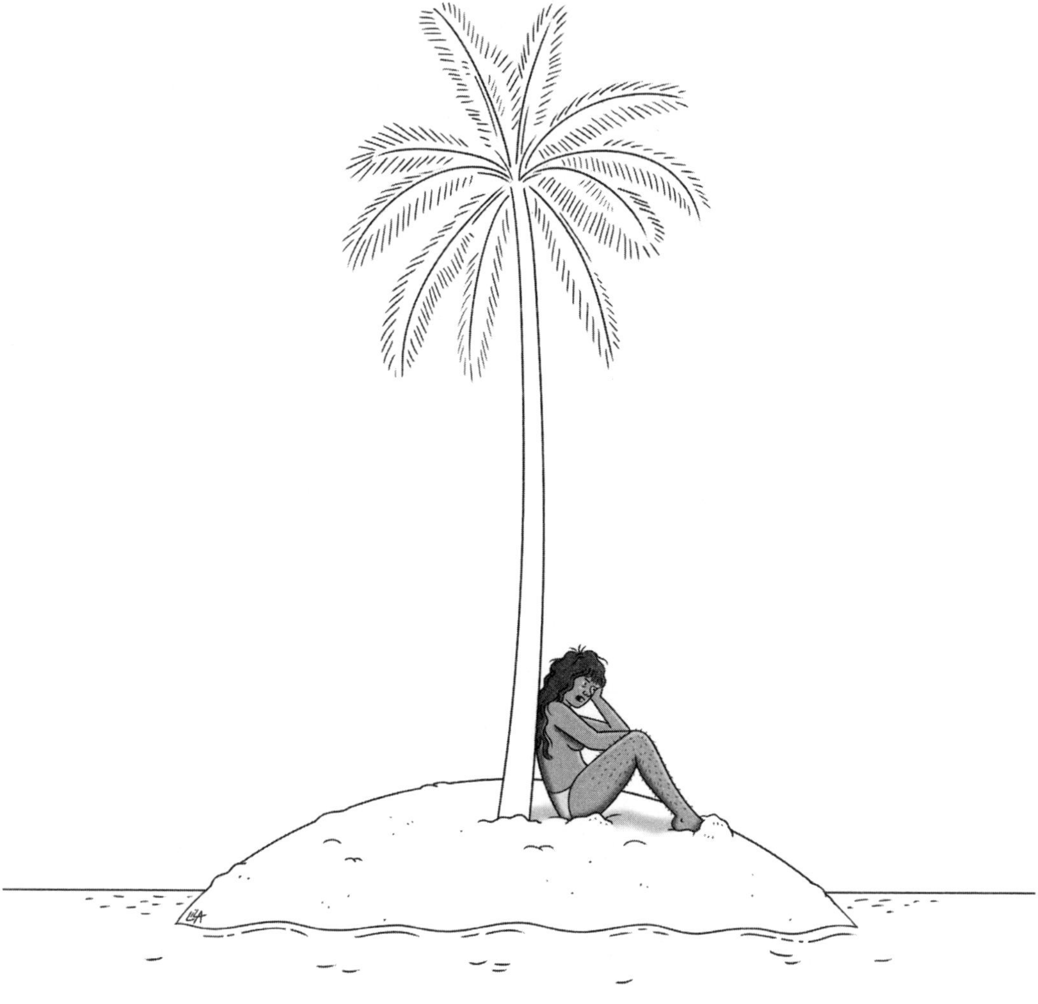

"At least I don't still live with my parents."

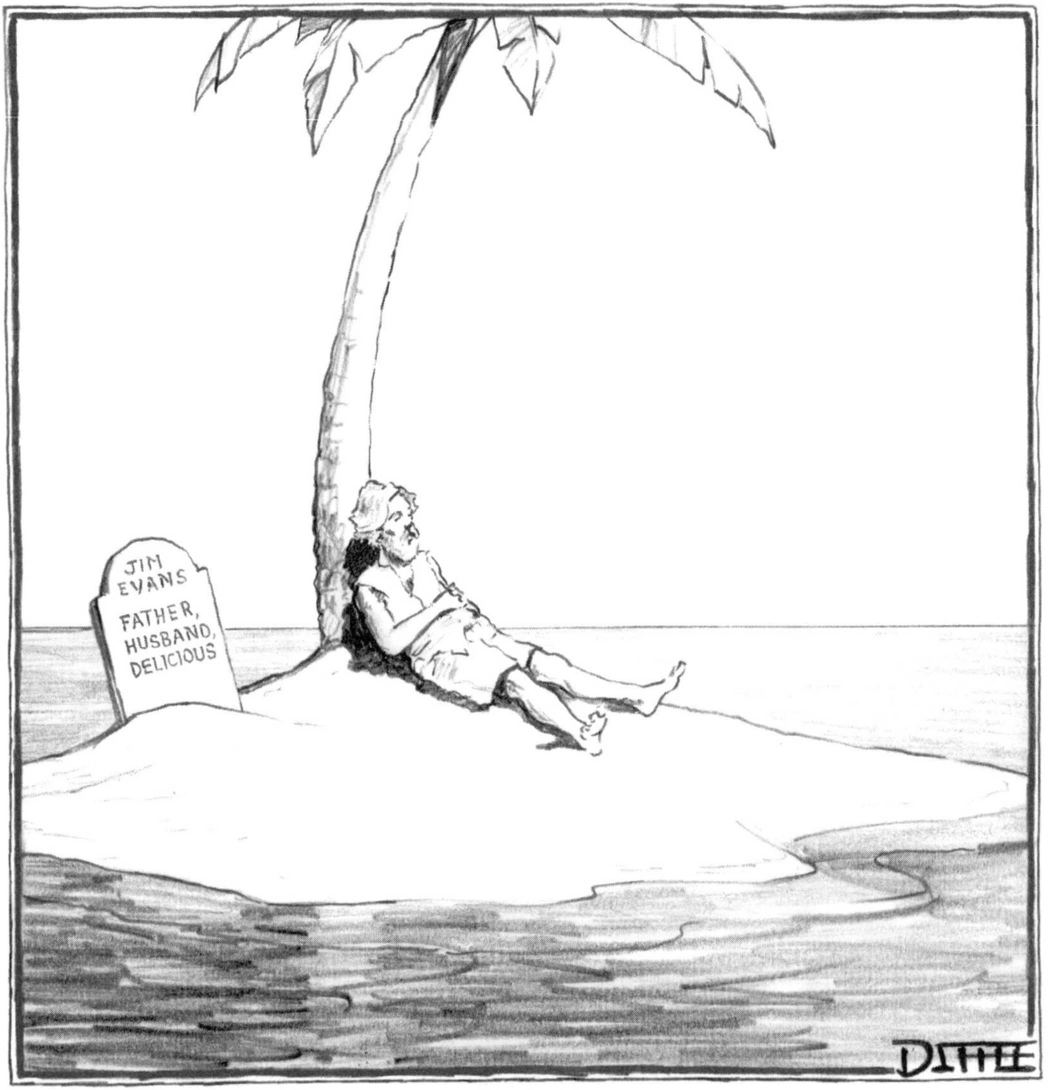
JIM EVANS
FATHER, HUSBAND, DELICIOUS
DIFFEE

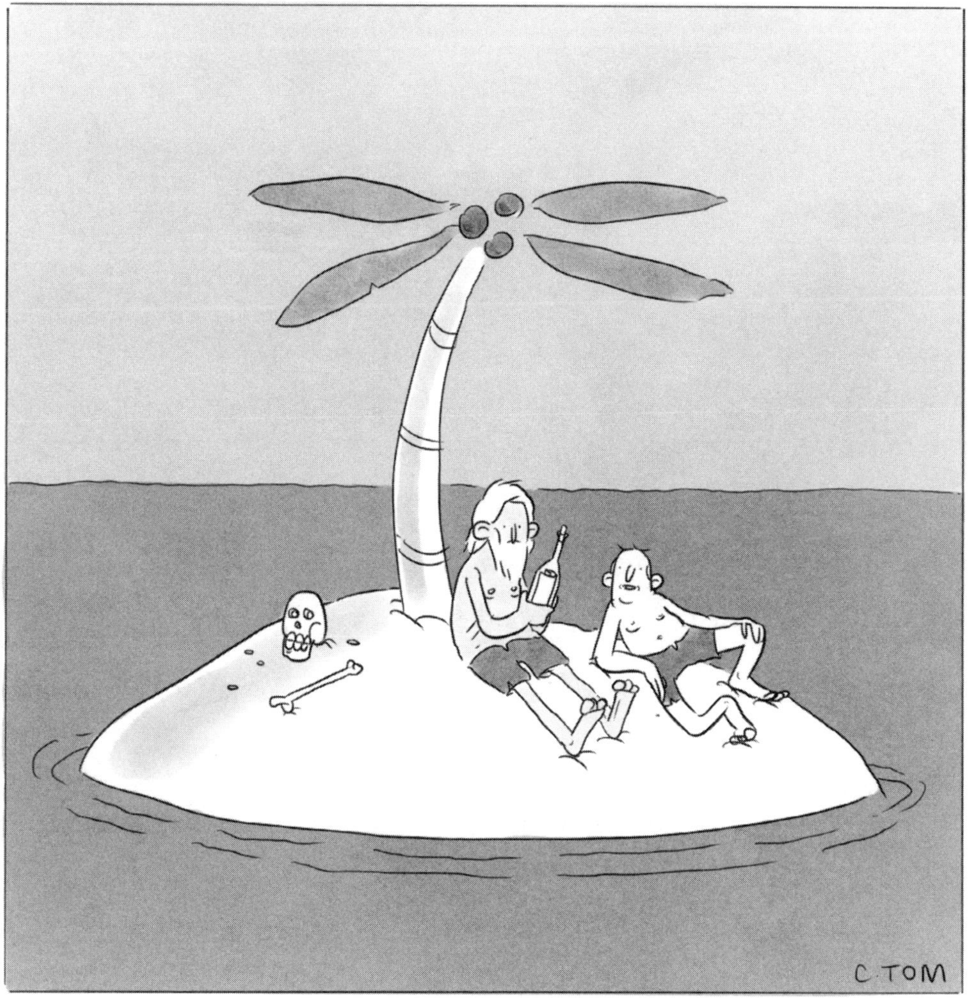
C.TOM

"If you send a second message without a response to the first, you'll look desperate."

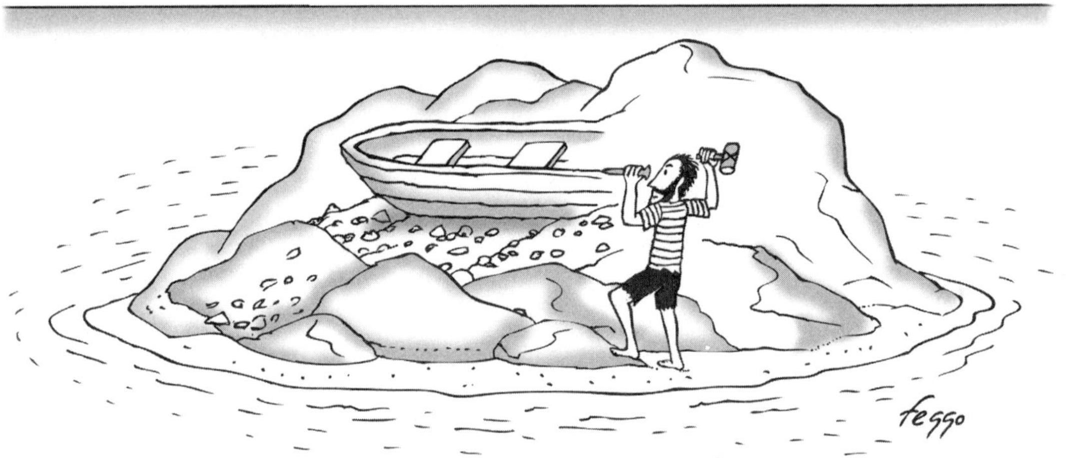
feggo

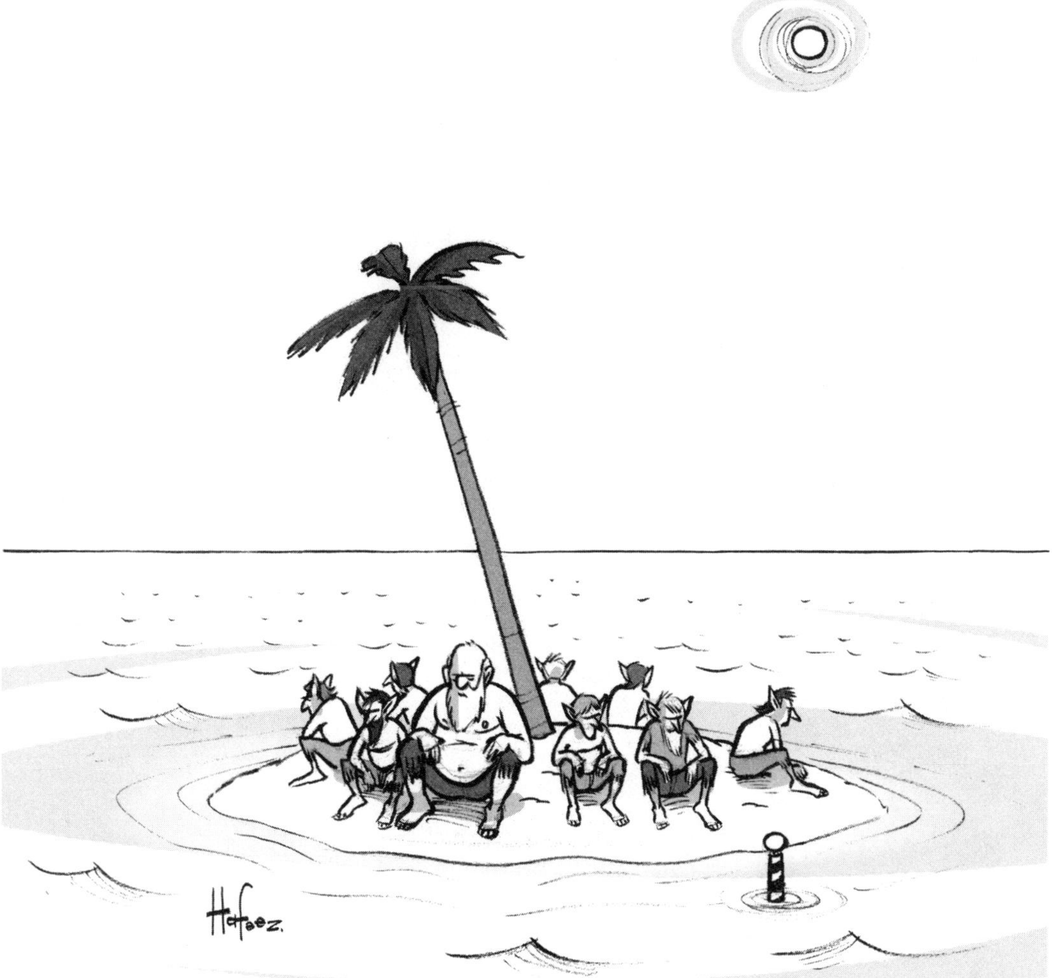
Hafeez.

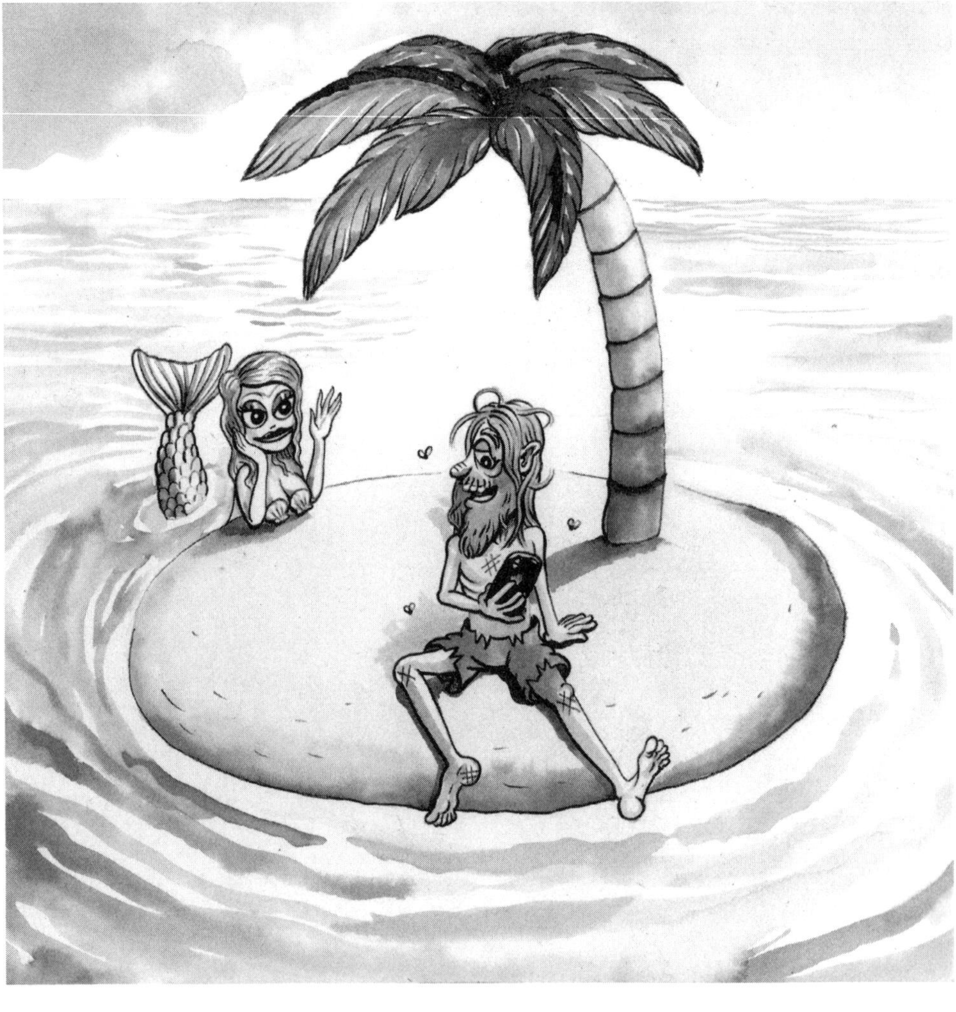

"Hey, you got a charger? My phone is about to die."

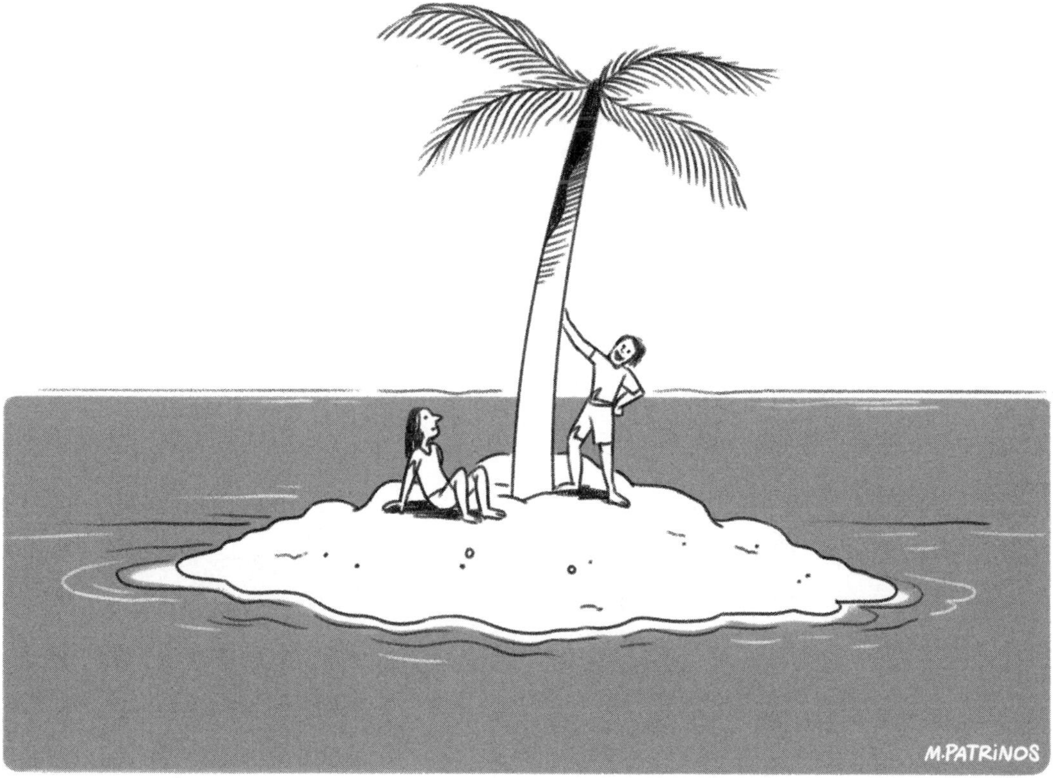
M.PATRINOS

"I've always dreamed of being someone's only option."

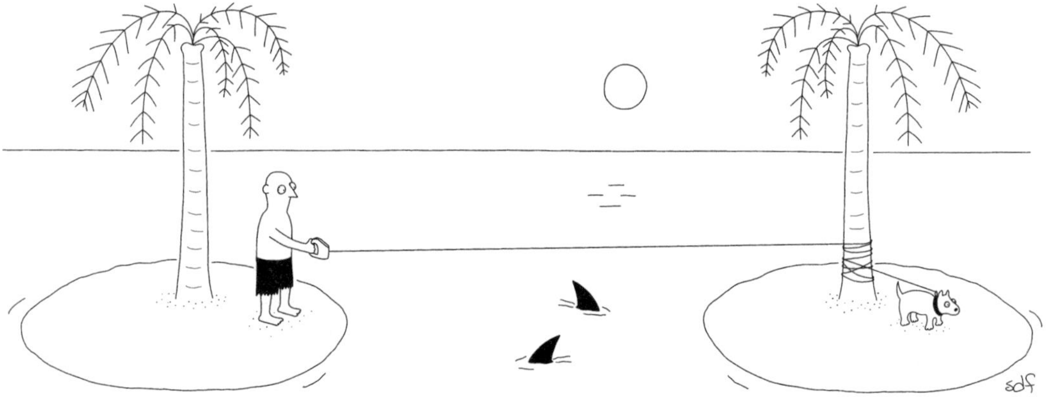
sdf

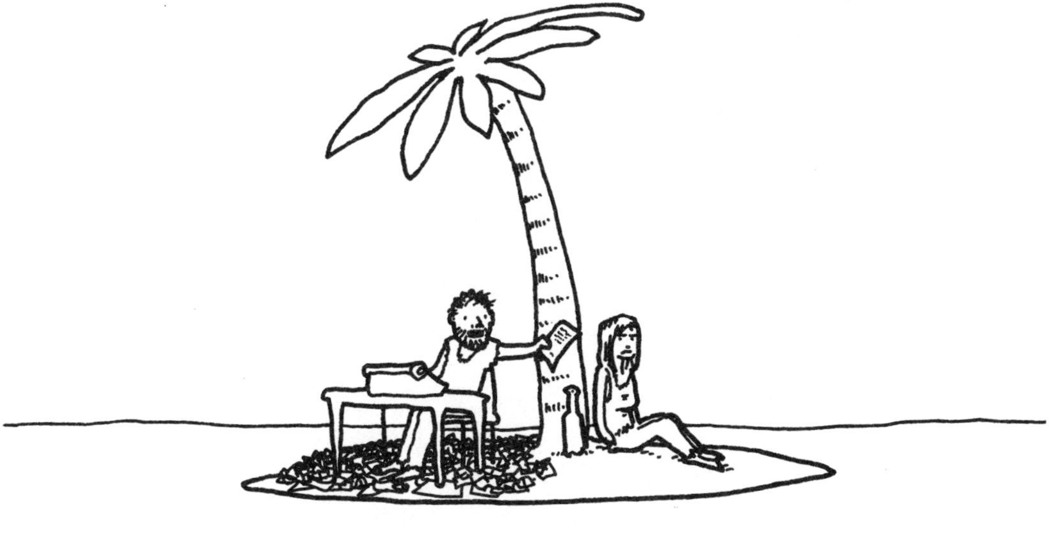
©SHANNON WHEELER

"Now you can send it."

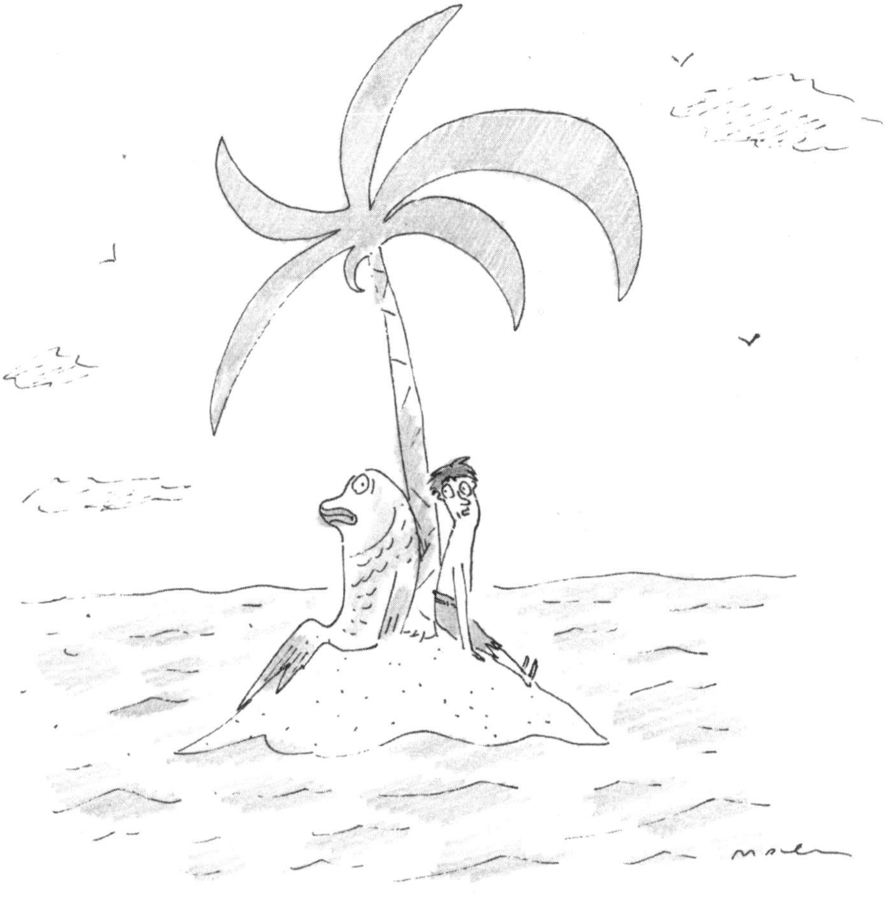

"You're here and you don't have to be. That tells me a lot."

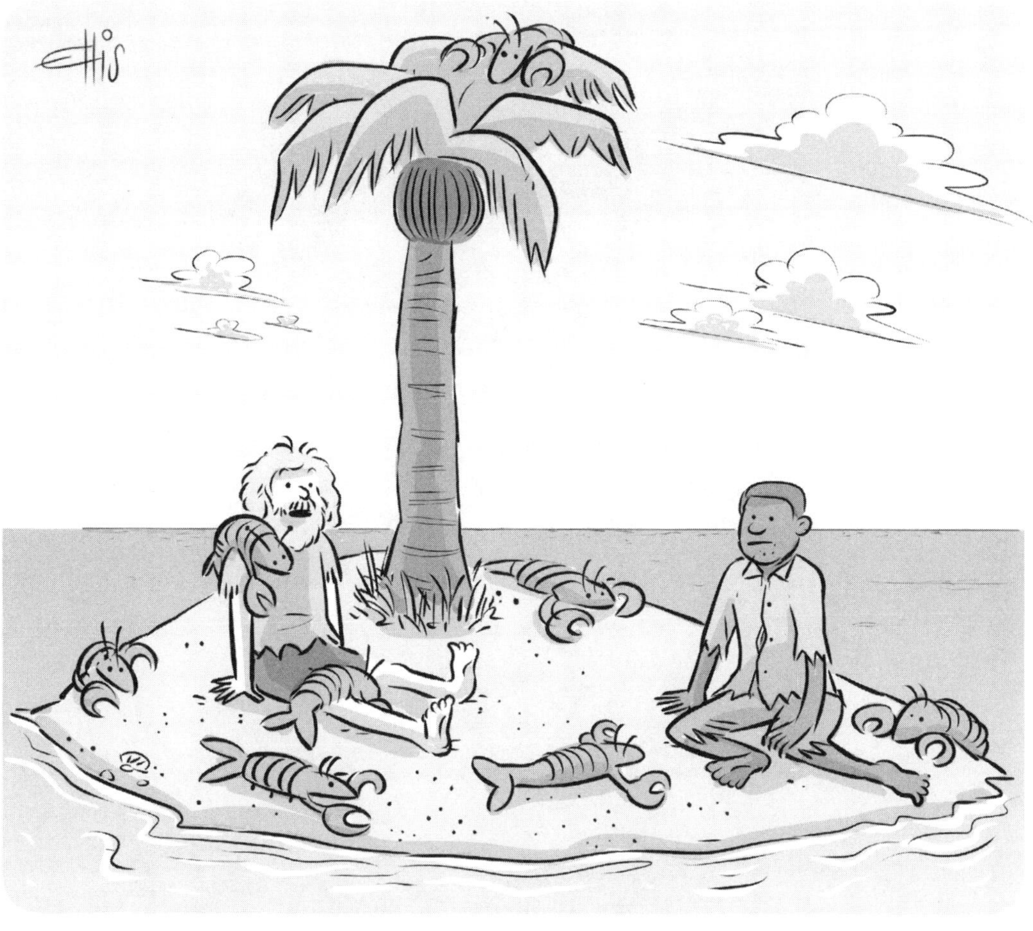

"I had one lobster, but he needed a friend. Then I saw another lobster that was just so cute."

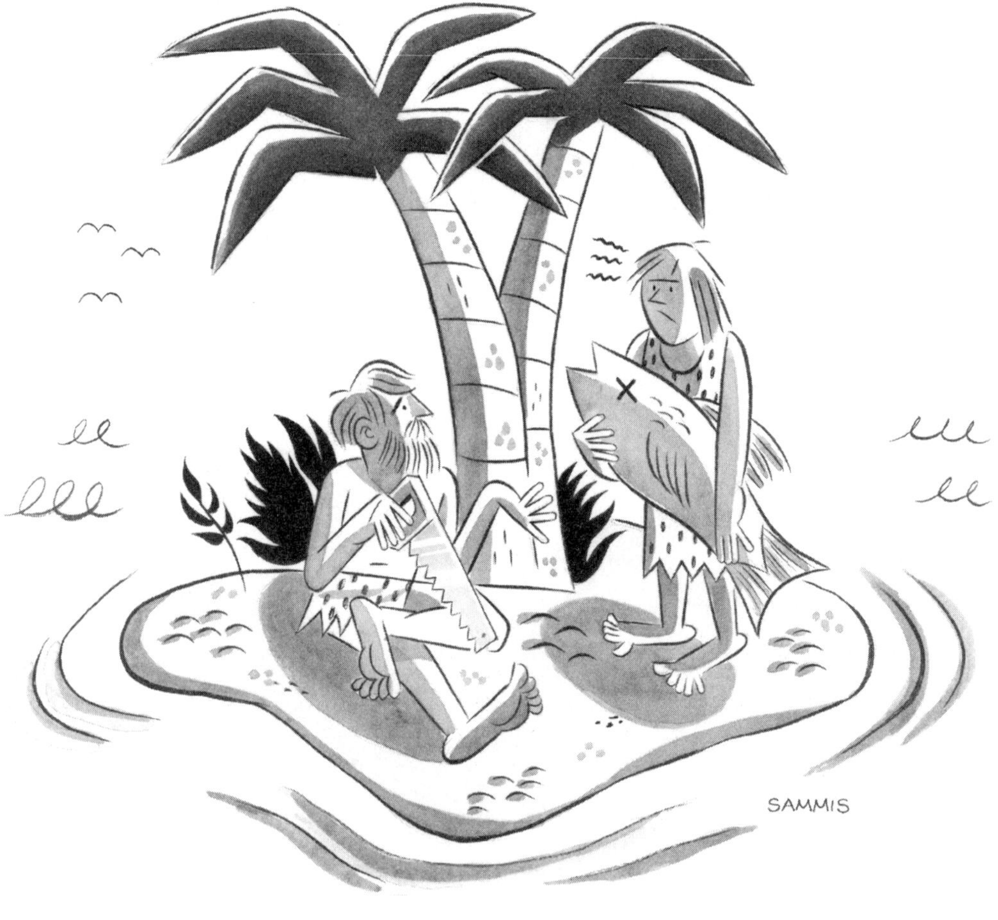
SAMMIS

"Honey, I never doubted your abilities."

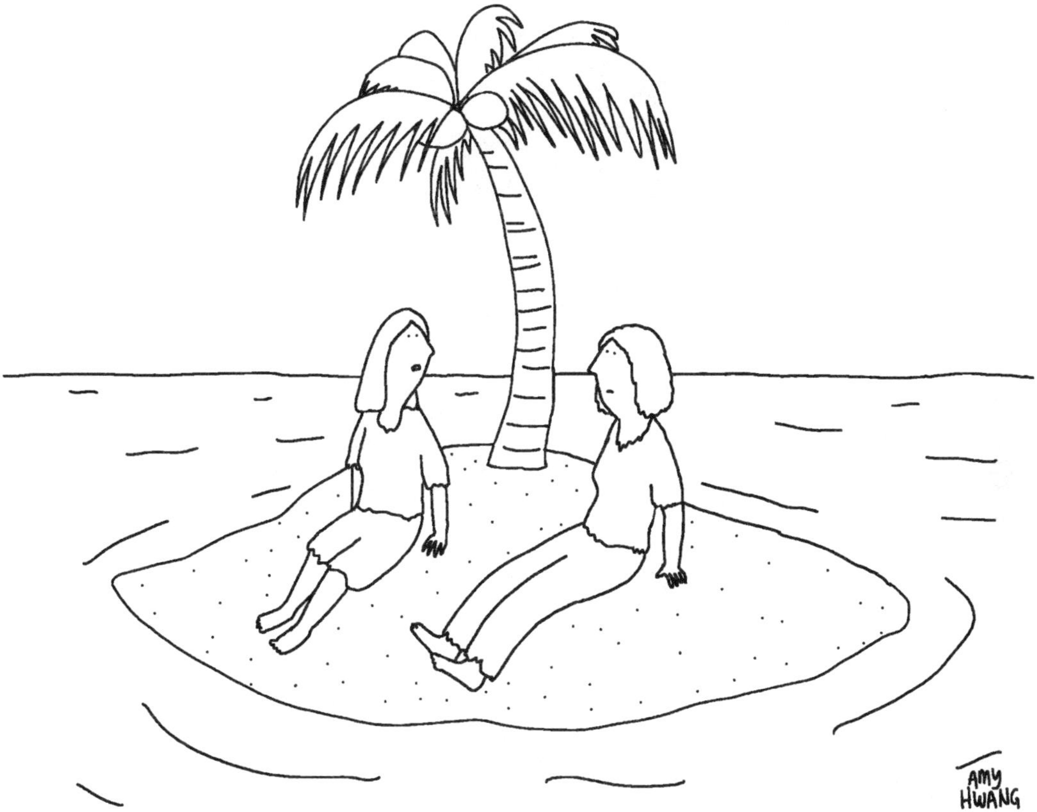
AMY HWANG

"What's the point of being rescued if we've lost the ability to digest cheese?"

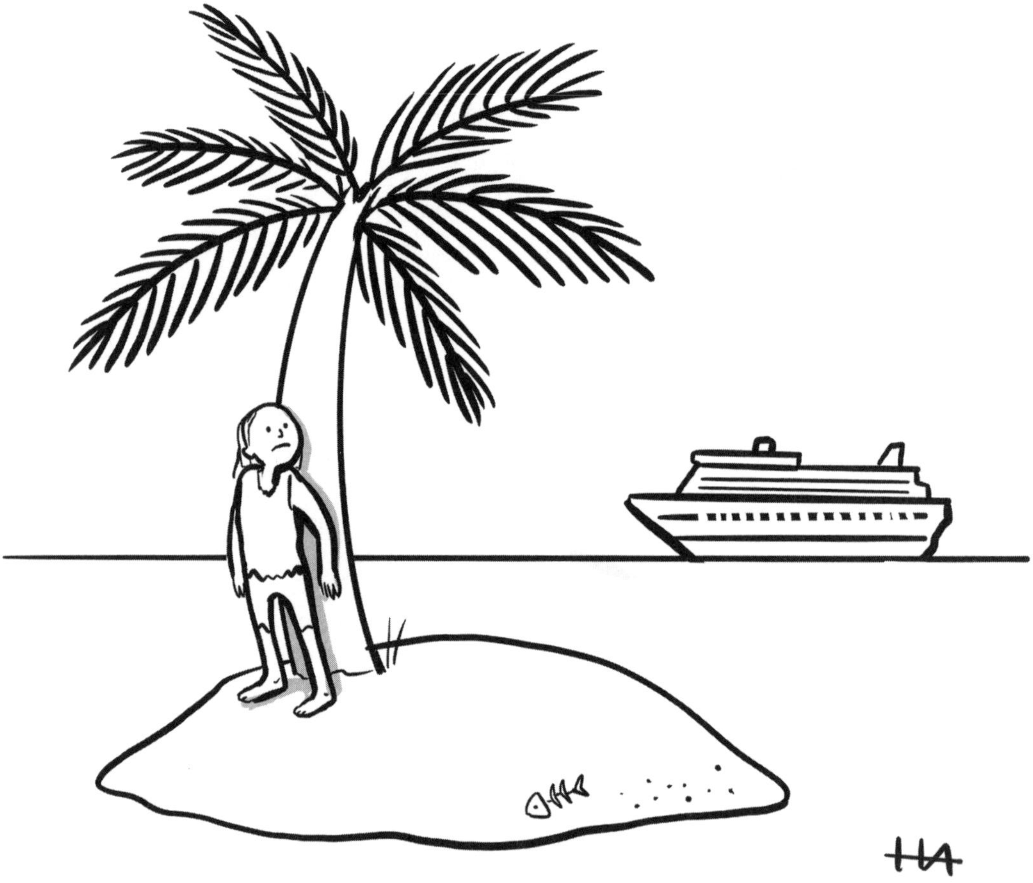

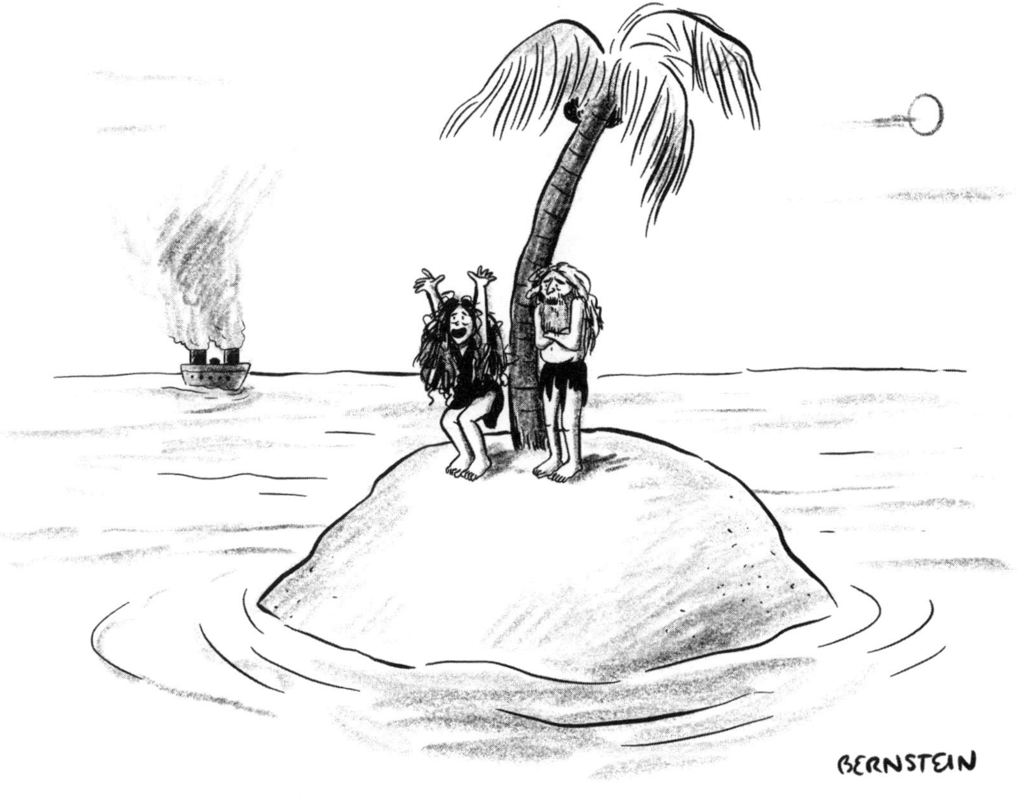
BERNSTEIN

"You don't have to look so happy."

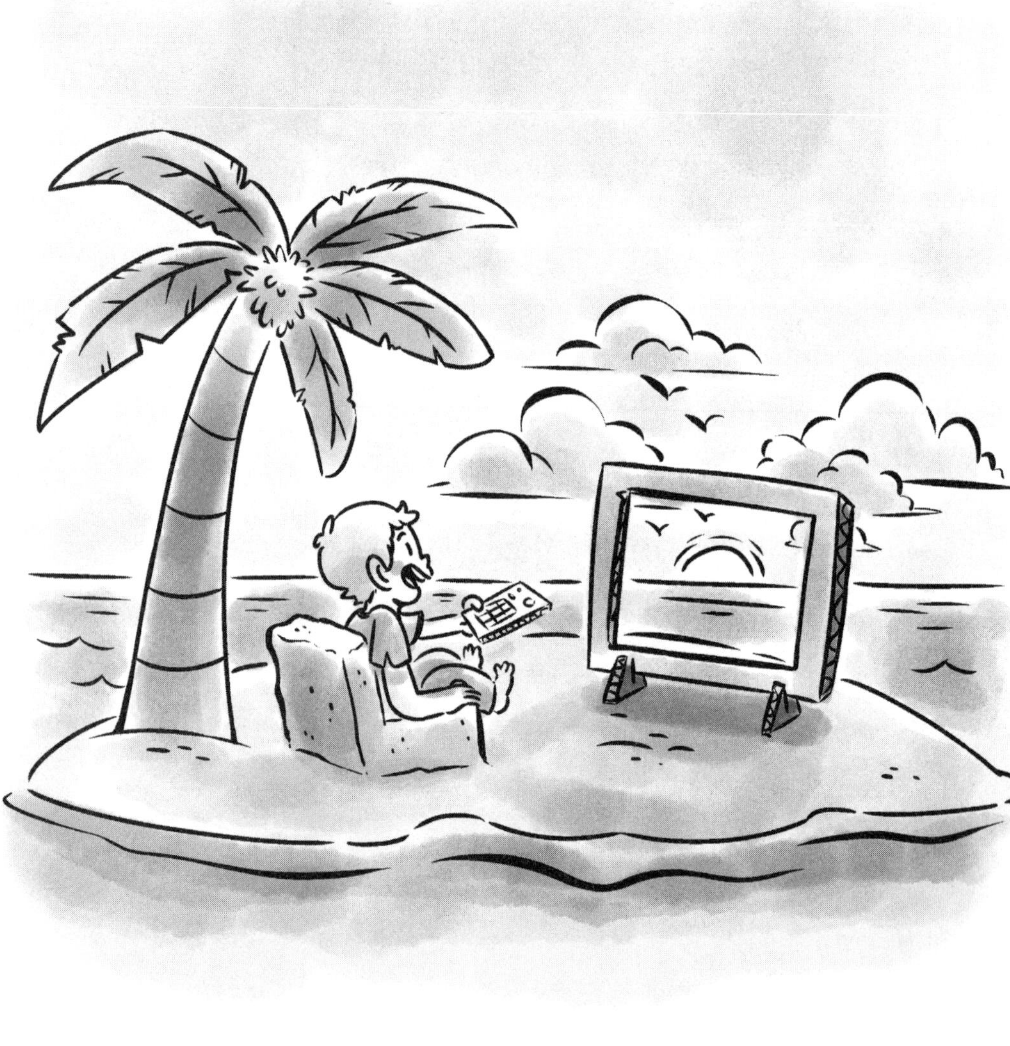

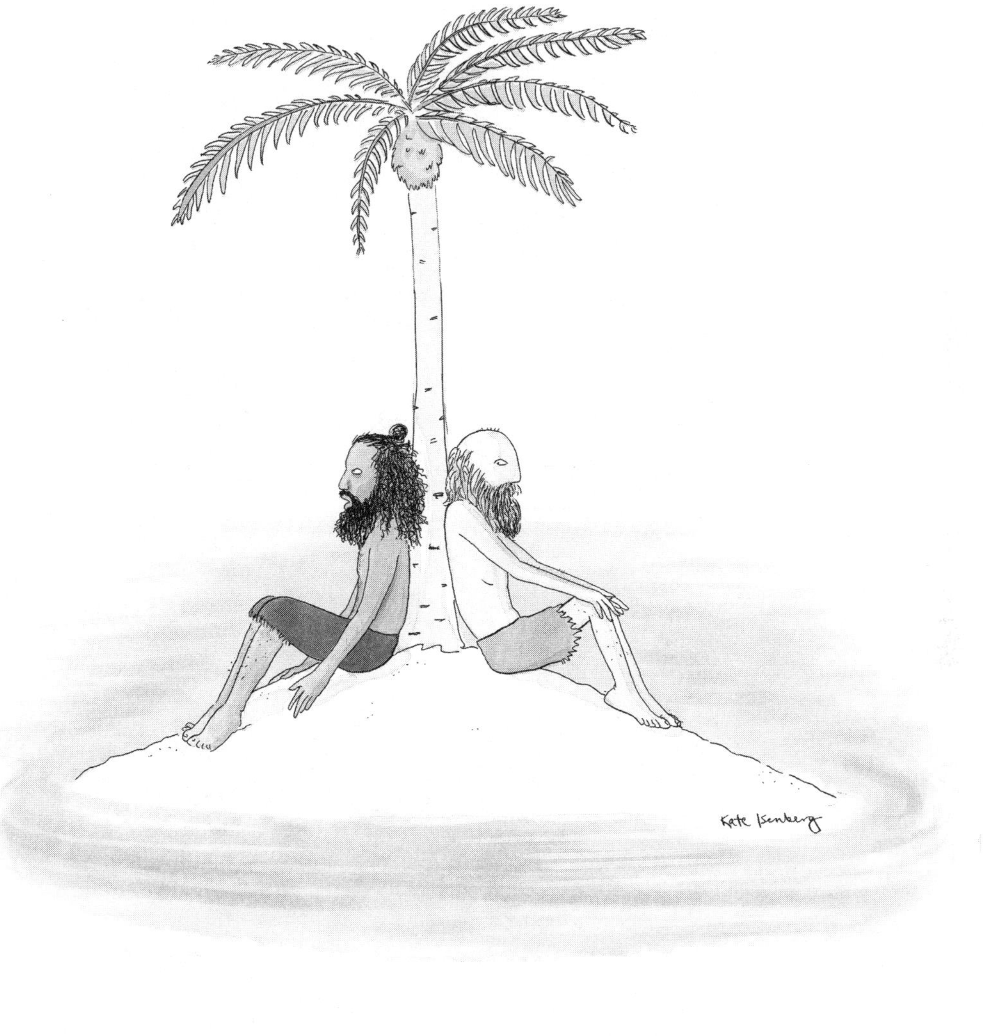
Kate Isenberg

"When I reflect on the choices that brought me here, I mostly blame Debbie."

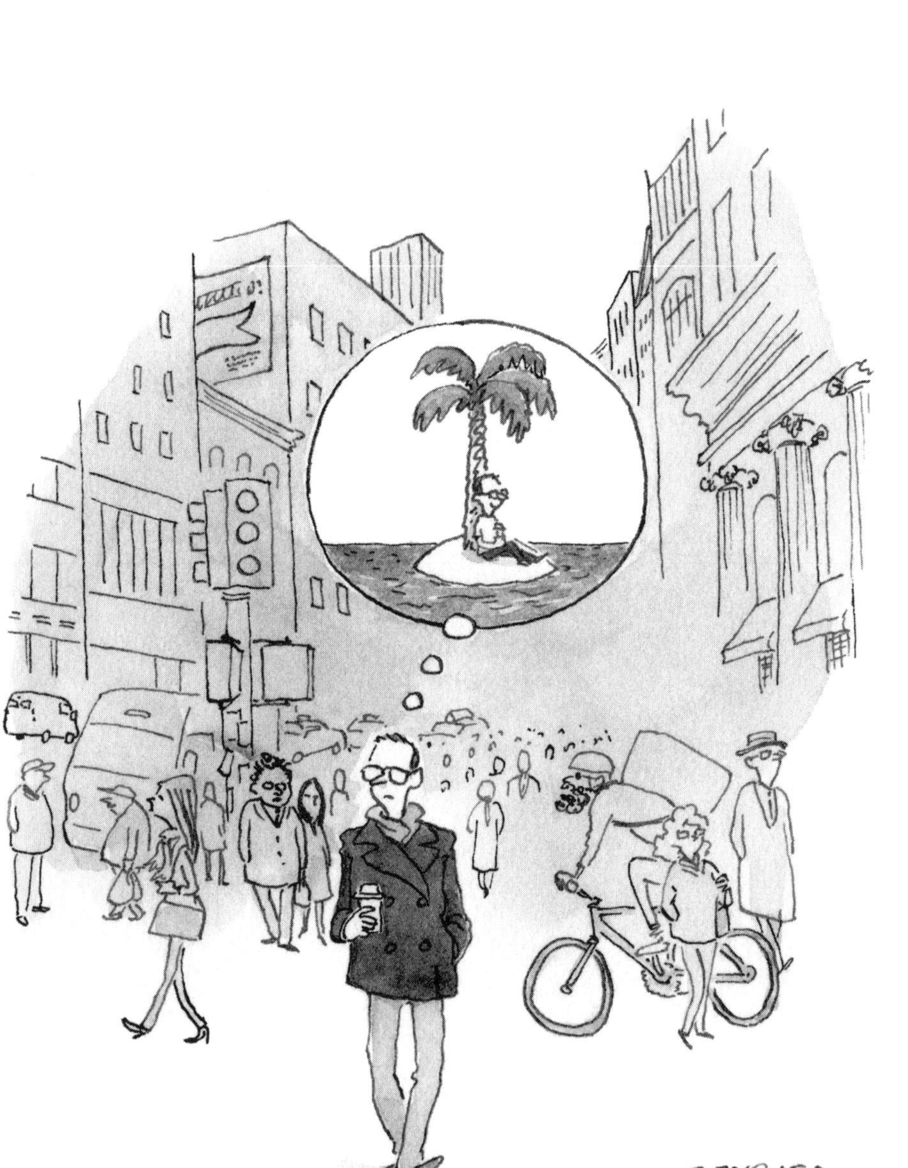
P. BYRNES.

The History of the Desert Island Cartoon

Bob Mankoff, president, Cartoonstock.com

If I were asked what books I would bring with me if I were stranded on a desert island my answer would be, "Short ones. I don't have much time. I'm going to die soon." Real desert islands are uninhabited by humans for good reason: they're uninhabitable. Centuries ago, when ships were the only means of overseas travel, shipwrecks did strand castaways on these tiny godforsaken specks and it was a cause for grief, not gags. Sure, tragedy plus time equals comedy, but during the aging process, the dramatic intervened with beached sagas such as Shakespeare's *The Tempest* in 1610 and the more relevant Daniel Defoe's *Robinson Crusoe* in 1719.

But the desert island cartoon was still waiting to be born. It would take a while. First the cartoon as we know it had to be born. That gestation could be said to start when the English humor magazine *Punch* in the mid-nineteenth century appropriated the word *cartoon*, which previously meant a preliminary sketch for a painting, to apply to its elaborate illustrated and captioned anecdotes.

On this side of the Atlantic, *Punch* spawned *Judge*, *Life*, *Puck*, the *Harvard Lampoon*, and a host of other humor magazines that fed a late-nineteenth-century appetite for laughs, which

NATURE-PRINTING.
THE NATURE-PRINTED BRITISH SEA-WEEDS.
PUNCH
PUBLISHED EVERY SATURDAY.
PRICE THREEPENCE.
No 948
VOLUME
THIRTY-SEVENTH
SEPTEMBER 10,
1859.
PUNCH OFFICE, 85, FLEET STREET.
A LITTLE TOUR IN IRELAND.
THE ENGLISH CYCLOPÆDIA OF ARTS AND

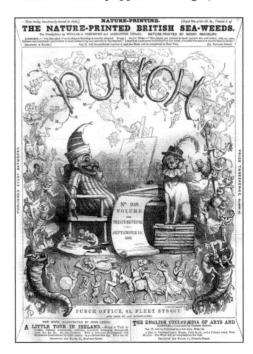

Punch *magazine, published September, 1859*

filled periodicals with jokes and cartoons and vaudeville theaters with audiences. What were these jokes? Unclear. Let's just say that comedy plus time equals *meh*. But time marched on, and cartoon humor was ready to march double time with it once *The New Yorker* came on the scene in 1925. *The New Yorker* didn't invent the magazine cartoon, but it did revolutionize it by paring it down to a compelling image with a single-line caption to convey a comic idea. That model would be extended to include comic sensibilities as diverse as Saul Steinberg's, but it's still the

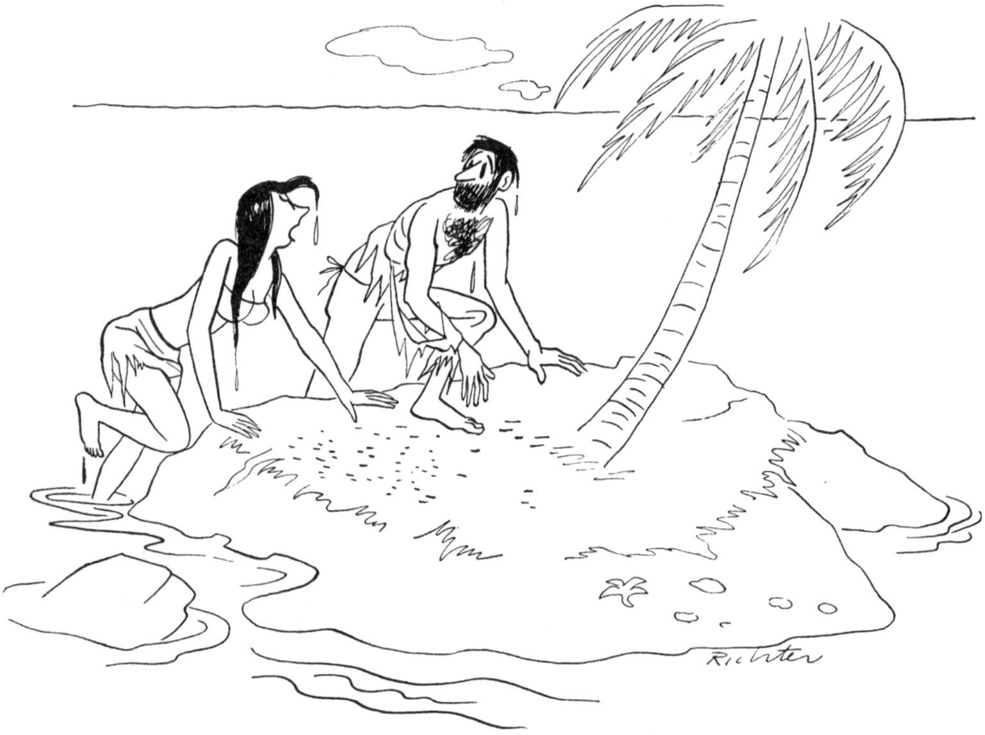
Richter

"Of course, you understand you can't possibly stay here tonight."

By Mischa Richter. Originally published in The New Yorker, *April 29, 1944*

template by which 90 percent of all single-panel cartoons get punched out.

"I claim this island for the U.S.A. and the Alfred R. Whipple Real Estate Company of Muscatine, Iowa."

But that oldest of the clichés (or tropes, if you want to get fancy), the desert island cartoon, has called to cartoonists like an SOS signal since its first incarnation in *The New Yorker* in 1931. The desert islands in these cartoons started out much larger than the iconic single-palm sand plots of today, with a shack and a raft or life preservers to provide some backstory, and occasionally some indigenous grass-skirted companions to ease the unbearable loneliness. These early iterations were often about erotic liberation, usually from the man's point of view. In one cartoon from that era, the woman asks the man, "But how can I be sure you're a millionaire?" In another, as both a man and a woman crawl onto the island, she says, "Of course, you understand you can't possibly stay here tonight." But the tables could be turned, as in a Peter Arno cartoon in which a voluptuous woman stares sultrily at a milquetoast character who says, "I think it's only fair to tell you, Miss Parsons, that I'm a happily married man."

Quickly, these desert island cartoons evolved to suit anything the cartoonist's imagination could connect with it. Here are some sample captions from *The New Yorker* archive for which I will let you conjure the image. Think of it as a reverse caption contest.

"I hope you're a music lover."

"I was hoping for a nice dry white wine."

"Well, there goes the last letter to my congressman."

"Junk mail."

"What's our immigration policy?"

Eventually the genre became so familiar to both creators and readers that the fuel for the cliché could be the cliché itself. Once self-referentiality was achieved, the desert island cartoon's immortality was assured. So when people ask me when the last desert island cartoon will be published, I say, "How about never—is never good for you?"

Desert Island Themes

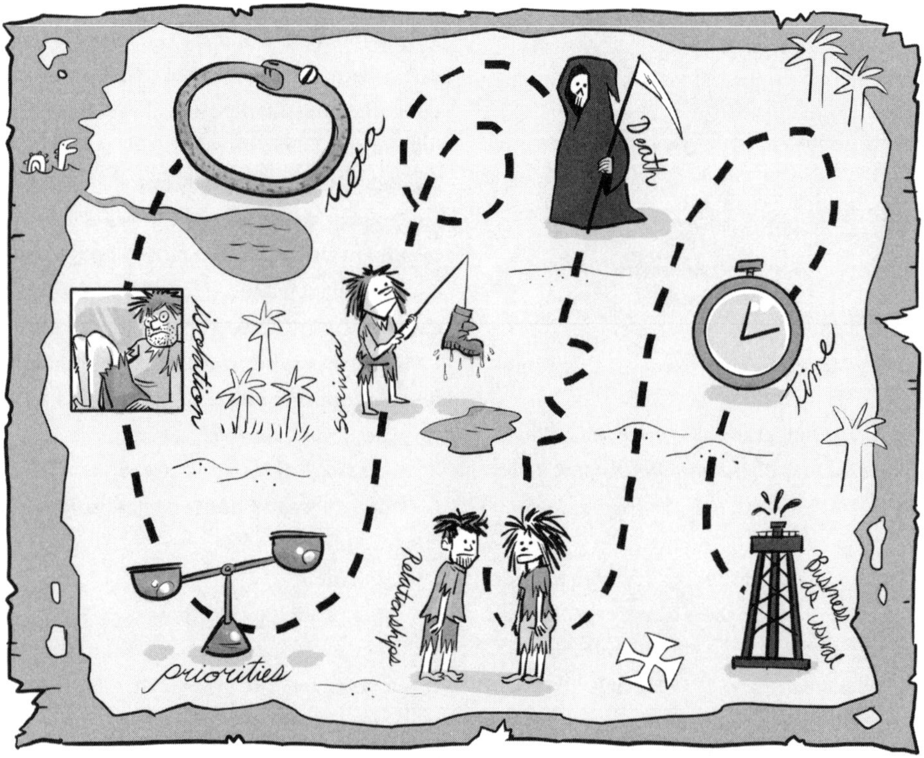
Meta
Death
Isolation
Survival
Time
Relationships
Business as usual
priorities

While perusing these great cartoons, you may have noticed certain themes creeping up from under the water like the fins of those murder-fish. What are they called? Shorks? Something like that. Anyway, we too have noticed them and felt compelled to jot them down. So here you have it: a handy-dandy guide to desert island themes!

META

You are reading this book. Ha! That's the fourth wall we just broke. Deal with it. Much like that mind-blowing trick we just played on you, the desert island cartoon is so ubiquitous that it's hard for a cartoonist to resist its self-referential temptations. You know you've read a desert island cartoon. We know you've read a desert island cartoon, so what's left to say? You've seen this joke before: that's the joke. Why make this kind of joke? It could be that the trope offers an excuse for the cartoonists' innate desire to deconstruct the very fabric of their chosen medium in an ongoing and futile attempt to better understand the profession and, in turn, themselves. Or it could just be low-hanging fruit. Regardless, you are done reading this paragraph.

ISOLATION

OK, this is a bit complicated, but bear with me. You know those cartoons with a person isolated on a desert island? They're about isolation. Got it? Isolation. The MOST isolation. Like, you can't get more isolated. Well, you *could* be floating in space, but never mind that. We all have days when we feel isolated. Cartoonists in particular spend most of their days alone in the dark, hissing when someone rolls up a window shade. This trope offers a perspective on that feeling. We live our lives being our own protagonist and antagonist, our own thoughts a guiding force that could turn on us at any moment. With all that drama, who needs other people? Whether you love being alone or hate it, isolation causes the tension that only a good punchline can break.

PRIORITIES

What top five albums would you bring with you to a desert island? The question is supposed to highlight your musical taste, but really it speaks to your questionable priorities. What the hell are you doing with albums on a desert island? Go find water, for Christ's sake! You're not going to be able to enjoy the timeless soundtrack to *Sleepless in Seattle* if you're dying of thirst. Listen, we get it, desert island or not, you're still you, flaws and all. For instance, if someone stuck a cartoonist on a desert island they would spend most of their time wondering if they'd said anything to offend the palm tree. That's what this kind of joke is about. Even in the most extreme situations, folks just can't help but be themselves. Maybe that's the whole point of survival. Can you really call living without the sweet serenade of Jimmy Durante living? Probably.

RELATIONSHIPS

People can be annoying! Right? Thanks so much, stick with us for more profound observations. Whether it's your lover, coworker, roommate, or whatever, they're all great at pushing your buttons. Don't worry, you're also great at pushing theirs. Now place both of you on a desert island, with nothing but tons of buttons to push all day. That's what we in the biz call a setup. These kinds of jokes are really about relationships; the desert island setting just raises the stakes. Personally, we would be great companions on a desert island. We could entertain you for hours with our two-man improv bits.

TIME

You're stuck on a desert island, with nothing to do, so all you have is time. And yet, all the time you're stuck on the island is time you are losing living your life. So do you have too much time or not enough? We don't know—that's why we're asking you. Time is weird and full of contradictions. Watch any time-travel movie and you'll know what we mean. After thirty minutes of expository dialogue explaining the rules of time travel, you'll develop the most pointless headache. You'll note that many of these cartoons feature characters wasting their time despite having all the time in the world. It's next-level procrastination.

SURVIVAL

Do you have what it takes to survive alone on a desert island, surrounded by endless sea under the hot, burning sun, dehydrated, probably a little gassy? We certainly would not. We barely survived putting this book together. Also, we're both in terrible shape. But honestly that's none of your business. What were we talking about? Oh right—surviving. The characters in these cartoons are doing just that: surviving any way they can. Some fail miserably, some take to it naturally. Some of them don't seem to have changed their lives much at all. There's something in all of us that wants to know if we have what it takes, but we don't want to actually find out. These cartoons do their best to answer that question without the whole "dire situation" part.

BUSINESS AS USUAL

You may be isolated from the world on your desert island, but the world is far from isolated from you. The wheels of capitalism keep spinning, and not even a clump of sand with a palm tree millions of miles out in the ocean is safe from it. Advertisements, drones, social media, and online shopping know no boundaries, so as alone as you may be, you'll still have plenty of ways to foolishly spend your money. In fact, if you ever do get rescued, it's only because some enterprising spirit found a way to make a profit from it. You'll take what you can get, though, because as with your internet service provider, you don't have a choice.

DEATH

One might say that all cartoons are about death. One might even say that all humor is about death. Or even that the human condition—encompassing each and every decision we make throughout life, and all of our insecurities and subsequent actions—is subconsciously driven by the unwavering fact that in every moment we spend on Earth, we creep closer to our inescapable demise. We wouldn't say that, though, because that's all a bit much. Regardless, those stranded on a desert island live with that fear close to the heart, spending each moment in a battle with mortality. How does one face such an existential threat? With a joke, of course. It's all one can do.

True Stories of Real-Life Castaways

As far as we know, most of the cartoons in this book are fictional. However, many people throughout history have found themselves stranded on an island, and lived to tell the tale. These are just a few of those stories.

Ada Blackjack

Born Ada Delutuk, she was an Iñupiat woman who traveled in 1921 as part of a small expedition to cross the Chukchi Sea to Russia's Wrangel Island in an attempt to claim it for Canada, which apparently didn't already have enough islands.

She'd joined out of desperation, due to several unfortunate circumstances, not the least of which was being alive in the early 1900s.

The group had planned to stay for two years, but when rations ran out and they weren't able to survive off the land, things got dire.

Three of the men who really wanted to eat, but not badly enough to eat each other, decided to see what would happen if they tried crossing seven hundred miles of frozen ocean to get back home. The fact that we'll never know what happened to them means we probably know what happened to them.

The fourth man stayed behind so Ada could take care of him since he was suffering from scurvy.

Having come along as a seamstress, because none of these men ever learned to sew, Ada had little experience hunting. But like any immigrant in a new land, she figured it out.

The man's scurvy later developed into a severe case of death, leaving Ada all alone, except for the polar bears.

It wasn't until 1923 that she was finally rescued, which seems like kind of a long time to have to wait when a bunch of people already know exactly where you are.

Likely annoyed by the whole ordeal, especially the media circus that followed, Ada moved on with her life. Though likely not receiving any overtime, she took the money she earned from her trip and used it to help cure her son's tuberculosis.

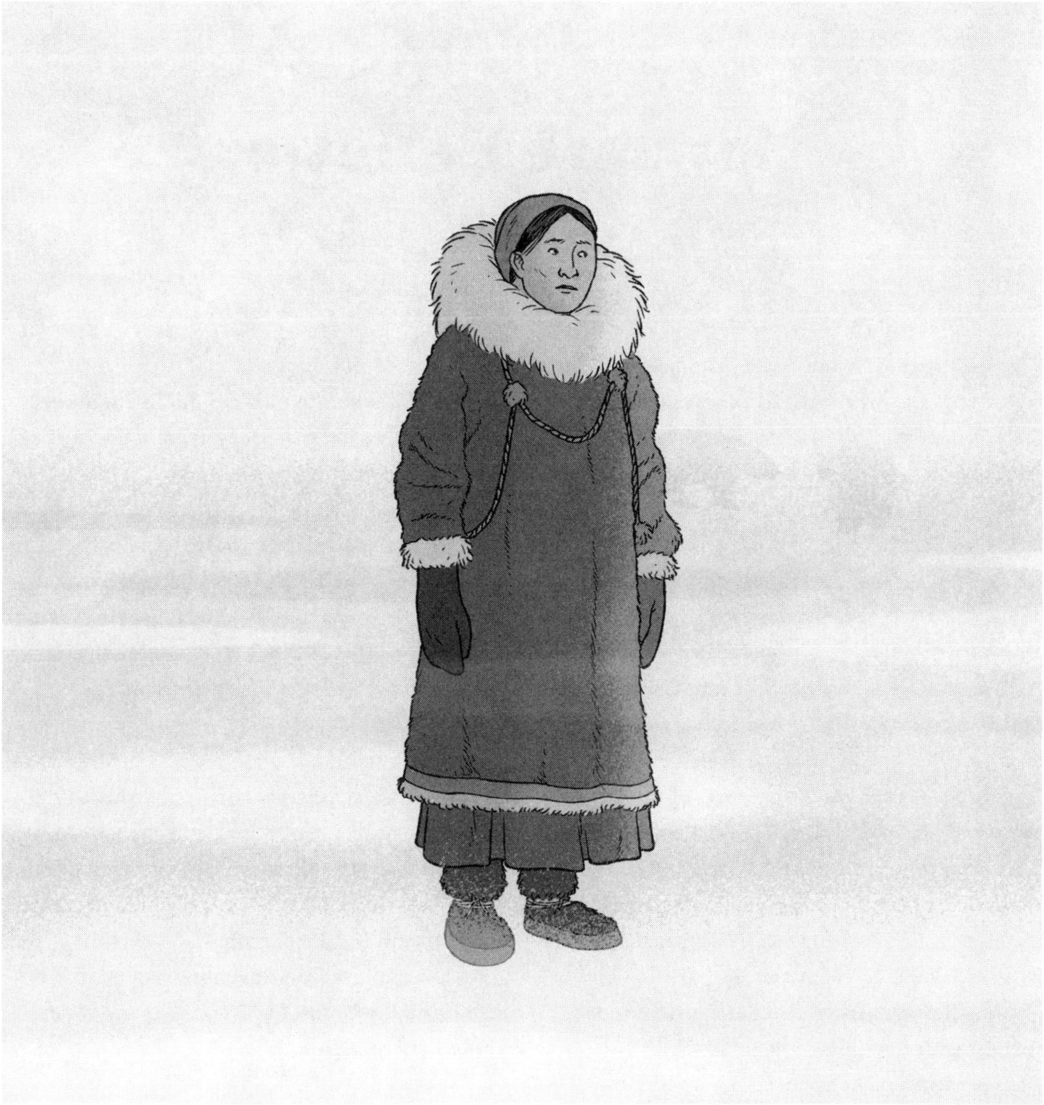

Narcisse Pelletier

When a cargo ship headed to Australia in 1857 ran low on supplies and became stuck on a reef, the crew found themselves trapped on a small island with a teenager, fourteen-year-old cabin boy Narcisse Pelletier. Their two top priorities were to find water and to find a way to not be stranded with a teenager, who was likely just blathering on about how cool scrimshaw was or the hottest new sea chantey artist.

Desperate, the captain sent Narcisse and a few others on a small boat to a nearby island in search of water.

The island turned out to be inhabited, and the party was attacked and most of them were killed. Unfortunately for the crew of the ship, Narcisse was among those who survived. He returned having only been hit in the head with a rock, and he wouldn't shut up about it.

One night under cover of darkness, the crew tried to escape on a longboat without Narcisse, who—unable to take the hint—scrambled on board at the last minute.

After twelve days on the ocean, drinking urine (presumably their own, but maybe each other's?), they finally reached the Australian shore.

At the end of this arduous journey, the crew finally succeeded in their goal of no longer having to hang out with a teenager. They ditched Narcisse, who was too weak to follow. He survived alone for a period of time before eventually being rescued by three aboriginal women of the Uutaalnganu people.

No doubt thrilled by the promise of fresh water, food, and a chance to complain about his parents to someone new, he gladly went with these women. They brought him into their group, where he was adopted, eventually indoctrinated with septum and ear piercings, scarring, and given the name Amglo. Seventeen years later, he was kidnapped ("rescued") by the French and underwent an exorcism.

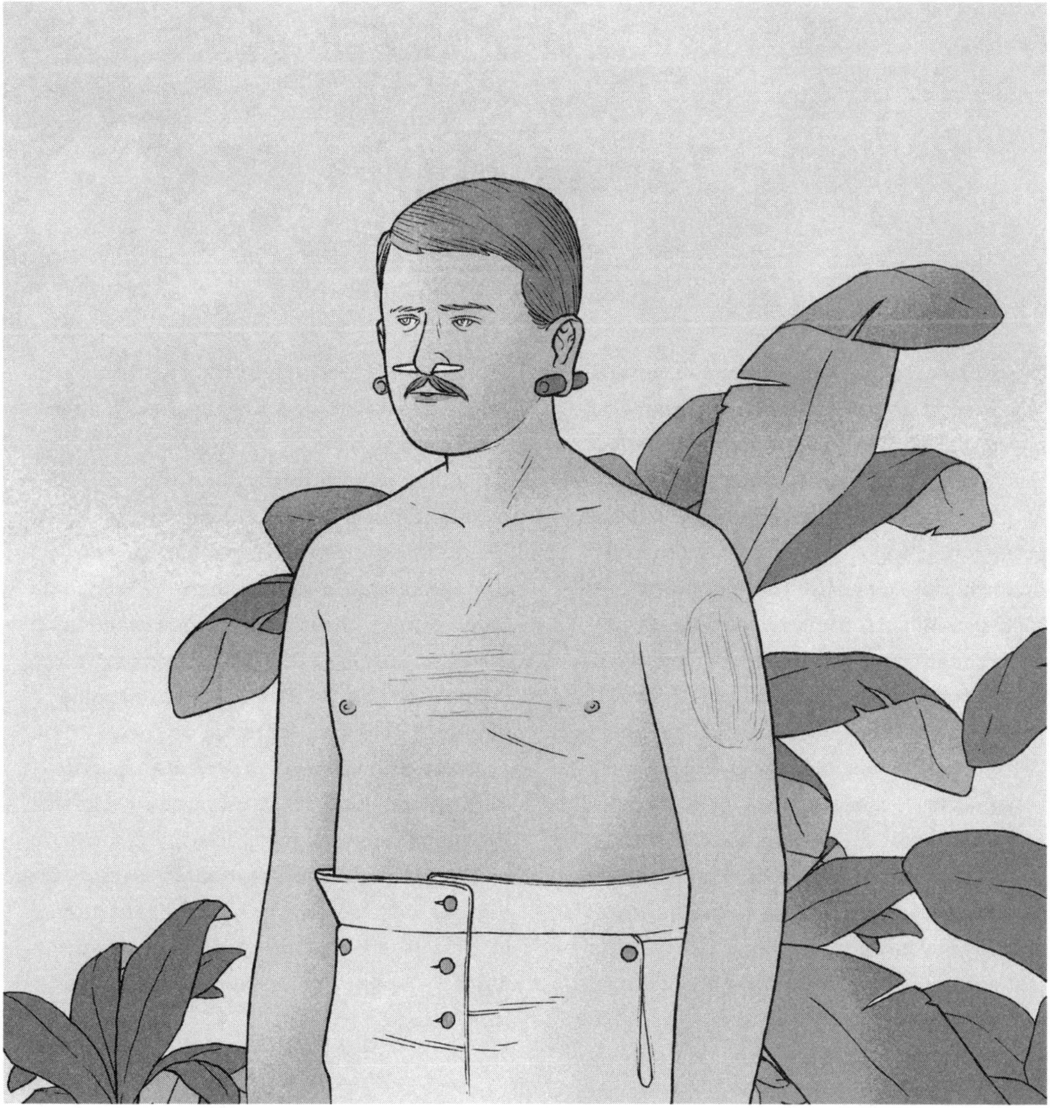

Juana Maria

The year was 1835. It was a different time. A time when people loved fur so much they didn't ask questions like, "Was anyone murdered to make this hat?" Questions we still don't ask today.

A group of Russian fur traders who had long occupied San Nicolas Island, off the coast of California, had decimated most of the native Nicoleños. When the Russians eventually left, fewer than a dozen Nicoleños remained.

The friars of the Santa Barbara Mission decided the Nicoleños could have super fun lives if they were kidnapped from their home and brought to the mainland. So that's what they did.

All except for one woman, whose name we'll never know because when she was found eighteen years later, everyone who spoke her language was dead. So the missionaries decided to call her Juana Maria, because they could all pronounce that pretty easily.

There are stories of people landing on San Nicolas throughout those eighteen years and seeing signs of life. In one instance, visitors were said to have found a woman and captured her, but she escaped.

In 1853, she was finally discovered, then in her fifties, living in a small home made of whale bones. She was taken to Santa Barbara and was by all accounts as happy to be there as she could be, given the realization that all her friends and family and her entire culture were gone. That is, until—in a turn of events that no one could have predicted when introducing a person from an isolated tribe into a town full of people rife with diseases—she fell ill. Just seven weeks after leaving the island, she was dead.

But her story doesn't end so tragically, because a statue was erected in her honor, bearing her made-up name, and for some reason, also the name of the guy who kidnapped her from her island home.

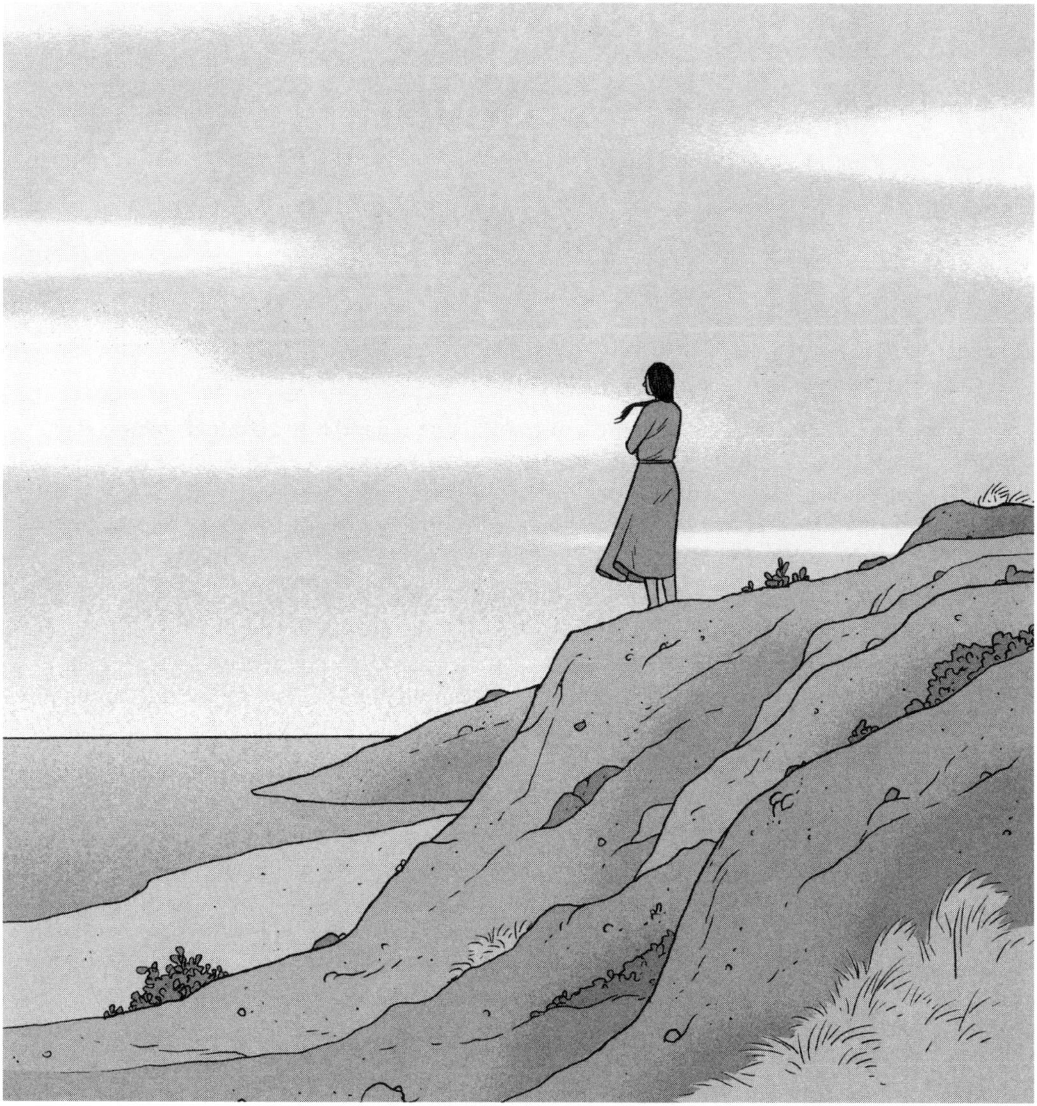

How to Survive on a Desert Island

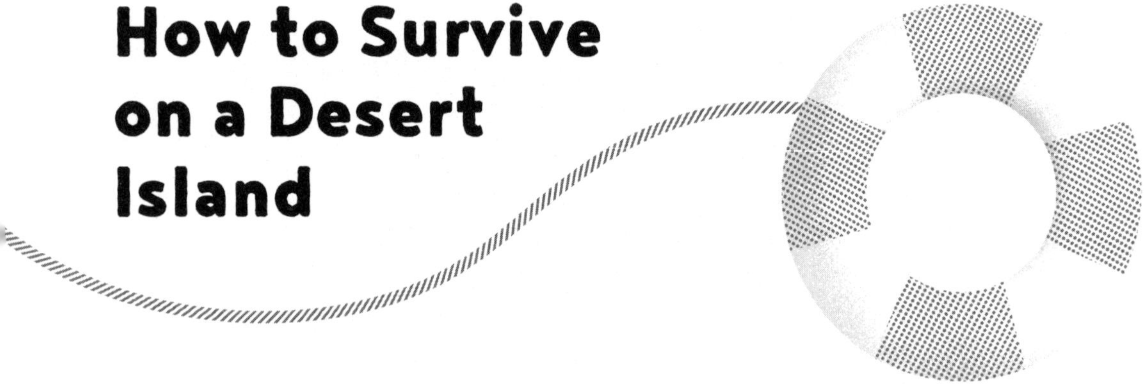

To survive on a desert island, there's one thing you'll need more than anything else: emotional fortitude. Despite all evidence to the contrary, you'll have to convince yourself that hope exists, and that one day you'll find your way off the island. You'll also have to convince yourself that your pre-island life is one worth returning to. If you can do this, the rest should be a piece of cake, provided you follow these simple tips.

WATER

Where will you get water? Well, according to science, up to 60 percent of the human body is made of water. That means that even a child who weighs a measly hundred pounds contains a sixty-pound water reserve. That should last you long enough, but if you start to really dry out, the inherent moistness of your body is not your only option.

Ask yourself, "Where is that palm tree getting all its water, and why isn't it giving any of it to me?" Then ask yourself, "Am I really going to let a palm tree steal my water?" Then answer, "No." Then fell the palm tree and mince it into pieces so fine you can squeeze the water right out of it. (Your sock will make a handy strainer.)

If you still want even more water, you can wait for some rain. Most people cup their hands to collect rainwater, but your feet are larger. Use those instead.

In times of true desperation people have been known to drink their own urine. You can definitely do that, but doing so without a cup can be a challenge. That's why we suggest drinking your own spit. Simply salivate until your mouth is full, and swallow. The more you swallow, the less thirsty you'll be.

FOOD

If you're worried that finding food will be hard, relax. It turns out you don't need as much food as you've been led to believe. The human body can go up to eight weeks without any food whatsoever. A coconut here, a dead fish washing ashore there. You'll be fine. If you're really in a bind, you can still live a normal, happy life with one or two fewer fingers.

Some people will tell you not to eat rocks because they will break your teeth and are "hard to digest." The only people who say that are people with other available food options. The scientific fact is, no clinical studies have been done to see what happens to you if you eat a bunch of rocks. On a desert island, rocks are plentiful and crunchy and require zero preparation.

COMPANIONSHIP

Contending with the isolation of the island can be tough. In some cases, you won't have anyone to talk to, or anything to do to pass the time. It will be just you and every thought you spent your life suppressing.

Fortunately, sand can be shaped into a friend. Someone who will listen to everything you have to say and never talk back. Someone who will never betray you, try to one-up you, tell you you're not good enough, or make out with someone you were hoping to make out with. And if that friendship should eventually grow old, you can destroy that sand friend and build a new one.

HYGIENE

Fortunately, the coarseness of rocks is great at stripping grime off your teeth, so no need to brush. For a really deep cleanse, just plop a handful of sand into your mouth and swish it around.

Cleaning the rest of your body won't be an issue because your skin will be so sunburned you can just peel off the filthy, burned outer skin to reveal perfectly clean skin beneath.

RESCUE

The laziest way to escape a desert island is to sit and wait for someone to spot you. It might work, but everyone's going to know you didn't really try. They may not say it out loud, but they'll be thinking it.

Humans have been building rafts for thousands of years. There's no reason you can't figure that out. All you need are some sticks. Or if rafting isn't your style, what about sea turtling? Those things are big and very easy to ride. Plus, you'll look pretty cool commanding a wild animal.

Another option is to move the entire island one handful of sand at a time. Just pick the direction that you think home is, or that you'd like your new home to be.

THE
DESPERATE
CASTAWAY'S

ACTIVITY
SECTION

A collection of games, brainteasers,
and other activities perfect for
anyone trapped on a desert island,
or feeling like they are

Picture Search

Find the hidden objects in this picture: A palm tree? Sand? The endless, forbidding sea? A reason to stay alive another day? The voice in your head that will inevitably turn on you? More sand?

Do-It-Yourself Mini Flipbook

Cut along the dotted lines and staple together on one end.
Then flip away to see the exciting action of the castaway spring to life!

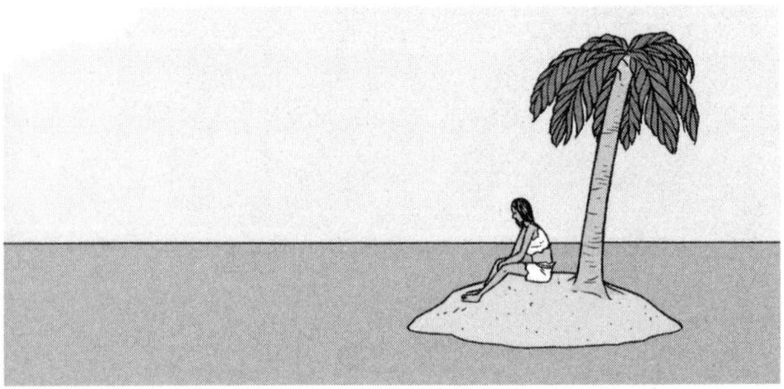

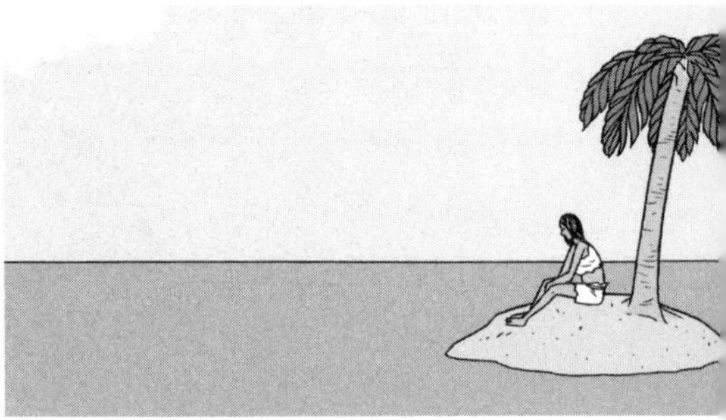

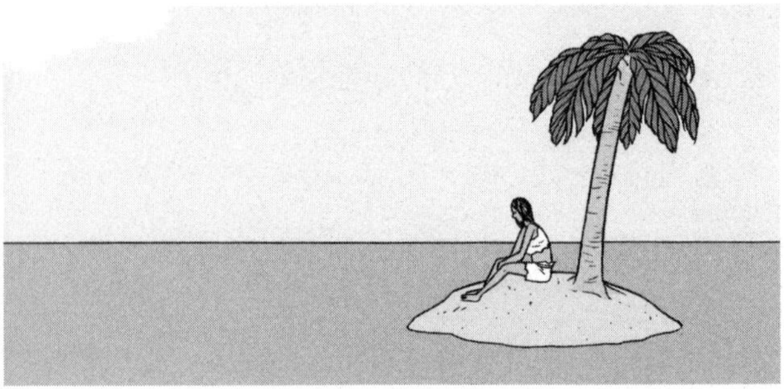

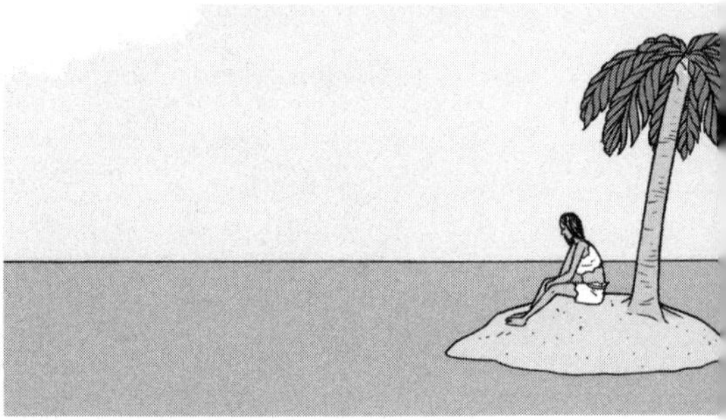

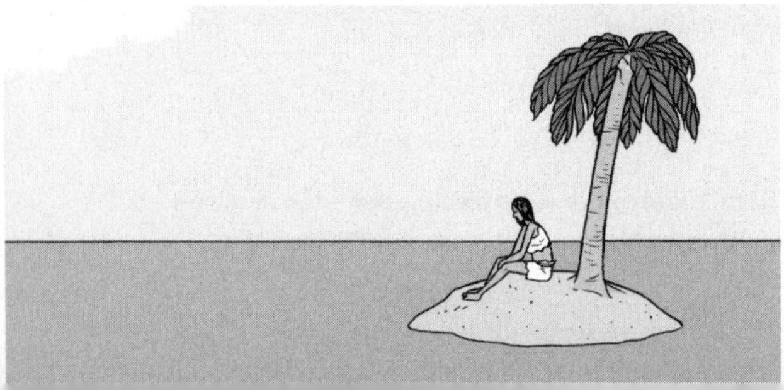

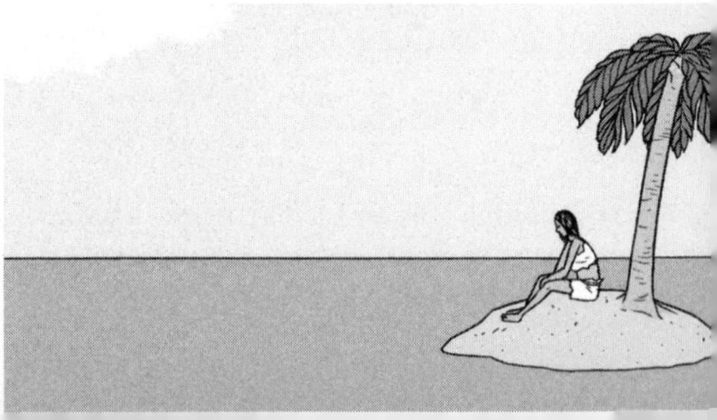

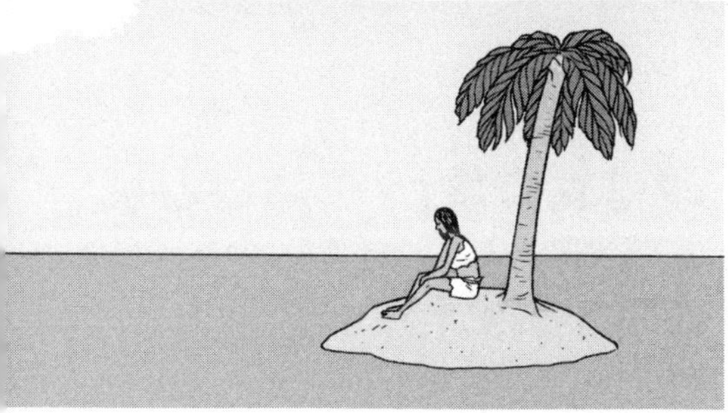
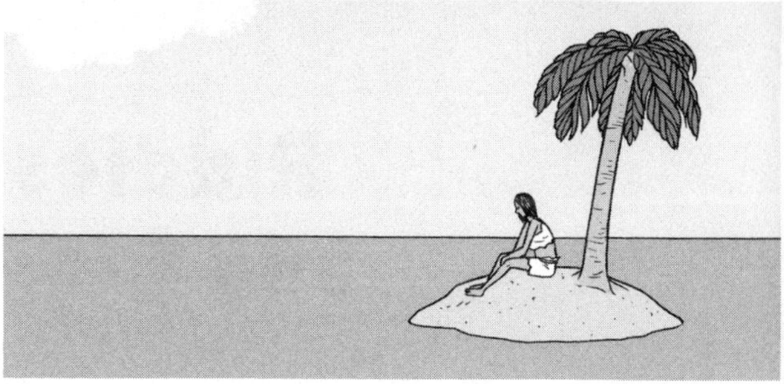
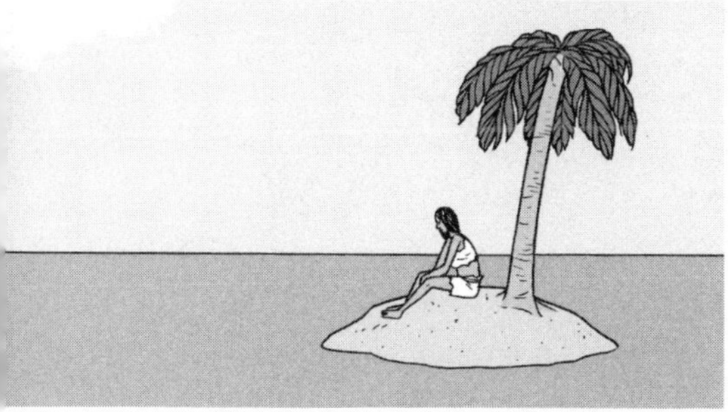
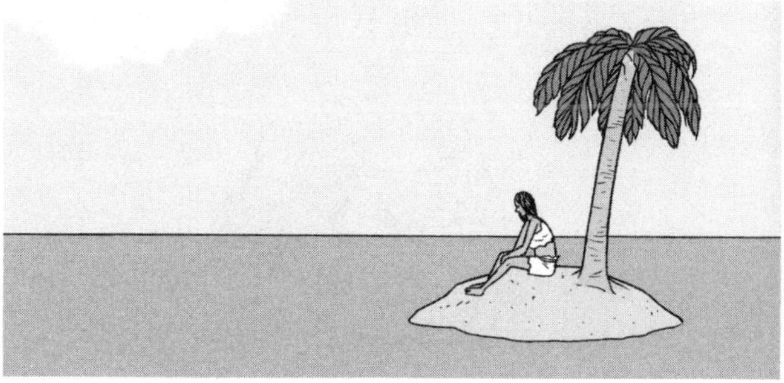
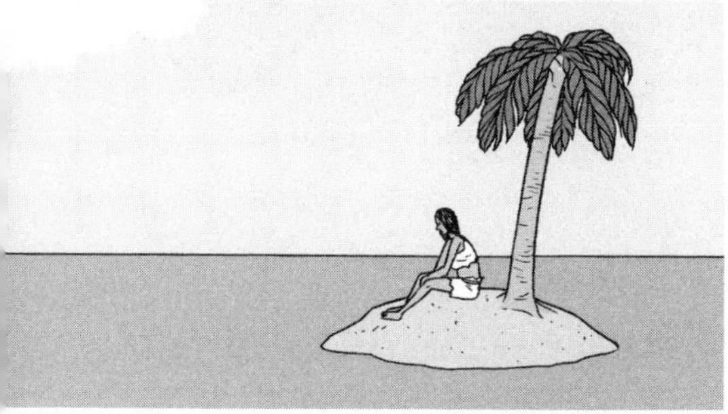
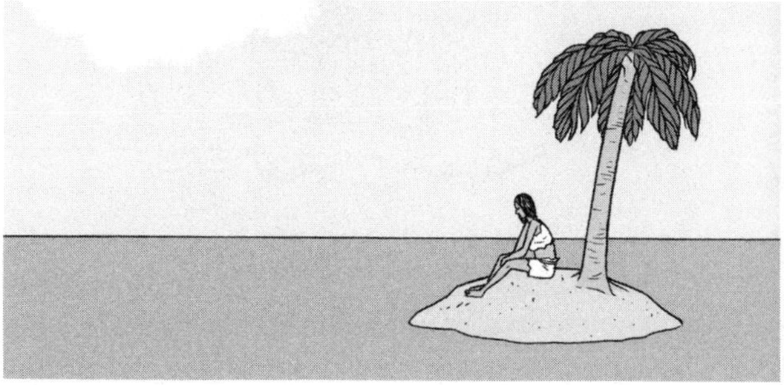
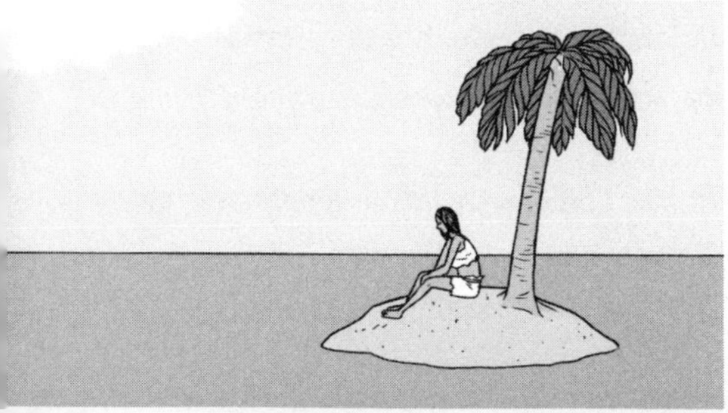
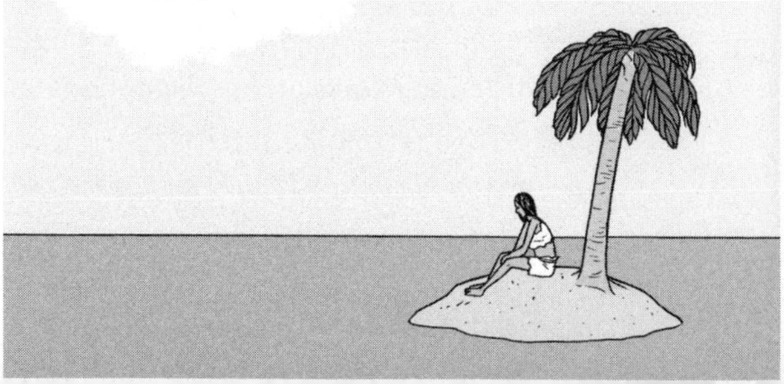

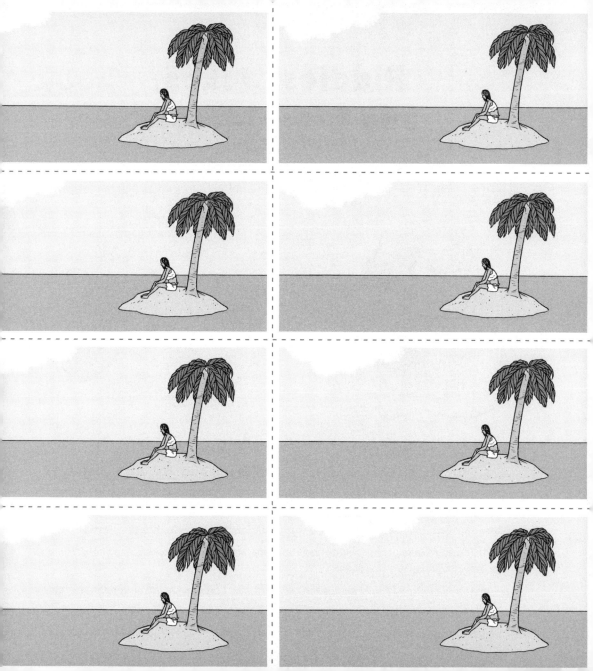

Riddles, Jokes, and Brainteasers

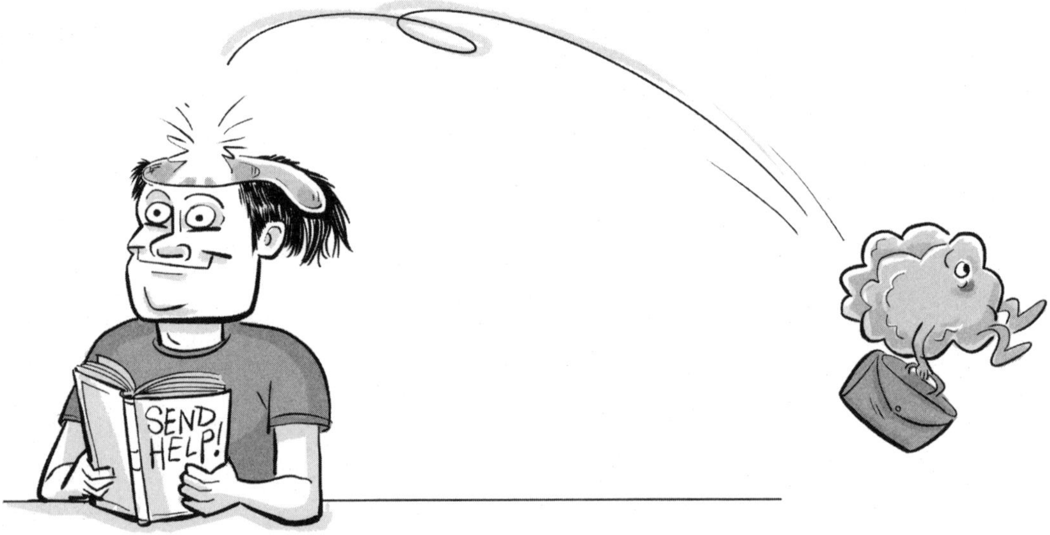
SEND HELP!

THE YACHT PROBLEM

A runaway yacht is barreling across the sea. Ahead of it are five castaways on a raft, and the yacht is headed straight for them. You are standing on a desert island, holding a button that if pressed, will redirect the yacht toward you, killing you.

You have two options (but keep in mind you're in international waters where no law exists):

1. *Do nothing and allow the yacht to kill the five people on the raft, and possibly some of the millennials partying on the yacht.*
2. *Press the button, and finally escape this hell you weren't brave enough to escape on your own.*

What is the right thing to do?

THE CASE OF THE MISSING SAND DOLLAR

Three castaways arrive on a desert island already inhabited by one castaway. The resident castaway agrees to not eat any of them in exchange for 30 sand dollars, so each of them pays 10 sand dollars. Later, the resident castaway realizes she would have been satisfied with just 25 sand dollars. She is unable to divide the difference of 5 sand dollars among 3 castaways, so she gives them each 1, and buries the remaining 2 as a treasure.

As each new castaway got 1 sand dollar back, they each paid only 9 sand dollars, bringing the total paid to 27. Adding in the 2 buried sand dollars, the amount comes to 29 sand dollars. If the new castaways originally paid 30 sand dollars, what happened to the remaining sand dollar?

ANSWER: There are no new castaways. The resident castaway has been driven mad by the sun and is hallucinating.

JOKE #1

"Knock Knock!"

"Who's there?"

"We're going to die on this rock."

JOKE #2

"How many people stuck on a desert island does it take to screw in a lightbulb? Any number! Really, even just one other person would be great. I'm so lonely."

JOKE #3

"What's dark and tunnel-shaped and has a light at the end of it? I don't know, but I'm going toward it!"

JOKE #4

"Hey, Sam, why did the chicken cross the road?"

"I don't know, Jim, why did the chicken cross the road?"

"..."

"Jim?"

"..."

"Jim? Jim? Oh, god, Jim, please wake up. Please, Jim, I can't do this alone!"

Escape from the Desert Island!

HOW TO PLAY: The player rolls two dice, and moves forward the resulting number. Roll any pair and the player moves backward one space. Roll any number over ten and the player must reroll. Roll an odd number and the game ends. Roll an even number between two and eight and the player loses a turn.

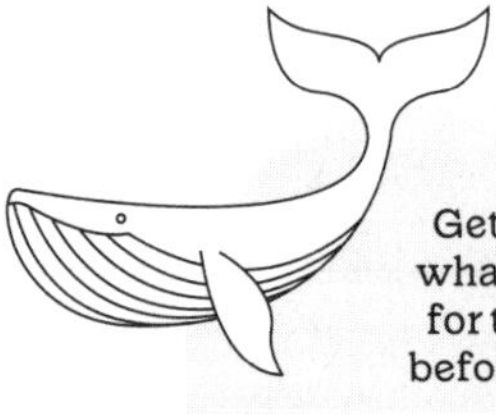

Get swallowed b
whale, survive in
for three weird d
before being diges

START OVER

Develop a poorly timed obsession with the taste of salt water.

START OVER

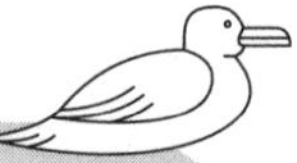

START

You've built a raft, now make your way home!

Befriend a seagull, eat it, be overcome with grief.

LOSE TURN

Test the limits of your e
staring at the sun, go bli

GO BACK 8 SPACES

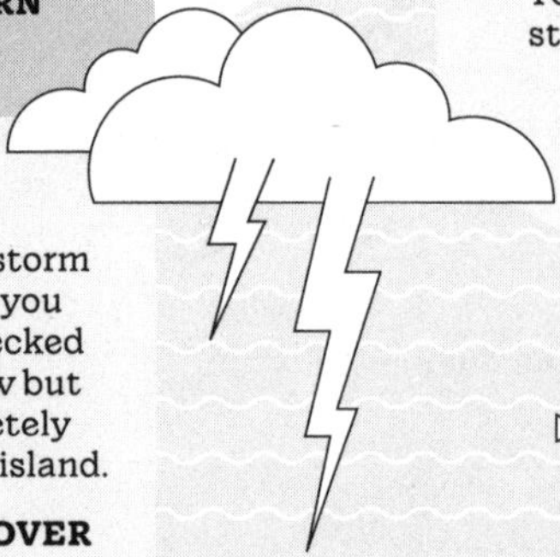

Violent storm leaves you shipwrecked on a new but completely identical island.

START OVER

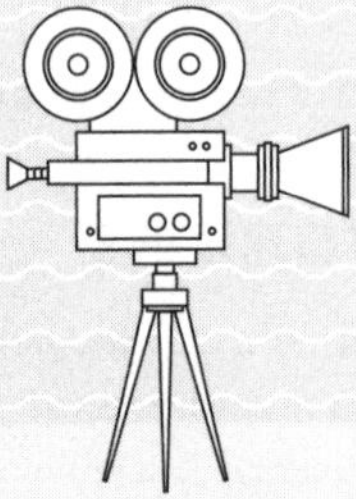

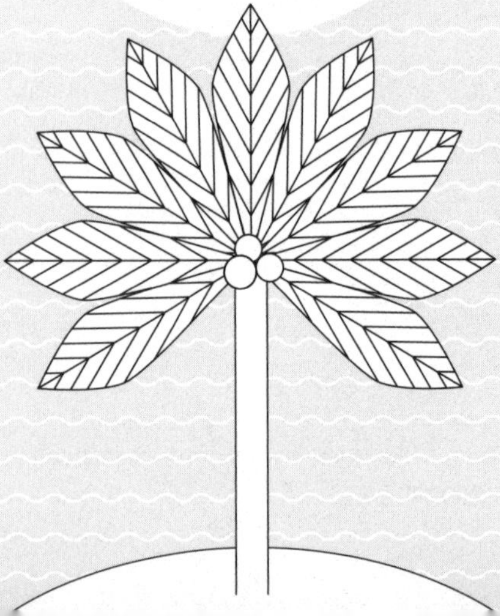

Fall off raft while yelling at the ocean.

GO BACK 1 SPACE

Spot the filming of *Waterworld Two* in the distance, wave frantically, go unnoticed until post production, be removed digitally.

GO BACK 3 SPACES

Get rescued by a yacht full of millennials, get absolutely wasted, wake up next morning back on your raft, unsure how you got there.

SKIP TURN

Approaching land, get swept away by undertow and pulled back out to sea, lost forever.

START OVER

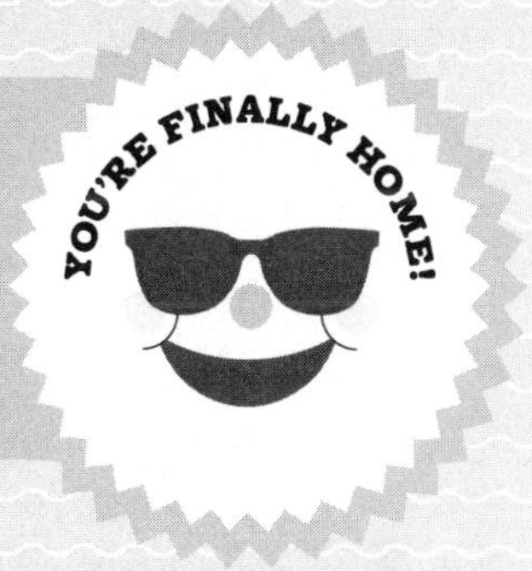
YOU'RE FINALLY HOME!

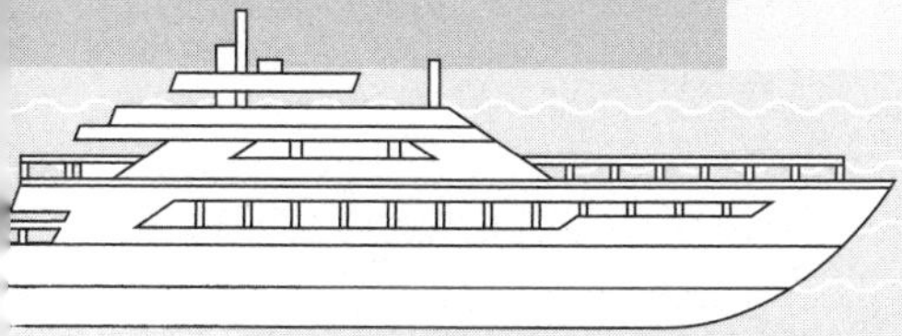

You did it! Thank god that ordeal is over. Now you can eat a warm meal again. Sleep in your bed again. Then get up out of that bed to go to work, earn a living, pay taxes, struggle with relationships, and wonder how and when it's all going to end.

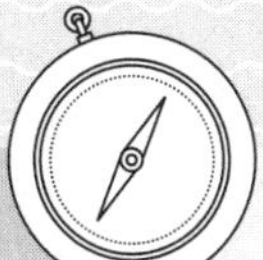

ud you
d drifts
forever.

BACK 2
ACES

Find a compass.

TAKE SHORTCUT

Meet another person adrift at sea, wrestle to the death.

START OVER

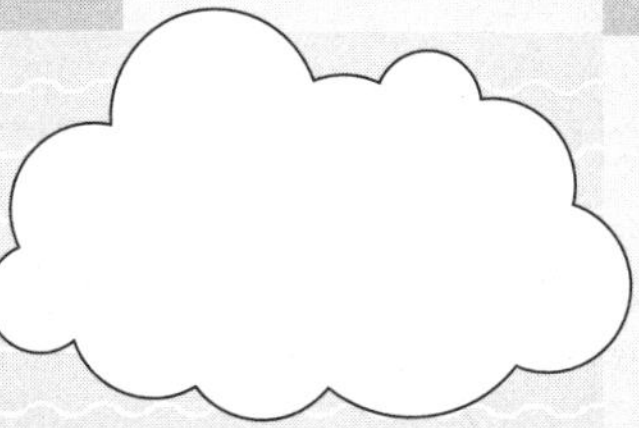

Begin emotional relationship with a cloud.

ADVANCE 3 SPACES

ger propels
ou into a
w state of
sciousness
oid of time.

VANCE 6
PACES

Convince yourself you will be rescued.

ADVANCE 2 SPACES

Get taken by a rogue tidal wave.

START OVER

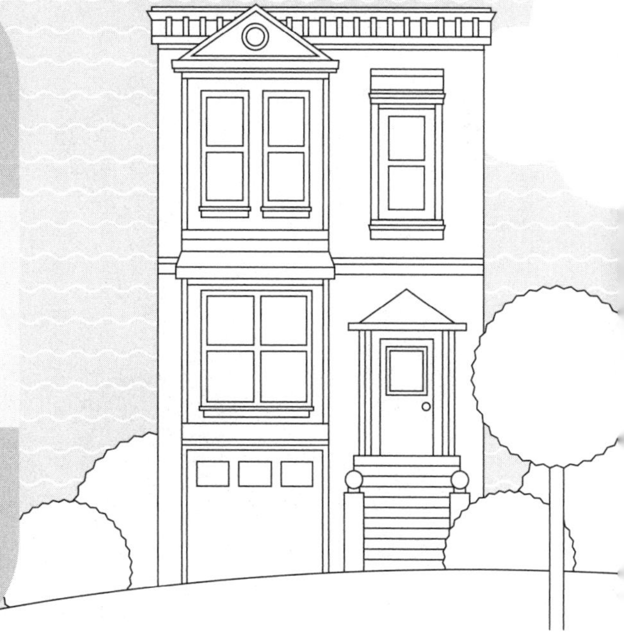

Matching Game

Match each person to the food they look most like.
If someone doesn't look edible, they will eventually.

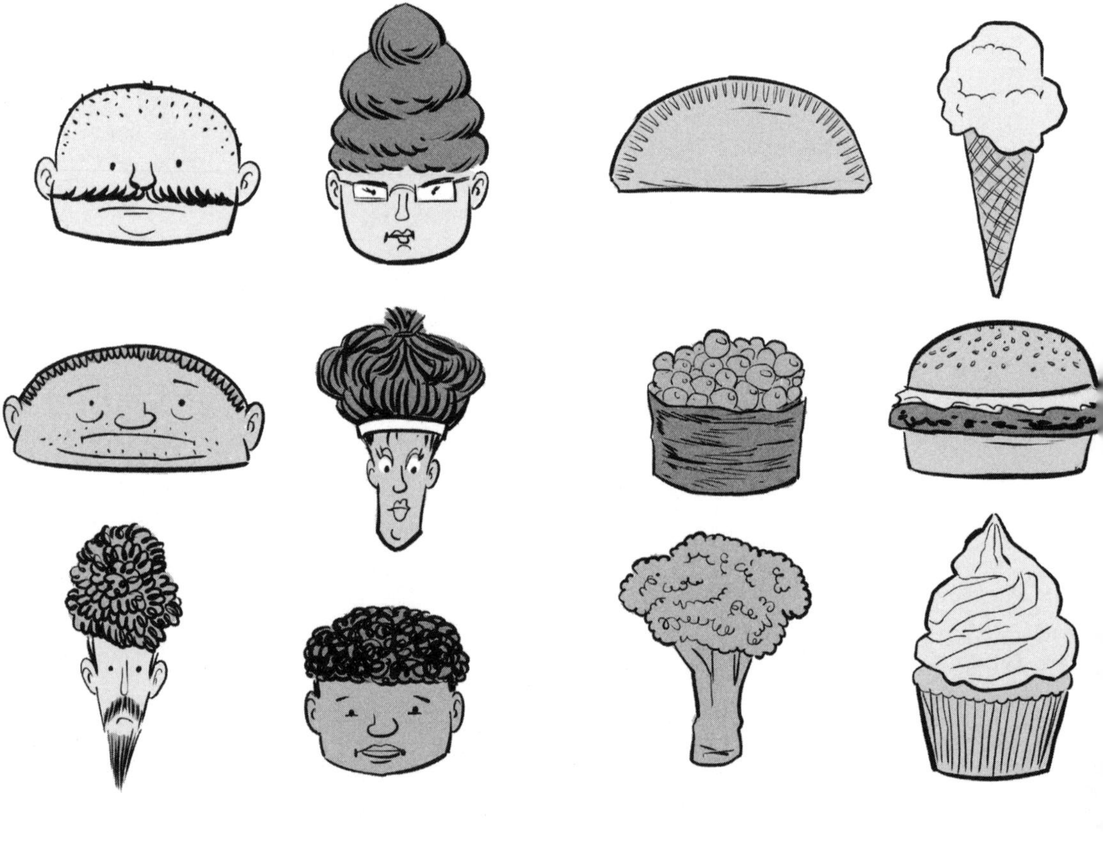

Crossword Puzzle

ACROSS
2. Last two words of a book, relevant to you
3. What you do first before the tears run out
6. Put a message in it, not that it will help
7. A song title for both ABBA and Rihanna
9. You won't get far trying this
14. There's lots of it
15. You're surrounded by it
16. It's not going to happen
17. There's exactly one with you on this island
18. Plenty of time to catch up on this
19. Abandon all of it
20. Sure, paint a face on it, but you're not Tom Hanks, so don't expect it to be your friend

DOWN
1. Boy, are they glad to see you
4. Unsightly editor of this book
5. Handsome editor of this book
7. Please buy a lot of copies of this book
8. There's one on the horizon—wait, no, never mind
9. It burns your skin, constantly
10. Put it in a bottle, not that it will help
11. Your fellow castaway is starting to look like this
12. You're dying of hunger, thirst, and this
13. What you yell, but no one is listening

Message in a Bottle Maze

Can you get your message in a bottle to someone willing to pick garbage out of the ocean? If so, help might eventually be on the way!

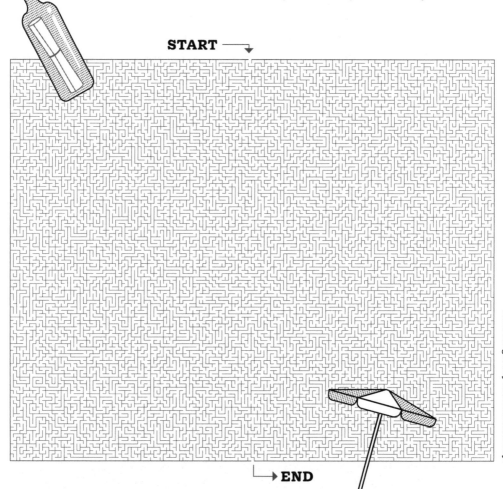

START ⟶

END

*Maze designed by an actual castaway.

Caption This Book

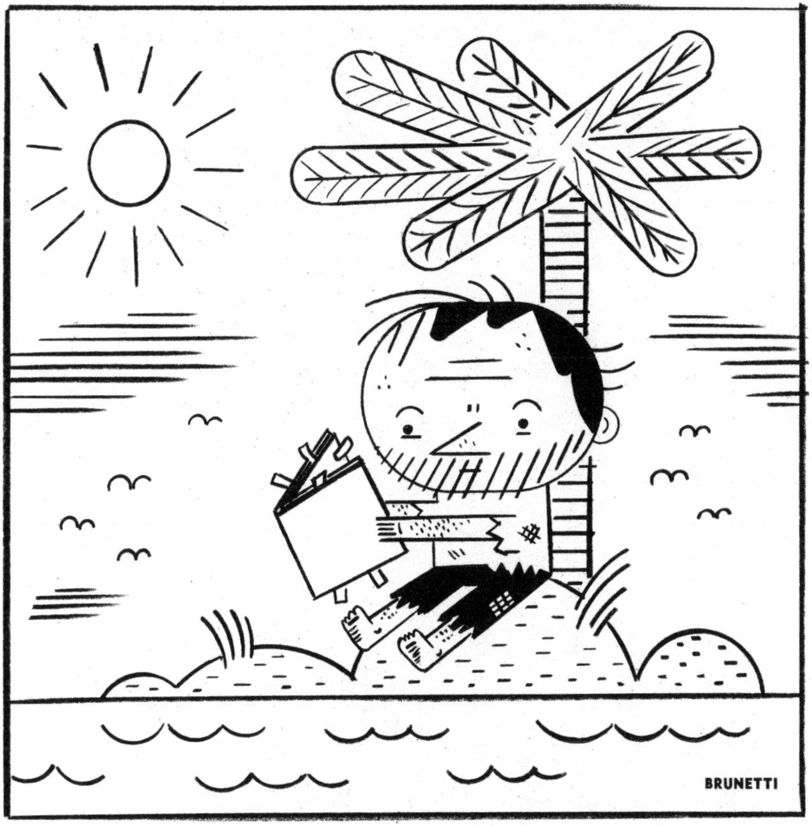
BRUNETTI

What book is this poor soul reading with such intense curiosity? Could it be the key to rescue? Perhaps it's a method for passing the time until rescue arrives. We'd love to know what you think! Write the title yourself and post it to social media with the hashtag #sendhelpcaption. We'll randomly select a winner to publicly acknowledge.

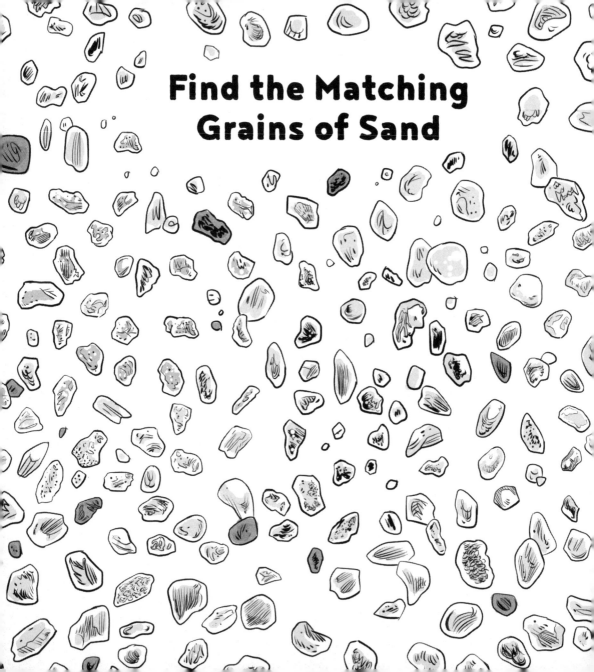

Find the Matching Grains of Sand

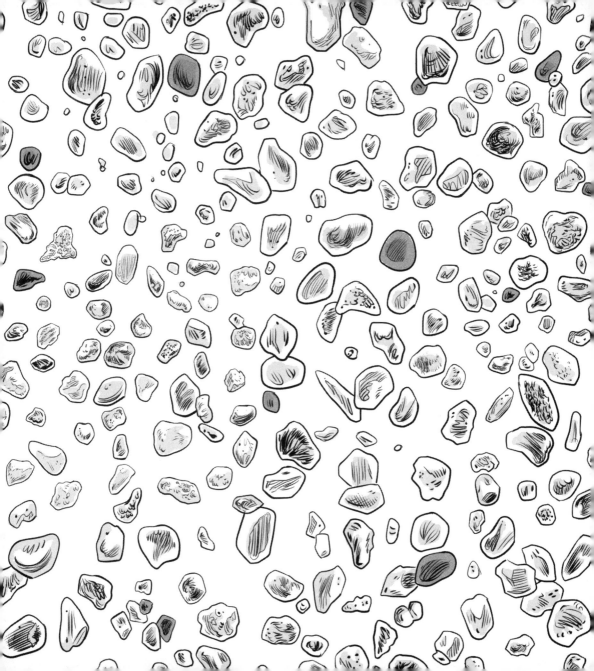

Castaway Paper Doll

What will your castaway wear today? Dress him up in a combination of up to nine different outfits! Or just go naked—no one is looking. No one will ever be looking. Perfect for any island event, from sitting, to standing, to lying facedown in the sand, waiting to die.

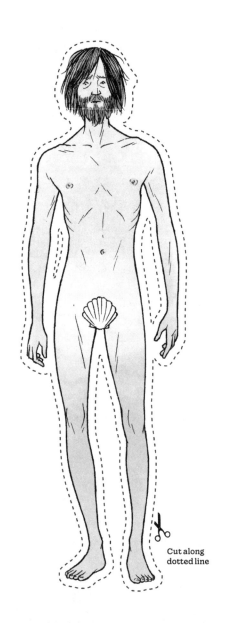

Cut along dotted line

Word Search

```
H E L P I M T R A P P E D O N A D E S E R T I S L A N D T H
I S I S N T A G A M E I V E B E E N S T U C K F O R S E V E
R A L D A Y S A N D I D O N T K N O W H O W M U C H L O N G
E R I C A N G O O N F O O D A N D W A T E R R U N N I N G L
O W I F Y O U A R E R E A D I N G T H I S I T W O U L D B E
V E R Y H E L P F U L I F Y O U C O U L D G E T T H I S M E
S S A G E T O A S E A R C H A N D R E S C U E T E A M N O T
S U R E E X A C T L Y W H E R E I A M S O M E W H E R E I N
T H E P A C I F I C O C E A N O F F A U S T R A L I A W H E
R E I W A S V A C A T I O N I N G T H E I S L A N D I S S O
S M A L L I T O N L Y H A S O N E P A L M T R E E I T S L I
K E S O M E T H I N G O U T O F A D U M B C A R T O O N P L
E A S E S E N D H E L P A N D F O R G O D S S A K E W H A T
E V E R Y O U D O P L E A S E D O N T T U R N T H I S M E S
S A G E I N T O A W O R D S E A R C H I H A T E T H O S E S
T U P I D G A M E S T H E Y R E J U S T S O C H I L D I S H
```

Can you find any words hidden above? We'll give you a start with a few of the easy ones:
SAND, COCONUT, SEAGULL, SCURVY, PIRATE. Now see what else you can find!

Draw the Passage of Time

A Fill-in-the-Blank Adventure

The cool ocean breeze blew through Carl's _____ as he leaned over the edge of the rail. It was his first
[hairstyle]

_____ fancruise without _____. He closed his eyes and
[fringe hobby]   [name of grown woman who decorates her home with tapestries]

dreamed of what lay ahead—a new and perfect life, full of _____.
[unattainable goal]

He walked back to his one-person cabin and crawled under his blankets to sob uncontrollably, as he had

every day at this time since the cruise began. About to cry, he wondered if _____ had
[aforementioned tapestry woman]

somehow installed a hidden camera in the cabin. "Forget this!" he yelled defiantly, as he ripped the covers off.

He then tried ripping his shirt off in more defiance, but it was too hard to do. He just unbuttoned it as fast as

he could. Another _____ was starting soon, and Carl wasn't going to sit this one out
[sports drink-branded singles mixer]

too. After changing into his best shirt, which was the one he had just taken off, he combed his hair for

_____ minutes.
[number greater than 10]

Staring at himself in the mirror, Carl was reminded of a TED talk about _____ that
[technology-based wellness trend]

convinced him anyone could do anything. Even becoming a _____. Feeling invigorated, Carl
[job that pays $45k a year]

decided to swim home to propose to _____.
[aforementioned tapestry woman]

Eleven weeks later, Carl was still on the desert island. He wondered if the search for him had been called

off. But there had never been a search, because no one had seen him dive off the deck, and no one had noticed

him missing. Not even _____.
[aforementioned tapestry woman]

Spot the Difference

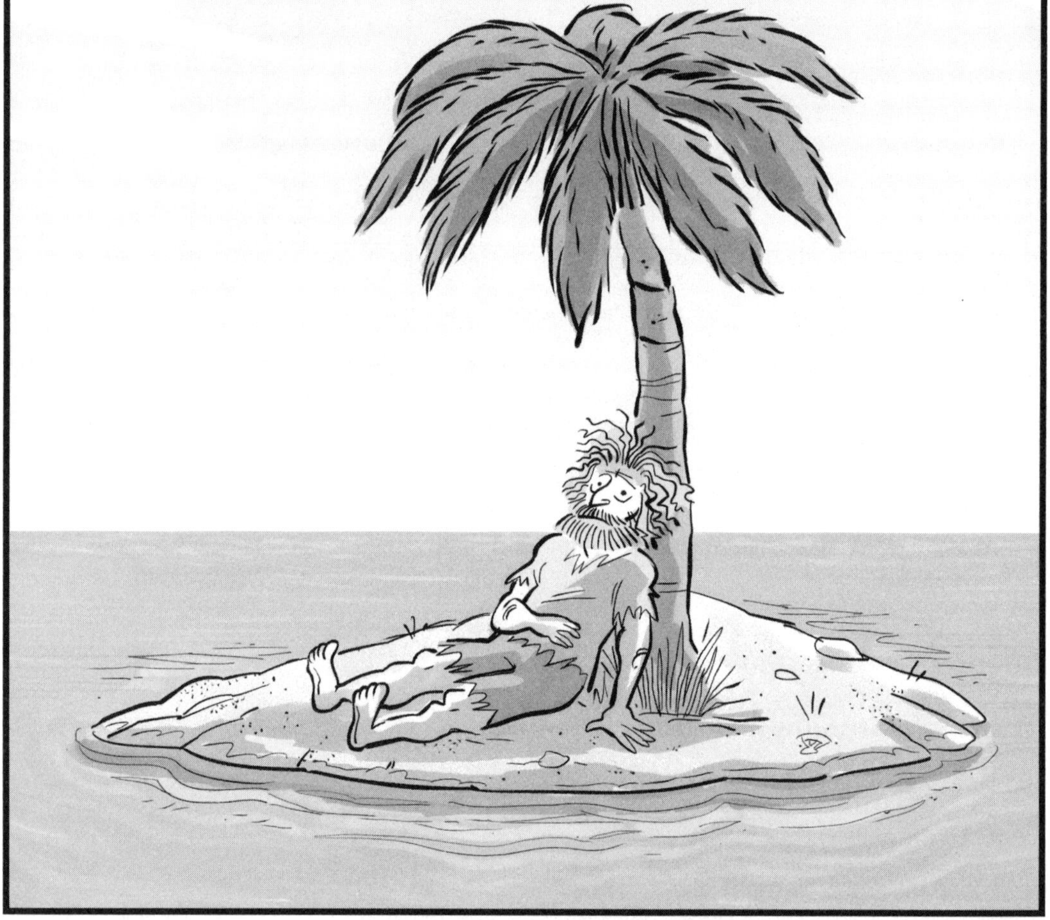

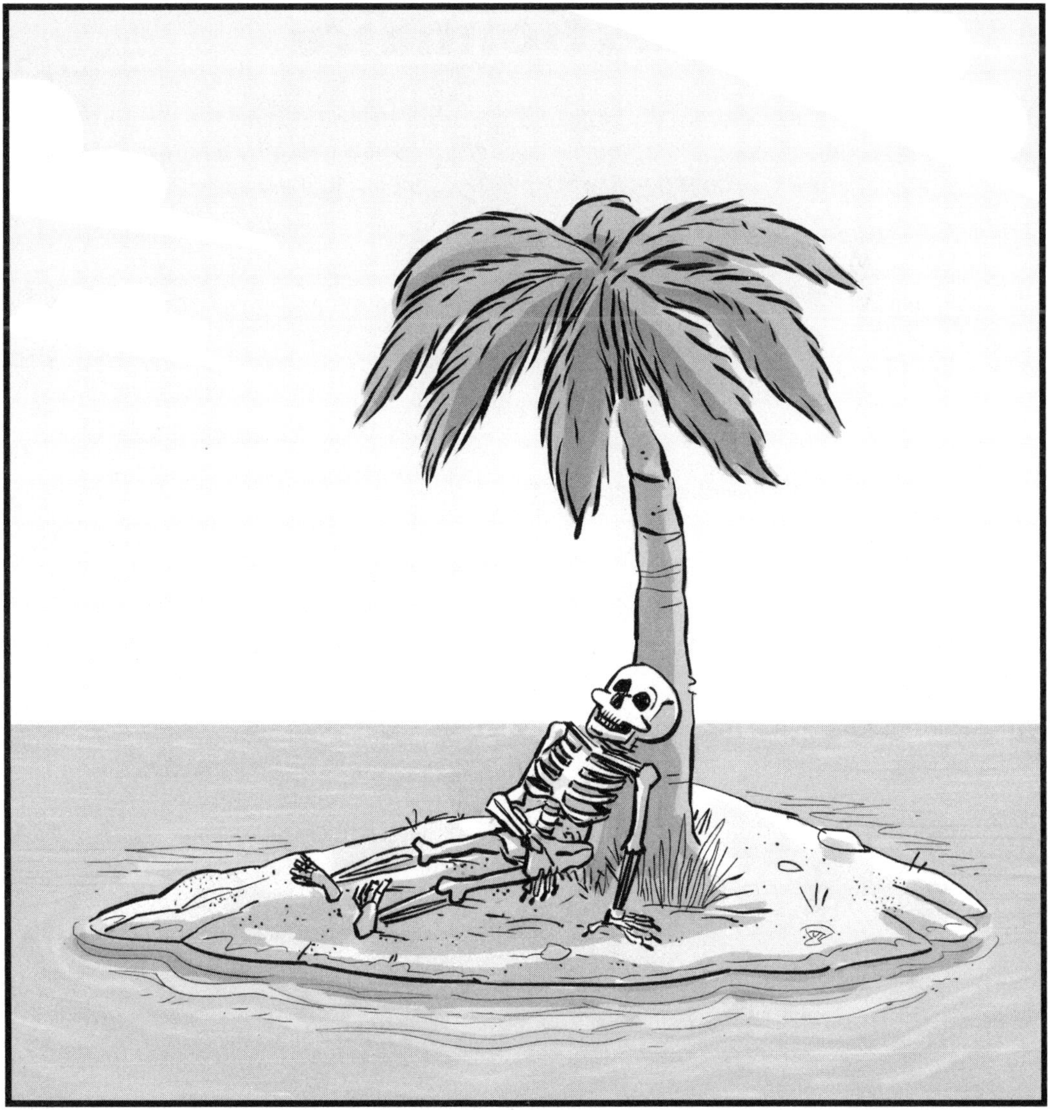

ANSWER: In the second image, the man's hair, clothing, skin, organs, endocrine system, and dreams of being rescued are all missing.

Questionnaire

It's estimated that one out of fifty people become desert island castaways. If that number seems high, consider all the people who have ghosted you. You may be the next to go missing, so use this questionnaire to prepare for your likely disappearance.

1. Which top ten Sarah McLachlan albums would you bring with you?

_____

_____

2. If stranded with your family, who would you sacrifice for the greater good, and how would you do it?

_____

_____

3. What would your top three reasons be for returning to civilization, and your top three reasons not to?

_____

_____

4. If you don't make it off the island, what would you like your epitaph to be, if anyone should ever discover your remains?

_____

_____

5. On a scale from 1 to 10, with 10 being "very likely," how likely would you be to recommend getting marooned?

_____

6. What issue would be most important to you if marooned? (check one)

☐ Help   ☐ Please help   ☐ Water   ☐ HELP

7. How would you prefer to find a desert island?

☐ Shipwreck   ☐ Plane crash   ☐ LinkedIn

8. In order of preference, place a number next to your preferred circumstances of island death.

☐ Starvation   ☐ Dehydration   ☐ Infection
☐ Seagull attack   ☐ Sand inhalation
☐ Self-strangulation   ☐ Drowning
☐ Rogue tidal wave   ☐ Fish attack

9. If, after being rescued, your story is turned into a movie, who would you like to play you?

☐ Tom Hanks   ☐ Rita Wilson   ☐ Colin Hanks
☐ Jim Hanks   ☐ Michaiah Hanks
☐ Olivia Jane Hanks   ☐ Chet Hanks
☐ Elizabeth Ann Hanks   ☐ Elizabeth Banks
☐ Banksy

Contributors

SARAH AKINTERINWA (pg. 61) is a British artist, writer, and *New Yorker* cartoonist and the creator of the comic *Oyin and Kojo*.

KENDRA ALLENBY (pgs. 30, 96) is a cartoonist for *The New Yorker* and other magazines. Whenever possible, she goes on months-long hikes and draws what she finds there.

HILARY ALLISON (pg. 160) is an NYC-based cartoonist and illustrator. Her cartoons have been featured in *The New Yorker*, the *Funny Times*, and other publications.

WESLEY ALLSBROOK (pg. 108) is an artist and writer who lives in Dubuque, Iowa.

LILA ASH (pg. 147) is an illustrator from Los Angeles who enjoys palm trees and living alone.

BECKY BARNICOAT (pgs. 28, 134) draws for *The New Yorker*, *New Statesman*, Netflix, BuzzFeed, and more. You can find her work @beckybarnicomics and on her website, beckybarnicoat.com.

EMILY BERNSTEIN (pg. 161) is an illustrator, animator, and cartoonist in Brooklyn. Her work has been published by Princeton University Press, *The New Yorker*, *Vice*, and more.

RODGER BINYONE (pg. 82) is an artist based in Philadelphia.

ELLIE BLACK (pg. 97) is a nice cartoonist. They live in Brooklyn.

DAVID BORCHART (pg. 46) is a cartoonist and illustrator. He has been a cartoonist for *The New Yorker* since 2007.

LISA BROWN (pgs. 72, 144) is a *New York Times* best-selling illustrator, writer, and cartoonist. She teaches at California College of the Arts but spends a lot more of her time staring into space next to a cup of coffee.

IVAN BRUNETTI (pg. 191) is a teacher, illustrator, editor, and cartoonist. He is the author of several books, including *Cartooning: Philosophy and Practice and Aesthetics*. His drawings appear in *The New Yorker*.

PAT BYRNES (pgs. 70, 164), former adman, actor, and rocket scientist (true), has been a cartoonist for *The New Yorker* since 1998 and is a winner of the National Cartoonists Society's Best Gag Cartoons.

KERRY CALLEN (pg. 67) has been a writer and artist for *MAD* magazine, the creator of the indie comic Halo and Sprocket, and a longtime art director and illustrator for Hallmark Cards.

HILARY FITZGERALD CAMPBELL (pg. 79) is a cartoonist, writer, and comedian in Brooklyn. Find her debut graphic memoir *Murder Book* in bookstores.

ROZ CHAST (pg. 99) is a longtime cartoonist for *The New Yorker*. She's not sure whether it's "desert island" or "deserted island."

TOM CHITTY (pg. 129) makes cartoons, illustrations, prints, and animations. He is a regular contributor to *The New Yorker*.

PAN COOKE (pg. 58) is an activist and cartoonist from Dublin, Ireland.

JOE DATOR (pgs. 77, 138) has been a regular contributor to *The New Yorker* since 2006. In 2018 his Imitation Vanilla Walnut Lemon Squares snagged Honorable Mention at the Dutchess County (N.Y.) Fair.

DREW DERNAVICH (pg. 63) draws. It would have been perfect to stop the bio right there, but we had to go and keep on writing, so we might as well tell you that he also writes children's books.

MATT DIFFEE (pg. 148) has been cartooning for *The New Yorker* for twenty years. His latest book is *Hand Drawn Jokes for Smart Attractive People*. It's not for everybody.

JOHNNY DINAPOLI (pg. 102) is a writer and cartoonist based in New York City. He's written for *The New Yorker*, Funny Or Die, and Upright Citizens Brigade.

LIZA DONNELLY (pg. 81) is an award-winning contributor to *The New Yorker*. She is the author of seventeen books, most notably *Very Funny Ladies: The New Yorker's Women Cartoonists*.

NICK DOWNES (pg. 57) dreams up desert island cartoons under a plastic palm tree in Brooklyn.

BOB ECKSTEIN (pg. 45) is a *New York Times* bestselling author and the editor of the Ultimate Cartoon Book series. He teaches at New York University.

IVAN EHLERS (pg. 8) is a writer and cartoonist out of Los Angeles. He has every intention to begin living la vida loca any day now.

LISA ROSALIE EISENBERG (pg. 137) is a cartoonist and teacher who has made comics for the *Nib*, the *Lily*, and Street Noise Books. Find more of her work at lisarosalie.com or @lisa_rosalie.

RUBY ELLIOT, a.k.a. Rubyetc (pg. 16), is a cartoonist and illustrator who likes dogs, jam, and shouting.

DEREK EVERNDEN (pg. 132) is the creator of the comic *Bogart Creek* and works as a commercial illustrator from his home in Canada. @bogartcreek

EVAH FAN (pg. 109) draws and paints, sometimes things the size of a pecan! Her name pronounced in Swedish means "what the hell." You can check out her work via evahfan.com or @evahscat.

REZA FARAZMAND (pg. 84) is a cartoonist and the creator of the comic series *Poorly Drawn Lines*.

LIANA FINCK (pg. 126) is a *New Yorker* cartoonist and graphic novelist.

EMILY FLAKE (pg. 36, 125) is a cartoonist, writer, illustrator, and performer living in Brooklyn. emilyflake.com

SETH FLEISHMAN (pg. 154) is a practicing musician and cartoonist. His cartoons have appeared in *The New Yorker*, *Esquire*, *Air Mail*, and *Narrative* magazine.

MATT FURIE (pg. 152) is a middle-aged artist who believes in the power of love.

FELIPE GALINDO, a.k.a. Feggo (pgs. 117, 150), creates humorous works in a variety of media. Born in Mexico, he has spent thirty-eight years on the island of Manhattan.

MORT GERBERG (pg. 31) has contributed to *The New Yorker* since 1965, drawn for television, and written or illustrated 45 books, notably *Cartooning: The Art and the Business*. In 2019 The New-York Historical Society presented his fifty-year retrospective.

E.S. GLENN (pg. 27) is a graphic novelist and cartoonist for *The New Yorker*.

ESTHER GOH (pg. 89) is an art director and illustrator based in Singapore.

MADDI GONZALEZ (pg. 106) is a comic artist from the Rio Grande Valley.

YAEL GREEN (pg. 53) is a writer based in Los Angeles. She has written for Netflix's *Space Force*, Apple TV+'s *Dickinson*, and Amazon Prime's *Upload*. @yaeluniversity

S. GROSS (pg. 14) has been appearing in *The New Yorker* for fifty years. He is very old.

PIA GUERRA AND IAN BOOTHBY (pg. 26) are married. Together they make cartoons, comic books, and excellent Halloween displays.

KAAMRAN HAFEEZ (pg. 151) is enjoying an insular, isolated lifestyle on provincial Gabriola Island, B.C. His cartoons have appeared in *The New Yorker* and more.

BRANDON HICKS (pg. 101) is a Canadian writer and cartoonist.

TREVOR HOEY (pg. 121) lives in Westhampton Beach with his wife, toddler, and two dogs—Cheeks and Buns.

LEISE HOOK (pg. 41) is a cartoonist and illustrator based in NYC. Her work has appeared in *The New Yorker* and the *Believer*.

MADELINE HORWATH (pg. 40) is a cartoonist who once ate five pounds of gummy bears in less than a week.

AMY HWANG (pg. 159) has drawn cartoons for *The New Yorker* since 2010.

MATTHEW INMAN (pg. 71) is the creator of The Oatmeal.

KATE ISENBERG's (pg. 163) work has appeared in *The New Yorker*, the *New Republic*, and elsewhere. Her animated film *Stewball* won a Matt Groening Fellowship. @thekateisenberg

KAYLANI JUANITA (pg. 54) is a California-based illustrator who illustrates inclusive picture books and editorial art. Her work has been recognized by the Society of Illustrators and the BBC.

CAROLITA JOHNSON (pg. 7) studied fashion, literature, medieval anthropology, and linguistics. She gave up academia to cartoon for *The New Yorker* in 2003.

MIRIAM KATIN (pg. 56) was born in 1942 in Budapest and emigrated to Israel in 1957. She served in the Israel Defense Forces as a graphic artist and worked in animation at MTV and Disney.

JASON ADAM KATZENSTEIN's (pg. 100) work has appeared in *The New Yorker*, the *New York Times*, and *MAD* magazine. He is the author of the graphic memoir *Everything Is an Emergency*.

MEGAN KELLY (pg. 66) has been a character layout artist on *The Simpsons Movie* and *Futurama* and is currently an assistant director on *American Dad*.

LARS KENSETH (pg. 90) is a *New Yorker* cartoonist whose TV writing credits include *Chuck Deuce* and *Norm Macdonald Has a Show*. He is developing *I Hate Mondays* for Amazon.

JOHN KLOSSNER's (pg. 62) cartoons appear in all the places fine cartoons can be found.

PETER KUPER (pg. 124) lives on the island of Manhattan. His work has appeared in *The New Yorker* and *MAD* magazine, where he's authored *Spy vs. Spy* since 1997.

AMY KURZWEIL (pgs. 91, 139) is the author of the graphic memoir *Flying Couch*. Her comics appear regularly in *The New Yorker* and the *Believer*.

TERRY LABAN (pg. 15) is a Philadelphia-based cartoonist who has worked in political cartoons, comic books, and syndicated strips.

MARY LAWTON's (pg. 116) cartoons have appeared in a gazillion publications since the 1980s.

ROBERT LEIGHTON's (pg. 49) work began appearing in *The New Yorker* in 2002. In addition to cartooning, he is a cofounder of Puzzability. robert-leighton.com

SHARON LEVY (pg. 78) is a product designer and *New Yorker* cartoonist.

JERALD LEWIS (pg. 74) is a character/prop designer and comic artist based in Burbank, California.

HARTLEY LIN (pg. 135) is a Montreal-based cartoonist. His graphic novel *Young Frances* won the 2019 Doug Wright Award for Best Book.

BRENDAN LOPER (pg. 122) is a cartoonist and painter living in South Carolina. His work appears in *The New Yorker* and *Playboy*.

NHI LUU (pg. 162) is a Vietnamese American illustrator, cartoonist, and designer from Baltimore.

NAVIED MAHDAVIAN (pg. 35) is a writer, cartoonist, and wannabe mountain man. His cartoons have appeared in *The New Yorker*, *Wired*, *Reader's Digest*, and more.

BOB MANKOFF (pg. 145) is an American cartoonist, editor, and author. He was the cartoon editor for *The New Yorker* for nearly twenty years.

SAM MARLOW (pg. 38) is a background designer for Titmouse and sometime *New Yorker* cartoonist.

MICHAEL MASLIN (pgs. 112, 156) is an American cartoonist for *The New Yorker*.

ELISABETH MCNAIR (pg. 107) is a *New Yorker* cartoonist and graphic designer in Atlanta. Her childhood was spent rifling through her dad's magazines, which inspired her to want to draw for *The New Yorker*.

LONNIE MILLSAP (pg. 47) is a frequent contributor to *The New Yorker*. Millsap's comic, titled *bacön*, is syndicated by Andrews McMeel. gocomics.com/bacon

DAN MISDEA (pgs. 69, 133) is a cartoonist and illustrator based in New Jersey.

SARAH MORRISSETTE (pgs. 18, 88) was reluctantly raised on a hippie commune. Hoarding pencils and scraps of old paper, she grew up lampooning everyone around her. morrissette.at

JEREMY NGUYEN (pg. 42) is a *New Yorker* cartoonist and illustrator, and created the comics series Stranger Than Bushwick.

AUBREY NOLAN (pg. 25) is a Brooklyn-based cartoonist.

PAUL NOTH (pg. 17) is a cartoonist for *The New Yorker* and the author of several books. He created the Emmy-nominated *Pale Force* for *Late Night with Conan O'Brien*. He has been a consultant for *Saturday Night Live* and developed shows for Cartoon Network, Adult Swim, and Nickelodeon.

DAVID OSTOW (pg. 73) has contributed to *The New Yorker* and *McSweeney's Internet Tendency*. He lives on the island of Manhattan, and awaits rescue.

RYAN PAGELOW (pg. 64) is the creator of the comic *Buni*. He lives in Chicago with his wife and kids.

DREW PANCKERI (pg. 48) is a cartoonist living in Philadelphia. Since 2015 he has been publishing work in *The New Yorker*, *MAD* magazine, and *Hustler*.

TERESA BURNS PARKHURST (pgs. 104, 140) is a cartoonist whose work has appeared in numerous publications and on greeting cards. She lives in Albany, N.Y., and enjoys not going places.

MARITSA PATRINOS (pg. 153) is a Brooklyn-based illustrator who works as a syndicated cartoonist for King Features and a designer for TikTok.

ASHER PERLMAN (pgs. 11, 65, 119) is a Brooklyn-based comedian, a writer for *The Late Show with Stephen Colbert*, and a performer with the Improvised Shakespeare Company. @asherperlman

LEUYEN PHAM (pg. 50) is the award-winning author and illustrator of more than a hundred children's books. She would jump at the chance to stay on a desert island if she weren't so afraid of water. leuyenpham.com

MALCOLM PHILLIPS (pg. 19) has retired in Florida and spends his days drawing cartoons to amuse his daughter. Find slices of this life @1989am.Comix.

ELIZABETH PICH (pg. 95) is a German American cartoonist who will most likely die from laughing at butt cracks. She is the creator of *Fungirl* and cocreator of *War and Peas*.

HILARY PRICE (pg. 114) creates the daily newspaper comic *Rhymes with Orange*, and teaches single-panel cartooning at the Center for Cartoon Studies.

SARAH RANSOHOFF (pg. 68) is a painter, illustrator, and engineering manager in Brooklyn. For seven years she performed improv comedy, where she learned to laugh and play.

ADAM REX (pg. 51) is the author and/or illustrator of about forty books for kids, including the bestselling *School's First Day of School*. He lives in Tucson and on twitter @MrAdamRex.

CRYSTAL RO (pg. 20) is a senior editor at BuzzFeed. She's written and drawn about everything from period problems to Baby Yoda as Disney Princesses.

AKEEM S. ROBERTS, a.k.a. AkeemTeam (pg. 128), is an illustrator from Brooklyn. If he could bring one thing to a desert island, it would be spicy honey mustard.

HANNAH ROBINSON (pg. 105) is an illustrator and cartoonist from London. Her love language is unsolicited offerings of oatcakes and carefully chosen dank memes. @robinsondraws

JOHN SAMMIS (pg. 158) is an illustration student attending Columbia College Chicago, where he regularly contributes editorial illustrations and comic strips for various publications.

JOHNNY SAMPSON (pgs. 22, 80) is an American cartoonist and illustrator based in Chicagoland. He likes to make funny pictures, posters, and songs.

BEN SCHWARTZ (pgs. 55, 141) makes cartoons for *The New Yorker* and does medical stuff for Columbia University.

SAM SHARPE (pgs. 10, 110) is an art educator and Eisner-nominated cartoonist. He is the cocreator of the comic Viewotron and creator of the graphic novel *Mom* from First Second.

SHERCHLE (pg. 23) is a Jakarta-based freelance illustrator who is often mistaken for being unemployed.

KAREN SNEIDER's (pg. 24) work has been in *The New Yorker*, *Nickelodeon Magazine*, SpongeBob Comics, and more. patreon.com/karensneider

ALI SOLOMON (pg. 52) is an illustrator and a regular contributor to *The New Yorker* and *McSweeney's Internet Tendency*.

MEREDITH SOUTHARD (pgs. 39, 130) lives with her husband and three incorrigible cats in Columbus, Ohio, and is a librarian by day, cartoonist by night.

EDWARD STEED (pgs. 87, 127) has drawn cartoons and covers for *The New Yorker* since 2013.

AVI STEINBERG (pg. 33, 93, 123) is the author of *Running the Books: The Adventures of an Accidental Prison Librarian*. He is a regular contributor to *The New Yorker*.

MICK STEVENS (pg. 9). Began existing: 1942. Began drawing: 1948. Sold first cartoon to *The New Yorker*: 1979. The rest is history!

JULIA ROSS SUITS (pg. 143) sold her first cartoon to *The New Yorker* in 2006. She lives in Austin, Texas.

ADAM THOMPSON's (pgs. 83, 92) work has been published in *The New Yorker* and the *Believer*. He has created large-scale art commissions, and his fine art has been exhibited in multiple galleries.

JAKE THOMPSON (pgs. 37, 75, 131) is the cartoonist behind *Jake Likes Onions*, a webcomic, and *The Book of Onions*, a book of comics. He's based in Brooklyn.

MARK THOMPSON (pg. 136) is a regular contributor to the *New Yorker*.

HAYLEY THORNTON-KENNEDY (pg. 118) is an interdisciplinary illustrator–educator working and adventuring in Baltimore.

COLIN TOM (pgs. 34, 149) has been a contributor to *The New Yorker* since 2015. He lives in Brooklyn.

TOM TORO (pg. 115) is a *New Yorker* cartoonist, illustrator, and author. His books include *How to Potty Train Your Porcupine*, *I'm Terrified of Bath Time*, and *Tiny Hands*. tomtoro.com

LARRY TREPEL's (pg. 12) work has appeared in *The New Yorker*, *National Lampoon*, and more. A lifelong classic car buff, he currently has a monthly feature in *Sports Car Market* magazine.

P.C. VEY (pg. 142) has been a regular contributor to *The New Yorker* since 1993. He has also worked for the *New York Times*, the *Wall Street Journal*, *Harvard Business Review*, and *MAD* magazine.

KIM WARP (pg. 111) is an award-winning *New Yorker* cartoonist. A Seattle native, she and her husband now live in Virginia.

SOFIA WARREN (pg. 59) was raised by a pair of sculptors in Rhode Island. She has been a *New Yorker* cartoonist since 2017. Her graphic memoir will be released in 2022 by Top Shelf.

JEAN WEI (pg. 85) is a Taiwanese American cartoonist and illustrator who is always in search of something sweet to eat.

CHRIS WEYANT (pg. 44) is a *New Yorker* cartoonist, children's book illustrator, political cartoonist, Harvard Nieman Fellow, and scribbler of scribbles.

SHANNON WHEELER (pg. 155) is best known for his Eisner-winning *Too Much Coffee Man* comics. shannonleowheeler.com.

WOULD YOU LIKE TO BE A CONTRIBUTOR TO THIS BOOK? IT'S NOT TOO LATE!

Here's what to do. First, come up with a cartoon idea. Ideas can be hard and may take some time. That's why we're not imposing a deadline. Once you have your idea, scribble it down furiously before you forget it. Then wait 24 hours and come back to it. If it no longer seems funny, that's because it never was. Restart this process, cycling through dozens of unfunny ideas until you find one that still seems mildly amusing after the 24-hour mark.

Next, draw your idea. Once it's done, show it to a friend and get ready to watch them double over in laughter. When they don't seem to understand the joke at all, retreat into an emotional coma, wondering how they can't see what you see. It's the exact same drawing you're both looking at! Convince yourself the idea is perfect and email it to us at sendhelpcartoons@gmail.com. If we like it enough, we'll reprint this entire book to include yours. Someone's cartoon will have to get cut, and we'll leave that decision up to you.

Acknowledgments

Thank you to the hundred-plus contributors to this book, who made it possible with their talents and collective wit. Heartfelt thanks to Stephanie Foo, Meghan Gerard, Shyama Golden, Amy Kurzweil, Chantel Tattoli, Miranda Tsang, and Sofia Warren, whose time and thoughts helped shape this book. And thanks for the additional support offered by Kendra Allenby, Joel Arquillos, Nick Bender, Hilary Campbell, Johnny DiNapoli, Benjamin Frisch, Emi Gennis, Jason Katzenstein, Brendan Loper, Navied Mahdavian, David Ostow, Joy Tutela, and Alvaro Villanueva. Jon would like to thank Tienlon for her patience, and Quin for her endless fascination with desert island cartoons.

About the Editors

JON ADAMS is an illustrator, designer, writer, art director, and dad living in San Francisco. He's a regular contributor to *The New Yorker*, and clients include *McSweeney's*, Marvel, DC, *MAD* magazine, *Wired*, Fantagraphics, MTV, and Netflix, among others. His work has appeared on *Late Night with Seth Meyers*, Comedy Central's *@midnight*, and *CBS Sunday Morning*. His first graphic novel, *Truth Serum*, earned him two Eisner Award nominations. His most recent graphic novel, *Chief O'Brien at Work*, earned him a cease and desist.

ELLIS ROSEN is a cartoonist and illustrator living in Brooklyn. His work has appeared in *The New Yorker*, the *New York Times*, *MAD* magazine, the *Washington Post*, *Wired*, the *Paris Review*, and *Air Mail*. He has also done several comics for the Daily Shouts section at newyorker.com. He is the illustrator of a children's chapter book, *Woundabout*, from Little, Brown and a contributor to the Eisner-nominated graphic anthology *Yiddishkeit: Jewish Vernacular and the New Land*.

Other Books by the Editors

Sand: An Investigation

Incredible Sand Facts

The Lure of Sand

How to Build a Lover Out of Sand

Let the Sand Become You

Sensuous Beach Mud

50 Wild Beach Activities That Are Only Misdemeanors

Footprints and Other Body Prints in the Sand

Sand: An Investigation, Vol. 2

Sand: An Investigation, Vol. 3

Sandcastles as Functioning Homes for Divorcées

Sand: An Investigation, Vol. 4

Sand Never Leaves You